THE LAST ACT

ALSO IN THE
History *of* Canada Series

THE LAST ACT

*Pierre Trudeau,
the Gang of Eight,
and the Fight
for Canada*

RON GRAHAM

ALLEN LANE
CANADA

ALLEN LANE CANADA

Published by the Penguin Group

Penguin Group (Canada), 90 Eglinton Avenue East, Suite 700, Toronto, Ontario, Canada M4P 2Y3
(a division of Pearson Canada Inc.)

Penguin Group (USA) Inc., 375 Hudson Street, New York, New York 10014, U.S.A.
Penguin Books Ltd, 80 Strand, London WC2R 0RL, England
Penguin Ireland, 25 St Stephen's Green, Dublin 2, Ireland (a division of Penguin Books Ltd)
Penguin Group (Australia), 250 Camberwell Road, Camberwell, Victoria 3124, Australia
(a division of Pearson Australia Group Pty Ltd)
Penguin Books India Pvt Ltd, 11 Community Centre, Panchsheel Park, New Delhi – 110 017, India
Penguin Group (NZ), 67 Apollo Drive, Rosedale, Auckland 0632, New Zealand
(a division of Pearson New Zealand Ltd)
Penguin Books (South Africa) (Pty) Ltd, 24 Sturdee Avenue, Rosebank,
Johannesburg 2196, South Africa

Penguin Books Ltd, Registered Offices: 80 Strand, London WC2R 0RL, England

First published 2011

1 2 3 4 5 6 7 8 9 10 (RRD)

Copyright © 2011 Ron Graham

Manufactured in the U.S.A.

LIBRARY AND ARCHIVES CANADA CATALOGUING IN PUBLICATION

Graham, Ron, 1948–
The last act : Pierre Trudeau, the gang of eight, and the fight for Canada / Ron Graham.

(The history of Canada)
ISBN 978-0-670-06662-9

1. Constitutional history—Canada. 2. Canada—Politics and
government—1980–1984. 3. Federal-provincial relations—Canada.
I. Title. II. Series: History of Canada (Toronto, Ont.)

KE4199.G73 2011   342.7102'9   C2010-907116-6
KF4482.G73 2011

Visit the Penguin Group (Canada) website at **www.penguin.ca**

Special and corporate bulk purchase rates available; please see
www.penguin.ca/corporatesales or call 1-800-810-3104, ext. 2477 or 2474

To Philippe
on the occasion of his marriage to Amanda
and
to his parents and grandparents
for their love of Canada and enduring friendship

"When Donald Smith drove that famous Last Spike one chilly November day in 1885, it was more than a symbol.

For the railroad built the reality of Canada—the nation proclaimed by our Constitution of 1867.

What a change Donald Smith would see today.

In fact—about the only thing in Canada that hasn't changed much—is the Constitution.

Now's our chance to make it right. Make it work. Make it ours.

Brought to you by the Government of Canada."

SCRIPT FOR A PROPOSED "SOFT SELL" TELEVISION ADVERTISEMENT, PRESENTED TO THE FEDERAL CABINET BY MACLAREN ADVERTISING, AUGUST 30, 1980

CONTENTS

INTRODUCTION TO THE HISTORY OF CANADA SERIES

Canada, the world agrees, is a success story. We should never make the mistake, though, of thinking that it was easy or foreordained. At crucial moments during Canada's history, challenges had to be faced and choices made. Certain roads were taken and others were not. Imagine a Canada, indeed imagine a North America, where the French and not the British had won the Battle of the Plains of Abraham. Or imagine a world in which Canadians had decided to throw in their lot with the revolutionaries in the thirteen colonies.

This series looks at the making of Canada as an independent, self-governing nation. It includes works on key stages in the laying of the foundations as well as the crucial turning points between 1867 and the present that made the Canada we know today. It is about those defining moments when the course of Canadian history and the nature of Canada itself were oscillating. And it is about the human beings—heroic, flawed, wise, foolish, complex—who had to make decisions without knowing what the consequences might be.

We begin the series with the European presence in the eighteenth century—a presence that continues to shape our society today—and conclude it with an exploration of the strategic importance of the Canadian Arctic. We look at how the mass movements of peoples, whether Loyalists in the eighteenth century or Asians at the start of the twentieth, have profoundly influenced the nature of Canada. We also look at battles and their aftermaths: the Plains of Abraham, the 1866 Fenian raids, the German submarines in the St. Lawrence River during World War II. Political crises—the 1891 election that saw Sir John A. Macdonald battling Wilfrid Laurier; Pierre Trudeau's triumphant patriation of the Canadian Constitution—provide rich moments of storytelling. So, too, do the Expo 67 celebrations, which marked a time of soaring optimism and gave Canadians new confidence in themselves.

We have chosen these critical turning points partly because they are good stories in themselves but also because they show what Canada was like at particularly important junctures in its history. And to tell them we have chosen Canada's best historians. Our authors are great storytellers who shine a spotlight on a different Canada, a Canada of the past, and illustrate links from then to now. We need to remember the roads that were taken—and the ones that were not. Our goal is to help our readers understand how we got from that past to this present.

Margaret MacMillan
Warden at St. Antony's College, Oxford

Robert Bothwell
May Gluskin Chair of Canadian History
University of Toronto

PROLOGUE

ONE

The Plot

For nearly 115 years, from July 1867 to April 1982, the constitution of Canada remained an act of the British Parliament, a remnant of the country's colonial past. Successive efforts over fifty years by five Canadian prime ministers failed to correct this humiliating anomaly, simply because no one could agree on how to amend the fundamental contract by which Canadians govern themselves once it was finally patriated. When the national government began to press the issue in the 1960s, all but a few of the premiers of Canada's ten provinces withheld their consent unless Ottawa agreed to give them more power within the federation.

In October 1980, following the failure of ten first ministers' conferences on the constitution since 1927, Prime Minister Pierre Elliott Trudeau decided to act unilaterally. Though his move was denounced by his opponents as a power grab that offended the principles of federalism, it in fact eliminated Ottawa's legal right to change the constitution on its own. Trudeau also proposed an amending formula that would give the final word to the citizens of Canada by means of referendum and introduced a charter of rights that checked the abuses of all governments, national and provincial alike. It was, for him, an exercise in nation-building that would overcome the divisive forces at work in the world's most decentralized federation—not least a government in Quebec dedicated to the province's independence.

Two provinces, Ontario and New Brunswick, went along with Trudeau's People's Package as fair, necessary, and long overdue. The eight others fought it in their legislatures, in the courts, and in London. Though each premier in the so-called Gang of Eight had his own principled, political, or personal reasons for opposing the reform, they all understood that its passage would spell the end of their strategic game. Worse, Ottawa's amending formula and its proposed charter threatened to shift power away from provincial governments to federally appointed judges and the Canadian people. Some termed it a constitutional revolution.

For a year and a half, in the midst of the worst economic downturn since the Depression, the prime minister and the premiers warred like the gods on Mount Olympus in a battle over their vision of Canada. In the House of Commons, the Official Opposition used every parliamentary tactic at its disposal to delay or derail the government's motion. The Gang of Eight came up with an alternative amending formula and attacked the draft charter in whole or in part. The Supreme Court ruled that the federal government's unilateral action, though technically legal, was a violation of constitutional convention. And so, to try to break the impasse and gain enough legitimacy to proceed rapidly to London, Pierre Trudeau felt compelled to make one last attempt to strike a deal with the premiers.

In cold Ottawa we lay our scene, November 1981, when eleven men and a couple of dozen advisers met in secret. There occurred a drama of intrigue and climax in which two feuding gangs fought for ultimate control of the country. It was a pivotal moment in the evolution of a nation, the stuff of history and of myth, the most significant meeting since the Quebec Conference of 1864, which had paved the way to Confederation. It was also a clash of philosophies and egos driven by intransigent players holding irreconcilable positions, presided over by a leader exercising one of the greatest acts of political will ever witnessed in a land renowned for conciliation and deference. The result was trumpeted in the press as Canada's spiritual coming of age. It was also bemoaned as a disappointment by those who had expected more, a treacherous "Night of the Long Knives" by those who had wanted less, and a matter of indifference by the many who hadn't cared. Heralded to last a thousand years, the new constitution came close to ripping the country apart within a decade.

TWO

A Can of Worms

Not long ago, *The New York Times* reported on the wedding of a young American couple who had met as history students at college. "The couple found, perhaps not surprisingly, that they shared an almost fanatical interest in current events, politics and law," the article noted. "They would stay up late discussing and debating the Constitution and the intent of the founding fathers."

Unlike the United States, Canada has been cursed—and blessed—with a supreme law about as romantic as a prenuptial agreement for an arranged marriage. The British North America Act, 1867—renamed the Constitution Act, 1867, in the aftermath of the momentous events of November 1981—is a thing that only a jurist or a scholar can truly love.[1] Far from being the emotive proclamation of an oppressed citizenry who rose up to seize their liberty, the BNA Act was a practical contract, drawn up behind closed doors by a few dozen colonial politicians and imperial officials for purposes that had more to do with parliamentary gridlock and expenditure reductions than with self-evident truths or inalienable rights. Legislated from above, it was rushed through as an act of the

Parliament of the United Kingdom before the MPs at Westminster, as though with a yawn, turned their attention to the more vexatious matter of licensing dogs.

Blunt-toothed compromise presided over the birth of this strange and ungainly invention called Canada, in which three of Great Britain's North American possessions were transformed into the four provinces of an improvised "dominion" within the British Empire. No longer fully a colony, but not quite a country either. The colonial pooh-bahs who crafted the union were the representatives of two European sub-cultures—one French-speaking, one English-speaking—that had rejected democratic revolutions in favour of tradition and moderation. Instead of *liberté*, *egalité*, *fraternité*, instead of life, liberty, and the pursuit of happiness, they aspired to peace, order, and good government. Thus the British monarch would continue to be the head of state. The motherland was to keep ultimate authority over foreign policy and defence. The highest court of appeal was to stay in London. The inhabitants of Canada were to remain loyal subjects of the Crown. British laws were still paramount. And to complicate matters for a long time to come, the ordinary piece of British legislation that was in effect the Canadian constitution could be amended only by the consent of the Parliament at Westminster.

Yet every country should be so fortunate as to have a constitution as dull and prosaic as Canada's. Blessed are the people who can agree to a set of values, principles, and rules by which to live and stick to it for generations. Within a hundred years of the signing of the United States Constitution, North and South were waging bloody civil war on the battle-fields of Gettysburg and Appomattox over the undelivered promises of freedom and equality. Canada's centennial, by contrast, was marked by a round of arcane federal–provincial conferences that led at a measured pace towards a legal referendum on a half-step towards a negotiated secession, which then was rejected. If the Confederation debates never reached the rhetorical heights or intellectual depths of *The Federalist Papers*, the BNA Act was nonetheless a declaration of independence based on ideals and experience. Buried beneath its technical verbiage, John Locke vied with Jean-Jacques Rousseau, Thomas Jefferson took on Alexander Hamilton, Edmund Burke quarrelled with John Stuart Mill, and English common law lay down beside the French civil code. The ambitions and arguments of Canada's founding fathers addressed the great questions of political philosophy from Plato to the present: Where should power be, and how much should be there?

The most crucial issue faced by the Fathers of Confederation and their masters in London was whether to make Canada a single state or a federation of provinces. There were many strong arguments in favour of the unitary model. The British taxpayer was fed up with footing the bills of separate colonial administrations. The railways, steamships, and telegraph networks necessary for bigger markets and greater prosperity required large pools of private and public capital. There would be strength in numbers, as well as a joint defence strategy to deal with any threat from the sabre-rattling republic to the south. The more visionary of the colonials even dreamed of forging Canada East and Canada West, New Brunswick, and Nova Scotia into one great people under a strong central government.[2]

One basic fact tipped the scales the other way. When Great Britain conquered New France in 1763, after a century and a half of skirmishes and seven years of war, there were some sixty-five thousand French-speaking Roman Catholics settled along the banks of the St. Lawrence River and in the Maritimes. With the imperial forces exhausted and overextended, and the Thirteen Colonies to the south already agitating for greater autonomy, the British authorities were in no position to aggravate the vanquished *Canadiens*. Instead, the Quebec Act of 1774 preserved the *ancien régime*'s civil law, tolerated its seigneurial system, restored its western territories, and allowed Roman Catholics to hold public office—fifty-five years before they were granted that same right in Great Britain. Seventeen years later, after more than forty-five thousand refugees had fled north from the American Revolution in order to remain under British law and British institutions, London was pressured into giving the two religious and linguistic communities their own governments. The Constitutional Act of 1791 split the old colony into Lower and Upper Canada, each with its own elected assembly and legal tradition, though a significant proportion of anglophone Protestants chose to settle among the French-speaking Catholics anyway.

For the next half century, French Canadians continued to outnumber the waves of Loyalist immigrants who poured into the two Canadas in search of a better life. They rallied with astonishing vigour to the defence of their homeland against the American invaders during the War of 1812. They remained essential to the economic development of the colony, as fur traders, lumberjacks, farmers, labourers, doctors, lawyers, and businessmen. And they produced a number of remarkably astute politicians, who proved adept at finding strategic and tactical ways to defend their language, their religion, and their culture.

That didn't mean, of course, that all was harmony and fair play. Far from it. The opportunistic carpetbaggers who arrived in Montreal from New York or London following the Conquest, feeling rather superior and entitled for being with the triumphant side, cast a covetous eye on the land and the commercial enterprises of the losers and wondered why to the victor shouldn't go the spoils. In the decades that followed the establishment of Lower Canada in 1791, a series of reactionary governors connived with the English-speaking merchants to keep power out of the hands of the French-speaking majority in the legislative assembly. The economic interests of the British Empire and a new breed of colonial capitalists clashed with those of the *habitant* farmers and the bourgeois professionals. The Protestant prejudice against Roman Catholics was deep and visceral. By 1837, the imperialist push led to a patriotic shove that escalated into a bloody rebellion.

Lord Durham, sent by the British government to report on the situation, found, as he famously put it, "two nations warring in the bosom of a single state," with both sides marked by hatred, animosity, grievances, and fear. His hastily conceived and impractical solution was complete assimilation. "Without effecting the change so rapidly or so roughly as to shock the feelings and trample on the welfare of the existing generation," he concluded, "it must henceforth be the first and steady purpose of the British Government to establish an English population, with English laws and language, in this Province, and to trust its government to none but a decidedly English legislature."[3]

On Durham's advice, Lower and Upper Canada were cobbled back together in 1840 under the Act of Union, with English the only language of government and the seats in the new assembly distributed in equal measure between Canada East and Canada West to keep power out of the hands of the more numerous French Canadians. Nevertheless, Louis-Hippolyte LaFontaine and his colleagues proved effective by acting as a single bloc. They struck ideological alliances across linguistic lines; reversed the ban on French in the assembly, the courts, and the civil service; and gained administrative control over most of the affairs of Canada East.[4] The roots of Canada's tolerance for diversity had been established early on—albeit for practical rather than philosophical reasons—and, once taken hold, proved impossible to extract.

As soon became obvious, the Act of Union was too haphazard, too makeshift, too inherently unstable to last. How could two majorities with competing social and economic interests avoid the inevitable struggle for domination? (Present-day advocates of sovereignty-association take heed.) It became even more dysfunctional after 1850, when the English-speaking population of Canada West began to exceed the French-speaking population of Canada East. Now the cry of "representation by population" went up from the very people who had opposed it, while French Canadians no longer wanted what they had been demanding for decades. The only way to break the deadlock was to once more put some distance between the feuding societies, yet somehow keep them together for practical purposes. The solution was found in the British North America Act, 1867.

Like it or not, because there were two European peoples locked from the start in a wrestlers' embrace of equivalent though different strengths—with the power of population able to hold its own against the power of empire for most of a century—the Fathers of Confederation were never able to achieve the degree of political centralization thought necessary to avoid the horrors of the American Civil War. They had to devise a constitution that accommodated difference, divided power, required negotiation, and balanced the rights of individuals with the rights of groups. Upholding diversity while preserving the nation, recognizing the parts while celebrating the whole, became the bane and the glory of Canada ever afterwards—never more so than during the First Ministers' Conference in November 1981.

"I have always contended," declared John A. Macdonald, the first prime minister, "that if we could agree to have one government and one parliament, legislating for the whole of these peoples, it would be the best, the cheapest, the most vigorous, and the strongest system of government we could adopt. But ... it would not meet the assent of the people of Lower Canada because they felt that in their peculiar position—being in a minority, with a different language, nationality, and religion from the majority—in a case of a junction with the other provinces, their institutions and their laws might be assailed, and their ancestral associations, on which they prided themselves, attacked and prejudiced."[5]

Even if there hadn't been a large French-speaking, Roman Catholic minority, heavily concentrated in the new province of Quebec but also present in significant numbers down east and out west, the vast new dominion probably couldn't have been that much more centralized. "We found, too," Macdonald added, "that though their people speak the same language and enjoy the same system of law as the people of Upper Canada, a system founded on the common law of England, there was as great a disinclination on the part of the various Maritime provinces to lose their individuality, as separate political organizations, as we observed in the case of Lower Canada herself."[6]

The same would be true—arguably even more so—when Manitoba joined the union in 1870, British Columbia in 1871, Prince Edward Island in 1873, Alberta and Saskatchewan in 1905, and Newfoundland in 1949. And so Canada was established as a highly centralized federation, in which the provinces kept control over what had been seen in 1867 as essentially local matters, while the new government in Ottawa was given the areas of general and greater importance, as well as all residual responsibilities and the lion's share of the revenues.[7]

The BNA Act, which set up the new national institutions and laid down the division of powers, quickly became a battleground. Much—too much, many would argue—of Canada's history, politics, and government during the next one hundred years was the saga of federal and provincial politicians trying to capture or retain a strategic height of jurisdiction here, a few yards of taxation there. The dry interpretations of section 92A or section 133 were the stuff of years of parliamentary debates, volumes of royal commissions, reams of bureaucratic analyses, shelves of academic studies, forests of newspaper reports, scores of court cases, and a host of federal–provincial conferences. The centralists pointed to Ottawa's right to veto provincial legislation by disallowance or reservation, to appoint the provincial lieutenant governors, and to spend money in areas of provincial responsibility as evidence of the founders' true intentions. The decentralists countered that disallowance and reservation had fallen into such disuse as to be rendered null and void, that the lieutenant governors had no significance beyond dedicating a new hospital or school with the snip of a ribbon, and that abuse of the federal spending power had violated the spirit of Confederation.[8]

Decade after decade, the push to centralization gave way to the pull of decentralization until the centrifugal forces threatened to undermine the unity or prosperity of the country and there was a reaction in the other direction. So constant was this sport, according to the hoary joke, that when an international conference was convened to talk about elephants, the British discussed elephants and cricket, the Americans discussed elephants and capitalism, the French discussed elephants and love, the Italians discussed elephants and food, the Indians discussed elephants and spirituality, and the Canadians presented a paper entitled "Elephants: A Federal or Provincial Responsibility?"

Just as every prime minister fought to preserve the union, the premiers became the passionate protectors of provincial rights and responsibilities. That was their job, after all, and there was often an advantage to be gained at the ballot box by blaming the federal government for the ills of the day, especially when that government was of a different political party. When Nova Scotia tried to pull out of the federation after only two years, Ottawa bought it off with more cash and a stronger voice at the Cabinet table. Oliver Mowat of Ontario and Honoré Mercier of Quebec emerged within the next two decades as particularly effective advocates of provincial autonomy, wrapping their ambitions inside the theory that Confederation had been a compact made by the provinces—or by two founding peoples—and was therefore unalterable without the consent of their premiers, a theory very much alive in the constitutional battles of 1980–81.[9] What had been relatively secondary provincial responsibilities for education, health, and social welfare in the nineteenth century became large, expensive, and hugely important areas of government activity in the twentieth century. The courts, especially in London, tended to side with the provinces in jurisdictional disputes, and the national parties became increasingly reluctant to pay the political price for using the weapons that Ottawa had been granted to compel the provinces to submit to the greater good. As distracting and exasperating as this squabbling often seemed to the average Canadian, it was rooted within the very nature of federalism, producing tensions that were often creative and affecting the lives of the people in a myriad of ways they never fully realized.

Caught in the crossfire was Canada's last important link to its colonial past: the British North America Act itself. As the country grew in wealth, population, and patriotism, especially after the disproportionate sacrifices it made during the Great War, it strove by itself and in common cause with the other five semi-autonomous British dominions around the world towards full independence.[10] The process was gradual and remarkably free of conflict or controversy—more a backroom bureaucratic exercise than a struggle for national liberation—not least because Great Britain was as eager to be rid of the financial liabilities of running an empire as its former colonies were to assume their rightful place among the nations of the world. The result was a familial "commonwealth," bound by history, tradition, the British parliamentary system, and in most cases, an abiding allegiance to the same constitutional monarch. Step by step, Canada claimed its right to sign treaties and declare war. British laws—with the one all-important exception of the BNA Act—ceased to apply in Canada after the Statute of Westminster in 1931. A distinct Canadian citizenship was established in 1947, and in 1949 the Supreme Court of Canada replaced the London-based Judicial Committee of the Privy Council as the ultimate court of appeal.

Unlike Australia or South Africa, however, Canada was unable to take complete control of its own constitution. Attempts to "patriate" the BNA Act met with failure at federal–provincial conferences in 1927, 1931, 1935, and 1950, primarily because there was no agreement on how it should be amended afterwards.[11] Under the existing rules, Ottawa and the provinces were allowed to propose unilateral changes within their own jurisdictions and to recommend bilateral or even multilateral arrangements with each other. But what about changes to the national institutions and the divisions of power that affect everyone? Should Ottawa and all the provinces have to agree? Or Ottawa and a majority of the provinces representing a majority of the population? Or eight of the provinces? Or 85 percent of the population? Or none of the provinces? Or each of the regions? Or just Quebec? Or should different amendments require different rules?

There was no clear answer. Technically every change to the BNA Act required a resolution from the Parliament of Canada to the Parliament of the United Kingdom, which had the legal right to refuse it or alter it. In its application, the process was confused, paradoxical, and seemingly ad hoc. In 1905, for example, Ottawa created Alberta and Saskatchewan out of the North-West Territories without seeking permission from any of the other provinces. Yet when the federal government took charge of unemployment insurance in 1940 and old age pensions in 1951, it obtained the consent of every province—without admitting that it had to.[12]

A good argument could have been made to leave the British North America Act alone. It was a tar baby, a can of worms, an irrelevant distraction from the meat-and-potato concerns of ordinary Canadians, who tended to regard their constitution not as a sacred text handed down from their ancestors but as a ready excuse for their politicians to ice the puck and bicker among themselves. Of course, it was a humiliation for a proud and successful nation to have to go cap in hand to the legislators of another country to ask for a change in its constitution, but hadn't Canada muddled along well enough with the status quo? The twenty-two amendments made between 1867 and 1964 somehow got through, and the BNA Act was surely no more anachronistic than the hereditary monarch of an overseas throne presiding over a modern North American democracy.

Nobody ever made that argument with greater lucidity or conviction than Pierre Elliott Trudeau, an iconoclastic Quebec intellectual who had personally witnessed the collapse of the federal–provincial negotiations in 1950, during his brief time as a junior civil servant in Ottawa. "As a professor," he once observed, "I was also being paid to know what enormous amounts of bile and wasted time constitutional conferences had produced since 1927, when Mackenzie King had first called the provinces together to look for a way of repatriating the Canadian Constitution from England, only to discover how impossible it was to get all of them to agree on a constitutional amending formula."[13]

THREE

Time for a Change

In the first week of November 1981, that same Pierre Elliott Trudeau, now prime minister of Canada, presided over the eleventh first ministers' summit on the constitution, trying once again to wrest an agreement on patriation and an amending formula from the ten provincial premiers. It was, as it always had been, a negotiation among politicians—all men, all white, all Christians—over legal and governmental issues of little interest and even less comprehension to the people they served. According to Ottawa's own polls, hardly 5 percent of Canadians put constitutional reform at the top of their list of priorities at a time when the country was going through the worst recession since the 1930s. Following the shock of two spikes in world oil prices, the jolt to the North American economy, the shakiness of the stock market, and the collapse of real-estate prices, unemployment in Canada was running above 8 percent, inflation was over 12 percent, and interest rates were approaching 20 percent. The last thing on the minds of those who were afraid of losing their jobs and their homes was the British North America Act.

Why, then, did Pierre Trudeau turn away from his earlier cynicism, not to mention the anger and impatience of voters, to devote so much of his time and effort to what many considered his obsession, magnificent or otherwise? ("He's not obsessed," said one of his advisers, "he's monomaniacal."[1]) The answer is to be found in the arguments that took place during a dramatic twenty-four hours, from the morning of November 4 to the morning of November 5, 1981, when the first ministers excused themselves from the day-to-day management of their governments to struggle over the fundamental questions of Canada, its founding principles, its values, its institutions, its ideals, and its very survival.

"Did Canadian sovereignty emanate from a people with a collective will to live as a nation, seeking a common good throughout the country and governing themselves under a federative form of constitution?" Trudeau asked, defining the central debate. "Or was it the creature of ten provinces (some would say two nations), dependent on them for its existence and governed by the consensus of its eleven governments—ten provincial and one federal? These two points of view hardened, crystallized and clashed throughout the series of constitutional conferences that began with the interprovincial meeting of 1967 and ended with the federal–provincial conference of November 1981."[2]

If the November conference was the last act, the curtain had risen in the early years of the 1960s, when Quebec emerged suddenly and irreversibly from *la grande noirceur*, the Great Darkness, as though propelled out of the Middle Ages and into its own Renaissance. Its five million French-speaking citizens, who made up more than 80 percent of Canada's francophone population, opened their eyes, looked around, and were infuriated by what they saw. From their proud status as the first European civilization in this corner of the continent and the co-authors of Confederation, they had slipped to an inferior position, both politically and economically.

Ever since 1867, English-speaking Protestants had been flexing the muscle of their new majority. Macdonald's Conservative Party soon sought to retain power by catering to the anti-Catholic, anti-French jingoists in the anglophone provinces, while at the same time relying on Rome's horror of liberalism to prevent Quebec from turning *rouge*. In 1871, New Brunswick abolished its separate Roman Catholic schools. In 1885, the federal government hanged Louis Riel, the mystic rebel who had become a folk hero among French Canadians by fighting for their schools and language rights in Manitoba and the North-West Territories. In 1890, Manitoba tore up the conditions by which it had joined the federation twenty years earlier, dropping the official use of French in its legislature and courts and removing equal funding for its predominantly French-speaking Roman Catholic schools. Two years later, French was demoted from being an official language in the North-West Territories as well. Wilfrid Laurier, a Liberal and the first French-Canadian prime minister, felt he had no political choice but to bend to the anti-Catholic legislation in the anglophone provinces. In 1912, Ontario enacted Regulation 17, a draconian measure to limit the teaching and use of French in the province's elementary schools. In 1917, Prime Minister Robert Borden decided to impose compulsory military service that would force French Canadians against their will to fight for the Empire in the killing fields of Europe. When Prime Minister Mackenzie King introduced conscription again during the Second World War, he did so despite the wishes of the overwhelming majority of French-speaking Quebecers, who had voted against the proposition in a national plebiscite in 1942.

No matter which party was in office, Ottawa retained all the trappings of a sub-Arctic Raj. The Crown's representative until 1952 was a British grandee who held court at Rideau Hall, and the first Canadian-born governor general was a millionaire anglophile so refined in manners and dress that he was said to have made a peer of the realm feel like a savage. The working language of the Cabinet and the senior civil service was English. The key economic portfolios were reserved for English-Canadian ministers. Government services, right down to pension cheques and postage stamps, were often in English only. Everything from the currency to the courtrooms to the corner mailbox was sanctified by a royal photograph, a royal coat of arms, or the Union Jack. The mint, the navy, and the mounted police were not just Canadian but *Royal* Canadian.

Even within the province of Quebec, English was the dominant language of commerce, industry, and high society. French-speaking Quebecers earned two-thirds the average income of English-speaking Quebecers. Francophones were rarely allowed to ascend to the management of major corporations or above the level of labourer in a factory. Four-fifths of the adult population hadn't gone beyond elementary school, and half of all Quebec youngsters dropped out of school before the age of fifteen. Unemployment was 2 percent higher than the national average. The destitute immigrants who had escaped the pogroms of Eastern Europe and Russia were soon better off than the old-stock Quebecers, who ranked twelfth in a list of fourteen ethnic groups in the province in terms of income.[3] In 1958, the largest hotel in Quebec, built in the centre of the second-largest French-speaking city in the world, was named in honour of Queen Elizabeth II. Four years later, the president of the Canadian National Railway, a publicly owned corporation headquartered in Montreal, declared that he couldn't find a single French Canadian qualified to be one of his seventeen vice-presidents.

"In the matter of education, as well as political rights, the safeguards so dear to French Canadians were nearly always disregarded throughout the country, so that they came to believe themselves secure only in Quebec," Pierre Trudeau observed. "Worse still, in those areas not specifically covered by the constitution, the English-speaking majority used its size and wealth to impose a set of social rules humiliating to French Canadians. In the federal civil service, for example, and even more so in the Canadian armed forces, a French Canadian started off with an enormous handicap—if indeed he managed to start at all. This was true also in finance, business, and at all levels of industry. And that is how English became the working language, even in Quebec, and at all levels from foreman to bank president."[4]

True, but as Trudeau was among the first to recognize, this wasn't exclusively the fault of the Empire-besotted Anglo minority, who seldom bothered to learn the language of the workers, the farmers, and the servant class. The Roman Catholic Church preferred to keep its parishioners poor, ignorant, obedient, and doing purgatory in the stony hinterlands, rather than exposing them to the Satanic materialism of modern, free-thinking Protestants in the cities. From 1936 to 1939, and again from 1944 until his death in 1959, Premier Maurice Duplessis presided over a corrupt and authoritarian regime like a tinpot Franco, bestowing contracts and favours on his supporters, suppressing his liberal opponents with threats and punishments, selling off the province's resources to foreign capitalists for a song, and striking a tacit understanding with the English-speaking corporate bosses to keep down wages and the unions in exchange for investments in the province and donations to his party.

Whatever the cause of the political and economic inequalities, there dwelled in the heart and soul of many French Canadians a deep sense of cultural insecurity and social inferiority. They shared both an atavistic fear that their language was drowning in the sea of English-speaking North Americans and stinging memories of discrimination at the hands of *les maudits Anglais*. But beneath the cliché of a placid, peasant people, there was a seismic shift taking place as francophone Quebecers moved by the hundreds of thousands into the cities and factory towns—or emigrated to Ontario or the United States—in search of work. Just as Duplessis and the priests had feared, the foundations of the old order were being undermined by the individual freedom of urban life. The expanded world of cars and films, the outside influences of radio and television, the technical training and consumer advertising of the branch-plant economy—all fed the growing desire to partake of the wealth, goods, and opportunities of other North Americans.

The inevitable quake occurred in 1960, when there came to power in the province a new generation of urban professionals, social activists, and union leaders determined to yank their conservative and relatively impoverished society into the twentieth century. The Quebec Liberal Party under Jean Lesage launched its "Quiet Revolution," from which there was no turning back. The means was an activist, interventionist state. The provincial government took over schools, hospitals, and welfare services from the Roman Catholic Church, which Quebecers proceeded to desert almost overnight. It bought eleven hydroelectric companies and merged them into the behemoth known as Hydro Quebec. It financed small business through a state-owned corporation and created a pension fund that grew into one of the largest pools of investment capital in Canada. It established a public steel company and a public mining company. It educated young Quebecers in commerce, engineering, and science, not just in the traditional professions of medicine, law, and teaching. It reformed the public service and gave public servants the right to strike. It built new highways, new dams, new colleges. It tried to strut on the international stage. And it demanded patriation of the constitution and an entrenched charter of rights.[5]

Consequently, to a degree never before seen in Canada, the ambitions of a provincial government bumped up hard against the programs and revenues of the federal government. Whereas Duplessis had been largely satisfied with defending his province's autonomy against the incursions of Ottawa, Lesage laid claim to large chunks of federal jurisdiction (not to mention the cash to pay for them). "It's time for a change," his election cry in 1960, became the old nationalist slogan "Masters in our own house" in 1962, and demands for a "special status" within the federation grew louder with each passing year.[6]

As fate would have it, Ottawa was particularly ill prepared to deal with the sudden release of suppressed dissent and energetic self-confidence in Quebec. The Progressive Conservative government from 1957 to 1963 was led by a Saskatchewan populist, John Diefenbaker, who mangled the French language and worshipped with a fervent devotion all things British—the parliamentary tradition, Winston Churchill, the Royal Family, the Commonwealth, the Union Jack—despite or because of his own half-German background. Diefenbaker's victory in 1957, when he managed to form a minority government in Ottawa with only eight of the province's seventy-five seats, sent a shockwave through francophone Quebec. His few French-speaking Cabinet ministers were notoriously incompetent, and he had no Quebec advisers with any skill or clout. He did little to redress the legitimate grievances of French Canadians, beyond appointing Georges Vanier as governor general, introducing simultaneous translation in the House of Commons, and setting his justice minister to work on patriation and an amending formula. In 1958, the Tories managed to elect fifty MPs in Quebec by arranging with Duplessis's bosses in the agricultural constituencies and small towns of the province a marriage of convenience based on their mutual hatred of Liberals. But by 1963, they had lost all that they had gained.

The federal Liberals, who subsequently tottered between confusion and crisis on the shaky base of two minority wins, made a more concerted effort. Their leader, Lester Pearson, was a former diplomat who had won the Nobel Peace Prize, after all, and he could hardly ignore the aggressive defiance of the Lesage government, the first serious talk of Quebec independence, the riots in the streets of Quebec City to protest a royal visit from Her Majesty, and a series of terrorist bombings in downtown Montreal. In short order, Pearson replaced the Union Jack with the Maple Leaf as the official flag of Canada and "God Save the Queen" with "O Canada" as the national anthem. He removed the royal coat of arms from mailboxes and federal buildings, and appointed a record number of French-Canadian Cabinet ministers and senior civil servants. He allowed Quebec to opt out of more than two dozen federal–provincial programs, trebled its share of income-tax revenues, and permitted it to establish its own pension plan apart from the national one. Not least, in July 1963, he established the Royal Commission on Bilingualism and Biculturalism, a groundbreaking public inquiry that found Canada to be "passing through the greatest crisis in its history."[7]

"Confederation may not have been technically a treaty or a compact between states," Pearson declared in a major address to the House of Commons on December 17, 1962, "but it was an understanding or a settlement between the two founding races of Canada made on the basis of an acceptable and equal partnership. That settlement provided that national political unity would be achieved and maintained without the imposition of racial, cultural or linguistic uniformity."[8]

For all his goodwill and sincere efforts, Pearson was like Canute confronted by the rising tide of Quebec's demands. In October 1964, he succeeded in initialling an agreement with all ten premiers to bring the British North America Act from London by accepting an amending formula that required unanimous approval on matters affecting the rights and powers of the provincial legislatures. For the first time since 1867, the federal government affirmed the provinces' legal right to have a say in changing the constitution. Not only did Pearson hope to satisfy the patriotic stirrings of Canadians and Quebecers alike, but he also wanted to demonstrate his willingness to negotiate a more up-to-date, more decentralized, more cooperative federalism, in which different provinces might even have different powers. However, the deal fell apart in January 1966 when Premier Lesage changed his mind, having been denounced back home as a traitor by those who believed that unanimity would prevent Quebec from ever getting the responsibilities and revenues it now sought.

When Lesage was defeated later that year by Daniel Johnson, who had inherited Duplessis's Union Nationale, the Liberals' *"maîtres chez nous"* was ratcheted up to *"egalité ou indépendance."* Lesage had wanted Quebec's share of personal and corporate income taxes to soar to 25 percent and its share of succession duties to double to 100 percent; Johnson demanded all of everything. Meanwhile, the idea of independence grew from the delusion of a few hotheaded pamphleteers and cranks to a mainstream crusade. In 1967, no less a world statesman than Charles de Gaulle, the president of France, gave it his blessing by shouting *"Vive le Québec libre!"* from the balcony of Montreal's city hall to an astonished and then delirious crowd. And independence, packaged for marketing reasons as "sovereignty" and sweetened with the promise of an ongoing economic association with the remnant of Canada, became the primary goal of a new political movement that quickly morphed into the Parti Québécois, an alliance of hard-core separatists and soft-core autonomists led by a popular, credible former minister in the Lesage government, René Lévesque.

Though Pierre Trudeau spent the 1950s as an academic opposing Ottawa's intrusions into provincial jurisdiction as a breach of Confederation, he now became alarmed by its concessions to what he saw as Quebec's insatiable demands—whether Pearson was motivated by a sense of justice or a sense of guilt didn't matter. Trudeau believed not only that the federal government's ability to manage the economy in the national interest was in jeopardy, but also that a tacit recognition of a privileged position for the province was the slippery slope to separation. Quebec didn't need any special status, he argued. As the Quiet Revolution was demonstrating, the province already had what it needed to build a prosperous, well-educated, culturally dynamic society.

"The present fad for constitutional change is keeping most politicians and opinion-makers busy, especially those whose knowledge of the constitution borders closest on ignorance," Trudeau wrote in 1964. "In the meantime, remarkably little is done to remedy the real disorders which plague the Canadian people, even though most of them could be righted under the present constitution."[9]

FOUR

The School
of Blackmail

By the time Pierre Trudeau entered federal politics in 1965, he could no
longer discount the pressure for constitutional change coming out of
Quebec. Traditional conservatives, secular liberals, and Marxist intellectuals alike were generally of one mind that Ottawa was an English-
speaking town under the control of the English-Canadian majority,
that the government of Quebec needed more control over fiscal and
legislative levers for the survival and advancement of the province's
French-speaking majority, and that Canada should finally cut its legal
and sentimental ties to the United Kingdom and her queen. In 1967, as
Pearson's minister of justice, Trudeau was instructed to embark on a
new round of constitutional reform, and he took the file with him when
he became prime minister a year later.

After six conferences and three years of negotiations at the political
and bureaucratic levels, Trudeau managed to get even closer to success
than Pearson had. In June 1971, all eleven first ministers, including the

new Liberal premier of Quebec, Robert Bourassa, reached a tentative agreement in Victoria on a deal that included, among other items, patriation, an amending formula, a bill of rights, and entrenched protection for the French language. Almost as soon as Premier Bourassa returned to Quebec, however, he buckled under the criticism that he hadn't come back with enough new power over social programs. He revoked his support, just as Jean Lesage had done, and the Victoria Charter collapsed.

"I felt the vise closing in on Quebec," Bourassa explained. "On the one hand we wanted to stay in the federal system; we wanted to profit from it. But on the other hand, we wanted to keep our pride, to assert ourselves, to have the maximum powers. The Quebec government is always caught between the two."[1]

"Okay," Trudeau said to himself after receiving the bad news over the phone, "we're going to put the worms back in the can and we're not going to open it again for a bloody long time."[2]

Yet as the strength of the *indépendantiste* forces mounted, he re-engaged in constitutional talks in 1975 and 1976. Again Bourassa pulled away, afraid that any agreement with Ottawa would weaken his chances of beating the Parti Québécois in the upcoming provincial election. He even encouraged Trudeau to propose something so that the provincial Liberals could look tough by shooting it down. And in an attempt to outflank the PQ on its own turf, he campaigned against a threat Trudeau had made in March 1976 to patriate the constitution unilaterally if the provinces wouldn't agree. Bourassa lost the election anyway on November 15, 1976.

René Lévesque was carried into office by a promise of good government and the public's desire for a change, but also bearing a commitment to put the question of sovereignty to the people of Quebec in a referendum to be held within his first term as premier. "We are going to show them that we are ready to play the game as long as Quebec's needs are respected," Lévesque said, referring to the federal government, "but we will constantly be reminding them that our ultimate goal is Quebec's independence."[3] So Trudeau was forced to focus on the constitutional issues once more, all the while knowing that he was even less likely to reach a deal with a separatist government.

"What made the negotiations seem all the more futile," he later observed, "was that the election of Lévesque was grist to the mill of the other provincial premiers. They obviously didn't like separatism, but they were only too happy to use Lévesque as a foil to try to get more for themselves."[4]

Though the quarrel over patriation and the amending formula had always been a power struggle between federal and provincial politicians, that now became increasingly and more transparently the case. The BNA Act proved a Pandora's box. Once opened, out flew a cacophony of demands, and until those ransoms were paid, Canada's constitutional coming-of-age was held hostage. Nothing was going to happen until the provinces got what they wanted. "Because if we are really serious in talking about renewal," Lévesque argued, "it is not that symbolic old paper that counts above all—it could even be left over there—it is the new contract that we are supposed to be negotiating."[5]

One by one, then all together, the other premiers saw the leverage to be gained by withholding their signatures. As Trudeau put it, "They had enrolled in the school of blackmail of which Quebec was the founder and top-ranking graduate."[6] Thus the feuding between the anglophone majority and the francophone minority was absorbed into the feuding between the federal government and the provincial legislatures, between the central provinces and the regions, between the energy-producing provinces and the energy-consuming provinces, between the haves and the have-nots.

On October 14, 1976, Peter Lougheed of Alberta, in his role as that year's chair of the Annual Premiers' Conference, wrote the prime minister of their unanimous agreement "that patriation should not be undertaken without a consensus being developed on an expansion of the role of the provinces and/or jurisdiction in the following areas: culture, communications, Supreme Court of Canada, spending power, Senate representation and regional disparities."[7]

The list was long and ever-changing. Alberta and Saskatchewan wanted more control over the development and regulation of their natural resources. Newfoundland and Nova Scotia wanted ownership of offshore resources and joint control of the fisheries. New Brunswick and Prince Edward Island wanted equalization payments to raise their government services to the level offered by wealthier provinces. British Columbia wanted to give each of the five regions equal representation in a more powerful Senate. Quebec, alone or in concert with others, wanted control over family law and immigration, provincial access to indirect taxation, the abolition of the federal authority to disallow or reserve provincial legislation, and the right to self-determination.[8]

At the First Ministers' Conferences in October 1978 and February 1979, Ottawa volunteered to hand over seven major items on the provinces' "shopping list," including a number of federal powers. "I've almost given away the store," Trudeau declared. But the premiers only came back for more. Certainly they had no incentive to reach an agreement with Trudeau when the odds were that he would lose the upcoming election—not least because voters thought him more attentive to the intricacies of the BNA Act than to the dismal unemployment statistics. Better to wait for a Progressive Conservative government, most of the English-speaking premiers calculated—one with a higher regard for provincial rights, a more decentralist view of the federation, and, in Joe Clark, a weaker leader. Meanwhile, Lévesque didn't want to commit to anything until after his promised referendum, which he kept postponing with the expectation that Trudeau's defeat would better his own chances of victory.

But the Canadian people, especially those in the swing ridings of Ontario, proved fickle. They did indeed throw Trudeau out of office in May 1979 for fiddling with the constitution and quarrelling with the provinces while the economy lurched from crisis to crisis, but they re-elected him in February 1980. Though energy prices and recessionary woes were the deciding issues of the election, most Canadians—including a vast majority of Quebecers—punished Clark for his inability to articulate a convincing national vision and his failure to rein in the demands of the premiers any better than Trudeau had.

On May 20, 1980, just three months after the federal Liberals' surprising resurrection, the Lévesque government finally held its historic referendum—but not, as it turned out, on independence, which, according to the PQ's own polls, would never garner more than 30 percent of the vote. Instead, the question posed in its place was carefully crafted, right down to the semicolons, to lure the moderates and discontents into the Yes camp: "The Government of Quebec has made public its proposal to negotiate a new agreement with the rest of Canada, based on the equality of nations; this agreement would enable Quebec to acquire the exclusive power to make its laws, levy its taxes and establish relations abroad—in other words, sovereignty—and at the same time to maintain with Canada an economic association including a common currency; any change in political status resulting from these negotiations will only be implemented with popular approval through another referendum; on these terms, do you give the Government of Quebec the mandate to negotiate the proposed agreement between Quebec and Canada?"[9]

The thirty-five-day battle for the hearts and minds of Quebecers was tense, brutal, and highly divisive. It tore apart families, wrecked friendships, stoked fear and fury, and spread anxiety across the country. The Yes side started out better organized and better focused, and it made better use of the three-week debate in the National Assembly that preceded the official campaign. The No side was weakened by a jockeying for control between the Ottawa Liberals and the Quebec City Liberals, who were now led by Claude Ryan, a dry-as-a-stick, ponderous, persnickety former editor of *Le Devoir* who bore no love for Pierre Trudeau as a person or for Trudeau's one-nation, one-people vision of Canada. There were strategic disagreements between those who wanted to emphasize the negative consequences of independence and those who wanted to offer Quebec more powers or a special status within the federation. At a key moment, to help clinch victory and summon the English-Canadian premiers to action, Trudeau vowed that a vote for Canada was not a vote for the status quo—the import of which politicians, journalists, and historians have debated ever since (though it caused no significant shift in the opinion polls one way or the other).

"I know that I can make a most solemn commitment," he told a rally in Montreal on May 14, in the last of his four major interventions, "that following a No vote, we will immediately take action to renew the constitution, and we will not stop until we have done that."[10]

When the federalists won with a decisive 60 percent, including more than half the francophone voters, Pierre Trudeau moved rapidly to act on his commitment. After ten attempts by five prime ministers in more than fifty years, including four major initiatives in the past decade, he was determined not to fail. "This time we're going to do it," he vowed.[11] He had to prove to Quebecers that Canada could change. He had to show Canadians that their system of government still functioned well. He had to finish the job, begun in 1867, of building an independent nation. What, he thought, could be more reasonable or necessary? Which other member of the United Nations, the Group of Seven industrialized powers, or the NATO military alliance would have left its highest law in the hands of a foreign power for more than a hundred years, simply because its provinces, states, cantons, or *départements* had refused to allow the national government to correct the absurdity?

"I was convinced that once the debate began, it had to be carried to a conclusion," Trudeau declared. "Canada was the only country in the world not in control of its constitution."[12]

PART 1
Wednesday Morning November 4, 1981

FIVE

The Players

The Centennial Room on the fifth floor of the Government Conference Centre in Ottawa could have been a set for *Twelve Angry Men*. The wood-panelled former courtroom atop the beaux arts extravaganza that was once the capital's grand railway station had been redecorated during a particularly unfortunate period of modern interior design when government-issue Scandinavian met garish seventies. Heavy dark-orange drapes were drawn across the four tall windows, a ring of spotlights beamed from the twenty-foot ceiling, and eleven flags hung limply on ceremonial poles at the back of the room. No art or photographs adorned the walls, just large squares of white stucco in frames of beige so bland it hardly qualified as a distinct colour. The leading men strolled into the room, as though onto a stage, and took their places around the table, which was in fact a dozen sectional desks assembled to form a jagged horseshoe.

The room smelled of the disinfectant and polish used by the overnight cleaning staff, the freshly photocopied documents set at each place beside silver trays of water jugs and glasses, cups of steaming coffee, and the first cigarettes of the day. The prime minister of Canada, nine of the ten provincial premiers, and a dozen of their ministers, all bobbing and swivelling on their burgundy bucket chairs, were like jury members who had been forced together far too long. The air was charged with testosterone, adrenaline, not enough sleep, and a growing impatience to be done. Just one more day, everybody was saying, and then, one way or another, it will be over.

To encourage frank, confidential discussion, only the political actors and their most senior advisers were allowed to enter the inner sanctum.[1] While close to one thousand officials, journalists, and staff were cooling their heels in the colossal Main Hall down on the first floor or in the delegation offices scattered throughout the building, left to starve for a morsel of rumour or news, a few dozen observers sat in a back row of upholstered frame chairs, chattering among themselves with the anticipatory murmur of an audience excited to have snagged a premium seat at the hottest show in town. They had been watching this real-life, high-stakes play unfold in public and behind closed doors for two days now. Many had been spectators and participants for more than a decade. They hushed the moment Pierre Trudeau brought the meeting to order, shortly before 10:00 a.m., on Wednesday, November 4, 1981.

Though each of the first ministers was a face on television, a name in the news, somebody to be reckoned with back home, Trudeau was unquestionably the superstar. A legend from coast to coast, even among those who loathed him. A celebrity abroad, if only because his wife's adulteries were the stuff of gossip magazines around the world. What he looked like, what he said, the red rose and Remembrance Day poppy he wore on the lapel of his elegant raw-silk jacket were noted by even the most jaded official, a tidbit on which to dine that weekend with family and friends, charisma by association. He was also the most intriguing man at the table—multifaceted, contradictory, unpredictable, inscrutable, perfectly bilingual, and widely travelled. Alternately charming and withdrawn, passionate and icy, scholarly and athletic, magnanimous

The first ministers and their senior advisers in the Centennial Room.

and petty, combining the rigid discipline of a Catholic intellectual with the sybaritic immaturity of a Don Juan.

There was always a bit of the ham in Pierre Trudeau. He had written and acted in plays as a young man, mounted elaborate pranks to shock the bourgeois, studied elocution and dance to refine his public style, and honed the classical arts of rhetoric and argumentation. To the end of his life, he loved reciting long passages of poetry, not least the famous Alexandrine soliloquies of Rostand's proud, belligerent, and eloquent hero, Cyrano de Bergerac. When invited by his television biographers to watch footage of himself as a neophyte politician, he said he saw a person who "was no longer me" but "somebody else, that I was acting, with my own lines."[2] Indeed, much of his success as a politician came from his skills as a performer. He spent hours memorizing important speeches to make them appear improvised, presenting them without any notes or a moment's hesitation. He delivered the best of them with dramatic pacing, oratorical tricks, and the talent of a professional thespian. He played to the cameras with a perfectly executed high dive into a swimming pool or a mischievous pirouette behind the back of the Queen. Though that pixie-like twirl wasn't premeditated, as some accounts had it, Trudeau intuitively anticipated the reaction, just as he understood the effect of wearing a flowing black cape to a football game or keeping his cool in the midst of an angry, bottle-throwing mob of demonstrators.[3]

Trudeau's self-conscious theatricality made him a formidable negotiator, though not a great conciliator. Often passive and indecipherable, as though awaiting his cue, he would suddenly explode in a fit of pique or break the tension with a witty remark. At times, when he dismissed a proposal out of hand or floated a trial balloon, even his own advisers weren't sure whether he was faking or following the detailed script included in his thick briefing book. The result was to keep everyone else off balance, on guard, while he maintained his aura of control and command right to the final curtain. Did he want the conference to succeed or fail? Was he ready to make a deal, and if so, on what terms? Or was he, in his dark and devious mind, preparing to precipitate a constitutional crisis the likes of which had never been seen in Canada? Nobody knew for sure.

Trudeau's mystery and charisma were enough to command attention that dull, chilly Wednesday morning. But of more relevance was his power. Few democratically elected heads of government anywhere have as much concentrated power as a prime minister with a parliamentary majority. As long as the Cabinet, the caucus, the courts, and the treasury are onside, there's little to keep a determined prime minister from getting what he wants—at least until the public gets what it wants at the next election.

Pierre Trudeau had been drawn into public life by mighty principles and the desire to do great things. Lesser politicians could content themselves with the housekeeping chores of government and the vanities of office; he had bigger fish to fry. "If we're just here to administer, what the hell are we wasting the best years of our lives for? Let Tories rule," he once told his caucus. "But we're here to try to give direction to the country."[4] But only now did he seem to understand his authority and how to wield it. In his first term, from 1968 to 1972, he dissipated the positive energy that had swept him into the highest office by allowing himself and his government to become bogged down in bureaucratic reorganization, policy papers, and crisis management. In his second term, which lasted only eighteen months, he was forced to submit to the restraints and alliances of governing with less than half the seats in the House of Commons. His third term, which dragged listlessly towards the humiliating defeat in May 1979, was beset by economic stagnation, the election of the Parti Québécois, and the collapse of his marriage. Though determined to never apologize, never regret, Trudeau took note of the refrains of disappointment and unfulfilled promise that had run through the political obituaries following his resignation as party leader on November 21, 1979. Yes, he had passed a few pieces of significant legislation and survived a decade in which television scrutiny, investigative journalism, dashed expectations, and public cynicism chewed up and spat out political leaders everywhere, but what had he really accomplished with his formidable intelligence and his three victories?

Having changed his mind about retirement following the sudden defeat of the Progressive Conservatives' accident-prone minority government in December 1979, Trudeau emerged from his close call with political death revitalized and transformed, leading the Liberal Party back to office in February 1980. He was aware that this was likely to be his final opportunity before he retired for good to look after his three young sons, and so he was full of resolve to make better use of his remaining time in office. If that gave him a sense of urgency, it also gave him a sense of freedom. At last he could do what he thought had to be done without being preoccupied with his own re-election.

Disparate and extraordinary circumstances converged to push him on towards a bolder, more strategic course of action. At sixty, but with the physical and mental strength of a much younger man, he had the experience of fifteen years as a member of Parliament, thirteen years as a Cabinet minister, and over ten years as a head of government. He had a cabal of veteran ministers, devoted staffers, and smart bureaucrats whom he trusted and respected. And most members of the Liberal Cabinet and caucus shared his feisty mood and felt emboldened to find themselves back in office so unexpectedly.

"This time I took quite a different approach to government," Trudeau recalled. "I told my staff to cut down on the amount of paperwork I had to handle, to give me fewer letters to sign, and to make their memos and briefing notes to me a little bit shorter. I decided to focus on just a few crucial issues—particularly the Quebec referendum, the energy issue, the economy, and the constitution. Above all I decided to take gambles that perhaps we would not have taken several years earlier, to achieve the results we wanted."[5]

No gamble was greater than his decision to tackle the constitution one last time—with the consent of the provinces, he hoped, but if that proved impossible, alone. As well as anyone, he understood the stress such a move would place on the political fabric of the nation and the risks for his party's prospects. On the other hand, he felt he had a just and noble cause. Canada had escaped its own political death with the referendum in Quebec. The centrifugal thrust of the provinces, made strong by the fiscal and legislative devolution that had taken place since the 1960s, was threatening the ability of the federal government to regulate the economy and establish national standards.[6] Canada had become the most decentralized federation in the world. Ottawa's share of the national revenues dropped from 67 percent in 1955 to 50 percent in 1969 to 43 percent in 1979. Province after province was busy erecting an array of protectionist barriers to the free flow of labour and goods, higher in some cases than those that existed in the European Union. Yet the premiers kept demanding more without offering anything in return. Moreover, Joe Clark's failure to achieve federal–provincial harmony through appeasement and soft words, despite the fact that most of the premiers were fellow Tories, had demonstrated to Trudeau's satisfaction that the root of the problem wasn't his personality or his politics—the federation was out of whack. Now was time to fight back to restore the proper balance.[7]

"What has been described as we look around the country?" Trudeau asked during an extraordinary two-and-a-half-hour address to his fellow parliamentarians. "We see alienation in Quebec, the West, and the Maritimes. It seems to me that makes it clear that the course of our national development cannot be left in limbo. After the Quebec referendum we on this side, at any rate, have promises to keep to change the constitution so that we can move out of the status quo. We intend to keep those promises. Even if we did not have any more time, lest the forces of self-interest tear us apart, we must now define the common thread which holds us all together."[8]

On Monday, June 9, 1980, less than three weeks after the Quebec referendum, the prime minister invited the ten premiers to meet with him in private at 24 Sussex Drive, his official residence in Ottawa. There, he handed them a list of twelve items that were to be examined by working committees of ministers and officials over the summer and brought back to a first ministers' summit in September.[9] Ten of the twelve belonged to the familiar grab bag of jurisdictional powers and institutional reforms: patriation and a bill of rights for Ottawa versus resource ownership, offshore resources, fisheries, family law, communications, reform of the Senate, appointments to the Supreme Court, and the principle of equalization payments for the provinces. But two items came as a surprise. This time, before giving away anything, Trudeau wanted a stronger economic union and a preamble of fundamental principles written into the constitution. If the provinces craved more autonomy, Trudeau was prepared to negotiate, but only if in return Ottawa obtained greater regulation over trade and commerce; a more open common market for goods, services, and capital; and most important, the free mobility of citizens to live and work in any part of the country.[10]

Startled and displeased by the federal government's new aggressiveness, as much as by its new demands, most of the premiers wanted the negotiations simply to pick up from where they had last left off. "Of course they did," Trudeau recalled, "because that was the agenda with the jurisdictional concessions I had offered them in 1978, when I said I had almost 'given away the store.' But they had turned down those proposals, we were back with our big majority, and it was a different world. 'That was then and this is now,' I told them."[11]

In advance of the meeting, Trudeau had been advised by André Burelle, his French-language speechwriter, to treat the premiers as statesmen rather than petty provincial politicians and let them rise to the historic challenge ahead. "I didn't see a lot of statesmen in there," he snapped at Burelle on the way out. "They were behaving as if Lévesque, and not the federalist camp, had won the referendum."[12]

The meeting in June 1980 had set the tone and the pace for the threats and ultimatums that led to this make-or-break conference in November 1981, when eight of Canada's ten premiers arrived vowing to break Trudeau's will. They didn't see themselves as provincial satraps journeying to the capital to render homage to the grand potentate in exchange for favours and rank. Some of them presided over territories and economies that were larger than those of many members of the United Nations. At least one of them nursed the dream of becoming the first president of an independent republic. Most of them believed themselves to be, by law or custom, if not fully the equals of the prime minister of Canada, then at least partners in the governing of the country, sovereign within their own watertight compartments and subservient only to their own legislatures. Not a few of them despised Pierre Trudeau with an intensity brought on by years of perceived slights, deliberate insults, wounded feelings, partisan disagreements, conflicting interests, mutual contempt, and personal rivalry. They were never going to hand him what he wanted, if only out of spite.

Trudeau shrugged his famous shrug. "My answer is there had been a hell of a lot of nice guys since 1926," he later said, "and the constitution was never patriated. Maybe it took a nasty guy."[13]

The first day of the conference, Monday, was relatively civil. The first ministers were on their best behaviour during the morning session, no doubt because it was being televised live to two million Canadians from the Main Hall downstairs. The prime minister and the premiers made opening statements, each man forcefully recapping his position yet appearing amenable to negotiation. Ottawa, Ontario, and New Brunswick won the day by putting forth a couple of concrete concessions. The others appeared somewhat churlish when they refused Trudeau's invitation to have lunch with him, preferring to use the time to talk among themselves and prepare for the private meeting on the fifth floor.[14] When all eleven reconvened after two-thirty, both sides staked their ground, probed for weaknesses, watched for signals, and tried to smoke the other out. No one was ready to make a deal, and there were several sharp exchanges before the end of the afternoon.

On Tuesday, the old rudeness and rancour returned. The arguments became more heated and personal. Ad hominem barbs were thrown across the table. At one point, Trudeau, exasperated, stormed out. After lunch, instead of returning to the Centennial Room, the eight dissident premiers remained huddled in a suite at the Château Laurier, directly across the street from the conference centre, plotting their next move. When it came in the form of a delegation of three premiers presenting Trudeau with what he considered a poor excuse for a settlement, he berated them for playing into the hands of the Quebec separatists. Thus, after two days, the talks were at an impasse.

There was resignation in the prime minister's flat, controlled delivery on Wednesday morning, but also hints of anger and impatience, as if this was exactly what he had expected from a bunch of small-minded, self-interested provincial politicians: nothing much. Trudeau's eyes moved from one premier to another with the stern, judgmental look of the

constitutional law professor he once was. It was as if he were admonishing his seminar students for their unsatisfactory work and sloppy
attitude, cautioning them to pull up their socks or else. "We intend
putting our final position on the table before the coffee break," he said
at the start of the session. "I consider this as one final attempt. I can't be
party to a waiting game."[15]

To Trudeau's left, fidgety and furious, René Lévesque dragged
nervously on a cigarette. How could Lévesque, as the leader of a political
party dedicated to pulling Quebec out of Canada, ever agree to renew
the federation? Signing a deal with Ottawa would undercut his party's
raison d'être and refute its favourite argument that the country could
never be made to work.

Nor did Trudeau place much hope in the two bullheaded premiers
from the West, Peter Lougheed of Alberta and Sterling Lyon of Manitoba.
They seemed to be viewing the negotiations as a form of trench warfare,
digging themselves in to an impregnable position and never raising their
heads except to exchange fire. Lougheed, a straight-shooter but excep-
tionally stubborn, was still feeling the bruises from his year-long battle
with Trudeau over oil-and-gas pricing. While each man respected the
other's qualities, neither was ever going to accept the other's views. The
premier of Manitoba, more ideologically conservative than Lougheed
and much more pugnacious, had already locked horns on Monday and
Tuesday with the prime minister, whom he despised as a socialist trying
to ram an abstract French republicanism down the throat of British
parliamentary tradition. In fact, caught in the middle of a tough election
campaign, Lyon had already deserted the conference after breakfast
that morning to return to Winnipeg, leaving his attorney general, Gerry
Mercier, to speak on the province's behalf.

Their western colleagues, Allan Blakeney of Saskatchewan and Bill
Bennett of British Columbia, had shown some flexibility of late, but
Trudeau doubted that either would abandon Lougheed. Blakeney was a
smart, earnest, personable politician who, as a former Rhodes Scholar

and the only New Democratic Party leader at the table, might have found a kindred spirit in the prime minister, but he had been wary of Trudeau from their very first one-on-one meeting in 1971. Each was accustomed to being the most intelligent man in the room; neither liked to lose on a point of principle, especially in public. Bennett, by contrast, was an amiable, good-looking lightweight, despite his "tough guy" public persona; a down-to-earth businessman who had followed his father into politics as leader of the Social Credit Party; a Conservative in all but name. The B.C. premier, who would much rather have been dealing with the dire economic situation than debating the constitution, was feeling pulled in three different directions as defender of his province's interests, chum of Alberta, and current chair of the Annual Premiers' Conference.

As for Brian Peckford of Newfoundland, Angus MacLean of Prince Edward Island, and John Buchanan of Nova Scotia—Tories all— Trudeau dismissed them as marginal players, parochial, hostile, and unhelpful. Peckford, the youngest premier at thirty-nine, was a former high school teacher with a temper and tongue that ran to demagogic extremes. Cocky, strident, and a fiercely patriotic Newfoundlander, he considered the federal government merely "the agent of the provinces."[16] MacLean, a grandfatherly war hero and blueberry farmer just back from a month's vacation in Fiji, was set to retire at the end of the week. Full of common sense but hardly an intellectual powerhouse, he had unashamedly described himself as "an Islander first, a Maritimer second, and a Canadian third."[17] Buchanan seemed strangely dissociated from the entire process. A self-made lawyer fresh from an election in which he had increased his majority, he appeared either bored by the whole subject or anxious about making a wrong move. "We would not expect that what Premier Buchanan will say," the prime minister's advisers drily observed in their briefing book, "will push the meeting much one way or the other."[18]

Even Trudeau's two allies, Bill Davis of Ontario and Richard Hatfield of New Brunswick, appeared to be getting a little weak in the knees. Davis, a consensus politician—calm, avuncular, pragmatic—was evidently becoming uncomfortable with the prime minister's confrontational, take-it-or-leave-it negotiating style. And though Hatfield often looked as proud as Sancho Panza to be playing the role of Trudeau's loyal sidekick, not least because it joined his love of country to his sense of mischief, he was in the end yet another Progressive Conservative like Davis, and thus was already in deep trouble with his party's Loyalist constituency for supporting the Liberals in Ottawa.

Tant pis! Pierre Trudeau would take on them all. This was the role for which he had been training all his life: Cyrano de Bergerac marching against a volley of venom, tough, indifferent, and alone. The greatest compliment he could imagine when he was nineteen years old, with adolescent dreams of becoming a great man who would guide his country to great things, were the words "You have won because you are Cyrano!"[19]

SIX

The Pierre
and René Show

At the start of the Wednesday morning session, before Pierre Trudeau had begun to speak, René Lévesque jumped in to announce his intention to quit "this circus," as he described it, to return to Quebec City for the next day's opening of the National Assembly, which he had already postponed once.[1] He had to check out of his hotel by noon, he advised the other first ministers, and he laughed along with everyone else when Pierre Trudeau offered to put him up for the night at 24 Sussex. But it was no joking matter. With Lyon gone and Lévesque going, the conference was likely headed for failure, which was what the Quebec delegation wanted anyway.

"We further expect that at some point in the Conference, Premier Lévesque will push hard and try to bait you personally," the prime minister was warned in his briefing book. "He appears to believe that earlier contre-temps between the two of you have served him well in his relations with the other Premiers. Given the approach to the Conference you are taking and the general objectives of the federal government, there is nothing to be gained by taking the bait, certainly not until after the Conference has irretrievably broken down."[2]

Trudeau, it seemed, was incapable of heeding the advice. He and Lévesque had been sparring partners for more than twenty-five years, and the savagery of their jabs on Monday and Tuesday kept undercutting whatever small hope existed for a deal. At times, the prime minister couldn't resist taking a cheap shot at the Parti Québécois defeat in the referendum. At times, the premier of Quebec launched into emotional orations about the humiliation of French Canadians and the perfidy of Ottawa. At times, the English-speaking premiers had to remind the two of them that there were other people at the table, other interests, other voices wishing to be heard. Brian Peckford called it "The Pierre and René Show."

"Mr. Trudeau addressed unflattering remarks to Mr. Lévesque. Mr. Lévesque answered in kind," Allan Blakeney remembered. "They continued in increasingly rapid and vituperative French. Then they looked around the table and noticed that the French was too fast for the rest of us. We were not getting the full benefit of their remarks. So each switched to English and continued the pleasantries."[3]

Unlike Trudeau, who usually concealed his emotions under a stony, cerebral facade, Lévesque could rarely avoid displaying his fury and frustration on his face, in his voice, or through his body language. He was a jumping bean of shrugs, twitches, grimaces, and gestures. If that often made him seem more human and trustworthy than Trudeau, a Chaplinesque Everyman with a comb-over and a baggy suit, it also betrayed an impetuous, undisciplined core as surely as the addictive desperation with which he inhaled cigarette after cigarette. And no one rattled René Lévesque more than Pierre Elliott Trudeau. He had, Lévesque once said, "an inborn talent for making you want to slap his face."[4]

Trudeau was the rich, sophisticated playboy intellectual—"the princeling," Lévesque nicknamed him—who had grown up in a cosmopolitan household in an exclusive neighbourhood in Montreal and had obtained a rigorous Jesuit education at the most elite school in French Canada. Lévesque, the son of a bourgeois country lawyer in a small English-speaking town in the hinterland of the Gaspé Peninsula, was well educated but a law school dropout. Though each was a lone wolf, hard to get close to and scarred by the premature death of his father, Trudeau inherited a fortune that allowed him to study abroad and wander the world as a vagabond, while Lévesque parlayed his lively mind, earthy charm, and smoky voice into a successful career as a war correspondent on radio, a current-affairs host on television, and a star of Jean Lesage's dream team, *l'équipe du tonnerre*. Trudeau had the depth, inwardness, stealth, and logical precision of a chess master; Lévesque had the quickness, bonhomie, insouciance, and gambling instincts of a poker player. Trudeau was philosophical principles, small-circulation periodicals, and individual liberty; Lévesque was romantic visions, mass media, and collective action.

"I have never hidden the fact that constitutional law has always seemed to me to be eminently soporific," Lévesque once wrote, in a confession that revealed his self-deprecating candour as well as his cavalier disregard for detail, "and all too frequently I have demonstrated my sketchy knowledge of the subject."[5]

He and Trudeau had clashed like curs at their very first encounter, in a Montreal cafeteria in the mid-1950s. Lévesque hadn't even sat down with his coffee before being chastised for failing to produce an article he had promised to write for *Cité libre*, the influential little magazine that Trudeau helped found and co-edit. "Hey, Lévesque, you're a hell of a good speaker, but I'm starting to wonder whether you can write. We've been after you for a while."

"Writing?" Lévesque retorted. "How can I find the time?"

"And something to say," Trudeau volleyed. If he'd caught the barb about his being an Outremont dilettante who didn't have to grub for a paycheque, it only made him more aggressive. It was also within his character to feel a mixture of jealousy and shame that someone who hadn't had his advantages of money, education, and freedom should have become more accomplished and renowned than he had. "Television's all very well," he went on, while Lévesque puffed on his cigarette nervously, "but there's nothing solid about it, as you know. People watch it when they have time to kill. Now, if you knew how to write, maybe with a little effort now and then—"

"If that's what you think," Lévesque finally burst out, "you can go peddle your potatoes, you bloody washout of an intellectual!"[6]

For the next three decades, the two men continued to attract and repel each other. "Trudeau watched Lévesque in action with the spell-bound admiration one feels watching the tricks of a conjurer," wrote Gérard Pelletier, the journalist who had accompanied Trudeau into federal politics in 1965. "René's vitality, his lively intelligence, his verbal originality, the surprises in his mental processes, his imagination, the breadth and variety of his erudition, his extensive knowledge of history and his disconcerting memory for the slightest facts in current history— all this left Trudeau flabbergasted. He was, nonetheless, irritated by Lévesque's petulance, his biting assertions, his tendency to juggle figures that were more or less well substantiated or to allow his passion of the moment to distort the realities of which he spoke."[7]

"He was disorganized, confused, improvising," Trudeau himself said, in summing up Lévesque. "A good tactician, but not much of a strategist."[8]

Wealth and personality aside, the two men actually had much in common. Both had escaped the hothouse of Quebec in the 1940s, and had joined the struggle for democracy and reform in the 1950s. Both had believed in a secular, activist, modern state in the 1960s. Both wanted equality, justice, and prosperity for their people in the 1970s. Both were preoccupied with the survival of the French-Canadian minority in an age when English had become the *lingua franca* of multinational corporations, mass entertainment, and international diplomacy. Both were

Library and Archives Canada/e010768036

Jean Chrétien, Michael Kirby, Pierre Trudeau, Claude Morin, and René Lévesque.

the only French-Canadian leaders at the conference table, which meant they shared a mother tongue, a Catholic education, a civil-code training, a familial set of cultural references and personal associations, and a presumption that politics was about deadly serious issues, the course of history, and the fate of nations, not merely about budget priorities and legislative timetables. With a dash more Rousseau in their philosophies than the anglophone first ministers, both placed enormous trust in the will of the people. But their paths diverged, their arguments grew heated, their principles clashed over the question of Quebec nationalism.

The idea that the "pure wool" descendants of the French settlers in North America were a distinct people, *une nation*, had throughout the nineteenth century been nurtured by intellectuals, politicians, and priests as a defence against the sporadic efforts of the British conquerors to assimilate them, first as a liberal movement inspired by European nationalism, then as a conservative movement under the thumb of the ultramontane Church. During the twentieth century, nationalism was picked up by the premiers of Quebec as an instrument to extract money from Ottawa and votes at election time. Since the province of Quebec was the only significant jurisdiction in the world in which French-speaking Canadians formed a majority, they argued, it was the true homeland of the French-Canadian people, and its government was therefore the true guardian of the interests of the *nation*. The day after the hanging of Louis Riel in 1885, Honoré Mercier founded the Parti National in Quebec. Five decades later, Premier Maurice Duplessis called his alliance of farmers, small-town professionals, and Catholic conservatives the Union Nationale. The provincial parks became "national" parks. The legislative assembly became the Assemblée Nationale.

Le rattrapage, l'épanouissement, le déblocage—the catching up, the blossoming, the thaw that took place in Quebec in the 1960s—let loose, like a genie from the bottle, a celebratory blend of ethnic pride and individual opportunities, an artistic renaissance, a giddy intoxication of personal release and communal energy. At the same time and in every corner of the globe, conquered peoples and oppressed minorities were rising up to expel their colonial masters or take charge of their own destinies: in Egypt and Malaya, in Kenya and Cuba, in Algeria and Vietnam, even in the United States of America, where the rhetoric and protests of the civil rights movement inspired victims of poverty and racism everywhere. National liberation, anti-imperialism, post-colonialism, power to the people, freedom now—these rallying cries also served as calls for social justice. French Quebecers hardly counted among the world's oppressed, but their struggle for cultural survival became married to a "neo-nationalism" that saw itself as progressive, proactive, and secular.

Jean Lesage did not begin his political career as an ardent Quebec nationalist. On the contrary, the young and handsome star in Louis St. Laurent's Cabinet might have become prime minister of Canada had he sworn off alcohol and chosen to stay in Ottawa. He and his left-leaning reformers—not least his minister of natural resources, René Lévesque— routinely dismissed Duplessis's tribalism as the archaic tub-thumping of a demagogue who, in the words of one prominent critic, "defended provincial autonomy to make Quebec the paradise for monopolies, the kingdom of low salaries, and the land of slums."[9] Nevertheless, the more Lesage sought new legislative responsibilities and fiscal revenues to carry out his government's expansive and expensive agenda, the more the provincial Liberals appreciated the degree to which wrapping themselves in the Quebec flag was good politics at home and a weapon of intimidation in Ottawa.[10]

The "call of race," as the revered historian Lionel Groulx once unapologetically heralded it, was almost unbearably alluring. Louis-Hippolyte LaFontaine, George-Étienne Cartier, Sir Wilfrid Laurier, and Pierre Elliott Trudeau had all been unable to resist its siren song in their youth.[11] What, after all, could be more seductive than the sense of belonging to a history and a place in which everyone speaks the same language, reveres the same landscape, upholds the same values, and knows the words to the same folk songs? In that northern Eden, no strangers intrude upon the natural order and no outsiders threaten the eternal norms. It remains an earthly paradise, *entre nous*, one big happy family, such as had existed in the golden age of New France (if one believes the popular novels and history texts of Quebec), before the Conquest and the arrival of the English. Conversely, what could be more frightening than to set off into unfamiliar territory, to be encircled by enemies, to have to learn a new language and respond to different points of view, to embrace diversity, to overcome fear and defeat discrimination? Isn't it always safer, always cozier, to be a majority than a minority?

"*Nous sommes des Québécois,*" René Lévesque proclaimed. "What that means first and foremost—if need be, all that it means—is that we are attached to this one corner of the earth where we can be completely ourselves; this Quebec where we have the unmistakable feeling that here we can be really at home."[12]

Lévesque wasn't a fanatic or a bigot. He had grown up playing with Anglo kids. He had seen for himself the extremes of ethnic nationalism as a reporter at Dachau.[13] He was comfortable speaking English and travelling abroad. He frankly admitted that Quebec "was (as it remains to this day) the least ill-treated of all colonies in the world."[14] But as a Cabinet minister in the Lesage government, he became increasingly frustrated in his dealings with Ottawa and the English-speaking business leaders of Montreal. Federalism was like "two scorpions in the same bottle," he declared, and he compared Quebec's Anglo elite to the white settlers who once ruled Rhodesia. "If we had colours here," he claimed, "you'd feel it."[15] The only way for French Canadians to break out of the economic colonialism, social disadvantages, and psychological inferiority that held them back, Lévesque concluded, was to invest more power in the state of Quebec. Wasn't it "normal," as he often put it, for a people to have a state of their own, one in which they could manipulate all the levers of power in their own interests? Wouldn't separation liberate the rest of Canada to pursue its own destiny in its own language, unfettered by the fruitless bickering and exhausting negotiations that were a pain in the neck to both sides?

"As long as we persist so desperately in maintaining—with spit and chewing gum or whatever—the ancient hobble of a federalism suited to the last century," Lévesque argued, "the two nations will go on creating an ever-growing jungle of compromises while disagreeing more and more strongly on essentials. This would mean a perpetual atmosphere of instability, of wrangling over everything and over nothing. It would mean the sterilization of two collective 'personalities' which, having squandered the most precious part of their potential, would weaken each other so completely that they would have no other choice but to drown themselves in the ample bosom of 'America.'"[16]

Pierre Trudeau would have none of it. If English Canada refused to budge on linguistic equality or constitutional reform, then maybe separation made sense, but English Canada was budging and could be budged even more. Quebec already had enough legislative authority, in his view, to do almost everything the nationalists hoped to accomplish with independence.[17] Diverting half a billion dollars from education or medical care to nationalize the hydroelectric companies wasn't sound economics, he argued, but dumb emotion based on nationalist pride and *la politique de grandeur*. And the most likely result of special status or independence, Trudeau believed, would be the assimilation of French-speaking communities outside Quebec, the persecution of minorities inside Quebec, the weakening of French Power in Ottawa, and the impoverishment of all Quebecers.

Independence, in Trudeau's eyes, wasn't the vision of a proud, courageous people, as Lévesque liked to portray it. It was the retrenchment of a small, timid, adolescent ethnic group within the boundaries of a petty state. True pride and true courage meant testing the confidence and competence of French Canadians to take on the best of the world in politics, in business, and in the arts. "Let's open the borders," Trudeau shouted. "This people is dying of asphyxiation!"[18]

Furthermore, though French Canadians could be considered a sociological nation bound by heritage and blood, much like the Scots or the Kurds, for example, Quebecers were not that French-Canadian nation, and neither was Quebec. Why? Because there were some 850,000 French Canadians living outside the province and about a million Quebec citizens who weren't French Canadians.

"Were we to leave the abusive tutelage of our Holy Mother Church and free ourselves from an atavistic vision, only to throw ourselves now under the shadow of our Holy Mother Nation?" Trudeau asked rhetorically. "We had fought for ten years on behalf of all Quebecers: white, black, yellow, Catholic, Protestant, and agnostic; were we now to neglect all those others and devote all our attention only to old-stock Quebecers? A province is not a nation but a mix of diverse people, differentiated by religion, culture, and mother tongue. Was it necessary to grind down all these differences and impose a dominating and intolerant ideology on all minorities?"[19]

Deep at the core of his position was an abiding hatred of all ethnic nationalism, the belief that the people of a particular race or culture should lay exclusive and collective claim to a political territory. Trudeau saw this as a primary cause of many of the greatest atrocities of human history, from the tribal battles of Africa to the gas chambers of Nazi Germany. Even an ethnic nationalism based on language and customs rather than blood could never be, in his view, a truly positive or progressive force. It would always attempt to coerce the individual into the group and attend to the welfare of some of its citizens over the welfare of all. "A state that defined its function in terms of ethnic attributes would inevitably become chauvinistic and intolerant," he wrote.[20] And since very few (if any) political states are perfectly homogeneous, persecution by the majority would compel every minority to demand a political state of its own, and on and on until the whole world was engulfed in liberation movements and "the last-born of nation-states turned to violence to put an end to the very principle that gave it birth."[21] Instead, different peoples, different cultures, different languages, and different religions had to learn to live side by side as individuals who freely consent to come together with equal rights and equal opportunities. And if a particular set of circumstances should make a unitary state either impractical or undesirable, he extolled the inherent diversity of federalism.

In 1965, Trudeau entered politics to break the fierce grip Quebec nationalism had on the hearts and minds of the province. At the same time, he pushed English Canadians to get beyond the inherited prejudices and ingrained superiority of their particular variety of ethnic nationalism. Canada isn't one culture, he reminded them. It isn't even bicultural. It's a multicultural society made up of citizens from all over the world. The founding fathers themselves had spoken of the British North Americans of 1867 as four distinct peoples: English, Scottish, Irish, and French. (They should also have included the aboriginals and the Métis, of course, and could well have recognized the German-speaking

Loyalists or the Black communities of Nova Scotia, among a host of other ethnicities already present in the colonies.)

"Each man has his own reasons, I suppose, as driving forces, but mine were two-fold," Trudeau once replied when asked why he had entered politics. "One to make sure that Quebec wouldn't leave Canada through separatism, and the other was to make sure that Canada wouldn't shove Quebec out through narrowmindedness."[22]

His dramatic, unyielding clash with Premier Daniel Johnson at the First Ministers' Conference hosted by Lester Pearson in February 1968 propelled the new minister of justice into national prominence and signalled that the days of appeasement were over. When Johnson went so far as to compare him to Lord Durham, Trudeau shot back, "Monsieur Johnson does not know his history very well. He seems to ignore the fact the Durham Report affirmed the existence of two nations, whereas I myself do not happen to believe in this thesis."[23]

There would be no more loose talk about *deux nations* or special status, no more lack of direction or of confidence, no more guilt and intimidation, no more identifying the interests of French Canadians with the interests of the government of Quebec. Trudeau knew what he wanted Canada to be, and as a French-speaking member of Parliament, he felt he was as much an advocate and defender of the rights and aspirations of French Canadians as Daniel Johnson or René Lévesque—more so, he argued, because no premier of Quebec could speak on behalf of the Franco-Ontarians, the Franco-Manitobans, or the Acadians of New Brunswick. "Masters in our own house, we must be," he told the Liberal convention that elected him leader in April 1968, "but our house is the whole of Canada."

The long and intense rivalry between Pierre Trudeau and René Lévesque was but the latest expression of the fundamental conflict that had coursed through and divided the French-Canadian family ever since its beginnings in North America in the first quarter of the seventeenth century. From the earliest days, the overarching question was how to survive in this barren place, cut off from the Old World by a huge and treacherous ocean, threatened by a long and bitterly cold winter, susceptible to famine and disease, and besieged by Iroquois warriors and English raiders. There were always two responses, both literal and metaphorical at the same time. One was to huddle together in a state of siege behind the walls of a well-defended fort, confined and destitute but sharing the workload and the store of provisions. The other was to go out in search of new lands and better opportunities, to risk more in order to gain more, to adapt to the challenges of the New World and learn from the ways of *les autres*.

Thus while the bishops and governors were ordering the *habitants* to hunker down on their farms rather than "roaming about in the woods in the hope of profits," as one court official put it, "which tends toward the utter ruination of the colony," explorers and fur traders journeyed west to the Rockies and south to the Mississippi to expand the riches and territories of the French Empire. After Louis-Joseph Papineau led his band of patriots in battle against the English oppressors, Louis-Hippolyte LaFontaine fought for the survival of his people by joining forces with Robert Baldwin in the legislative assembly of the united Canadas. While Antoine-Aimé Dorion attacked Confederation for creating "local governments whose powers will be almost nothing," George-Étienne Cartier asked, "Shall we be content to maintain a mere provincial existence, when, by combining together, we could become a great nation?"[24] When Honoré Mercier rose up as premier of Quebec in defence of provincial rights, Wilfrid Laurier got himself elected as the first French-speaking, Roman Catholic prime minister of Canada so that he could serve the interests of all Canadians. When Louis St. Laurent moved to rebuild Canada following the Second World War, Maurice Duplessis replied, "You shall not crucify the province of Quebec, even on a cross of gold."[25] When Pierre Trudeau brought French Power to Ottawa, René Lévesque founded the Parti Québécois.

What complicated the struggle was that French Quebecers weren't just divided into two camps, one against the other. They were often conflicted within their own selves. In 1974, Quebec voters gave Pierre Trudeau's Liberal Party of Canada sixty of their seventy-four seats; two years later they elected René Lévesque's provincial Parti Québécois with a majority. In February 1980, they gave Trudeau 68 percent of their votes and all but one of their seats; then they turned around in April 1981 and gave Lévesque another majority.

"What does Quebec want?" English Canada kept asking in a practical but somewhat peevish tone. "An independent Quebec within a strong Canada," the comedian Yvon Deschamps replied, and his joke became a cliché because it cut so close to the bone. In this fantasy, it seemed, Quebec would declare its independence and take its seat at the United Nations, as though to release French-speaking Quebecers from the shame of the Conquest, while at the same moment joining the rest of Canada in a new, truly confederal arrangement, a kind of Austro-Hungarian diarchy with a common currency, a customs union, one passport, and the free passage of labour and goods. When Daniel Johnson spoke of "*egalité ou indépendance*," he was imagining equality *and* independence. When René Lévesque campaigned on "*d'égal à égal*," he was proposing a Canada-Quebec governed by the consent of two equal majorities, one English-speaking, the other French-speaking, in matters of mutual interest.

"But was it necessary to cut all formal ties with Canada?" Lévesque asked the hardliners within the Parti Québécois. "Even though Confederation, which was never really a true one, gave us dangerously little breathing space at the very time we felt the need for ever-increasing room to manoeuvre, didn't it remain conceivable that the framework could be readjusted in such a way as to let Quebec live and develop freely?"[26]

Who could possibly object to such a neat and sympathetic arrangement? For those who yearned for a country of their own, there would be sovereignty, which Lévesque defined as "the complete mastery over every last area of basic collective decision-making."[27] For those who had too many psychological or practical attachments to Canada to wish to sever the connection, there would be association. For those who couldn't make up their minds one way or the other, there would be sovereignty-association (or sovereignty association, depending on whether you thought the hyphen meant something or not, an issue hotly debated in nationalist circles). Hence the nuanced and convoluted question the Parti Québécois government concocted for the 1980 referendum, with the help of extensive polling, to increase the odds of getting a Yes majority. Even the French press called it *"souveraineté-confusion."*[28]

At the same time, for those who viewed independence, sovereignty, or even sovereignty-association as too risky and traumatic, the nationalists offered to arrive at the same ultimate destination by means of a slower, less direct route, variously known as a special status, associate statehood, distinct society, two nations, or opting out with financial compensation. "With regard to all these concepts," Lévesque declared, "one idea stood out: equal rights for the two *collectivities.*"[29] He even called renewed federalism nothing more than a slow track to sovereignty-association, without ever admitting or recognizing that sovereignty-association was a sure route to independence. "Monetary system, economic system, all this is plumbing," he said dismissively. "One doesn't worry about plumbing when one fights for the destiny of a people."[30]

As ideal as the vision may have been on paper, it had one spectacular flaw: it was impossible. Talk about "two nations warring in the bosom of a single state." Talk about "two scorpions in the same bottle." Talk about a "hobble" and "an ever-growing jungle of compromises." Assuming there could never be a perpetual harmony of interests, how were conflicts to be resolved without trade-offs and, more often than not, a winner and a loser? How could Quebec take charge of its economy if it didn't have control of its currency exchange or interest rates? Indeed, what evidence was there that the rest of Canada was one voice, one ethnicity, one side of a duality, just because it spoke in one language? It was to get around just such a deadlock, created by the double majority in the 1850s, that the British North America Act was invented in the first place. And it was to prevent just such a paralysis that the English-Canadian premiers cautioned Quebecers that there would be no guarantee of association if they voted for sovereignty.

The 1980 referendum was the very first time the people of Quebec had ever been asked if they wanted to be a part of Canada, even though the question wasn't quite so clear. No longer were their wishes projected through the politicians, intellectuals, columnists, and priests who always claimed to be speaking for them, even while holding completely opposite positions. When forced to take a stand on whether to begin negotiating an association that might lead to independence, they answered with a resounding *Non*.

"If Quebecers are offered the chance to have their cake and eat it too, naturally they will accept," Trudeau concluded. "But as Canadians they also know that a country must choose to be or not to be; that dismantling Canada will not save it and the nationalists cannot be allowed to play the game of heads-I-win-tails-you-lose, or to hold referendums on independence every ten years."[31]

The lopsided defeat on May 20, 1980, was a blow for the Parti Québécois. It would have been better not to hold a referendum at all. Its bluff had been called. It had gambled and lost. For the moment at least, it could no longer use the threat of independence to blackmail the rest of Canada for more power and money. René Lévesque admitted as much when he returned to the bargaining table, though he continued to argue with Pierre Trudeau about the meaning of the vote. To Lévesque, Quebecers had interpreted Trudeau's promise of reform as one last chance for Canada to deliver on the province's traditional demands for special status and the devolution of responsibilities.[32] To Trudeau, meeting Quebec's traditional demands, as set down by Jean Lesage in 1960, meant patriating the Canadian constitution with an amending formula that included a veto for Quebec and a charter of rights that protected the language and culture of French Canadians forever.

"Some people in Quebec," he observed, "have the temerity to suggest that when I promised change during the 1980 referendum campaign, I meant that we would change the Constitution according to how the Yes side would have changed it, had they won. That isn't very logical. I had always fought special status. I had always fought the over-decentralization of a country that was already the most decentralized in the world. The Yes side had lost fair and square."[33]

SEVEN

Coup de Force

So how did it come to be that on November 4, 1981, less than eighteen months after the Quebec referendum, the Saviour of the Nation found himself ringed by a gang of eight premiers united in their determination to prevent him from delivering on his promise to those Quebecers who had voted for Canada? How was it that seven of the nine English-speaking premiers, some of whom had campaigned vigorously for the No side, were now allied in a battle against Ottawa with the leader of the *indépendantistes*? Some might think it improbable, even wondrous. Pierre Trudeau thought it disgusting.

The turning point had come the last time these eleven men had all been together, just over a year earlier in the second week of September 1980, in the same Government Conference Centre where they were presently gathered. That First Ministers' Conference had been a disaster. Its collapse was burned into everyone's memories, unacknowledged but present, like a lesson learned through pain. "Once bitten, twice shy," perhaps, or "Fool me once, shame on you; fool me twice, shame on me."

The 1980 summit was supposed to have been the culmination of the summer-long negotiations on the twelve items the prime minister and the premiers had determined in June. But whatever progress had been achieved among the more than three hundred officials during the two months of talking together in hotels, restaurants, bars, and meeting rooms in Montreal, Toronto, Vancouver, and Ottawa, it hit the rocks when they passed their reports to their first ministers on Monday, September 9, 1980. The conference hadn't even begun when Trudeau, enraged by the premiers' suggestion that Sterling Lyon of Manitoba co-chair the sessions with him, bolted from the opening dinner after barking at Governor General Ed Schreyer to hurry up and get the dessert served.

"The princeling is certainly in high dudgeon tonight," René Lévesque joked in a loud whisper to Ontario's attorney general, Roy McMurtry, who phoned his wife at the end of the debacle to tell her that the conference seemed doomed.[1]

Both at the time and in retrospect, the premiers put the blame squarely on Pierre Trudeau's combativeness, his arrogance, and a disdain that edged on utter contempt. They suspected that he actually wanted the negotiations to fail, a belief reinforced by the leak of two secret federal documents. The first, a memo to the prime minister from Michael Pitfield, the cerebral Clerk of the Privy Council, secretary to the Cabinet, and Canada's highest-ranking civil servant, had landed like a grenade right in the middle of the premiers' annual get-together in Winnipeg in the third week of August. "Without waiting for the first ministers' meeting in September," the *Ottawa Citizen* reported on its front page, "the government has drafted a Parliamentary resolution to patriate the constitution unilaterally." In the memo, which was in fact a routine contingency plan, Pitfield laid out a specific timetable by which a resolution could be tabled in the House of Commons before the end of September, passed before Christmas, and sent on to London early in the new year. "Premiers Shocked by Pitfield Memo," the newspaper headlined.[2]

The second document, which was slipped to the premiers on the eve of the meeting in Ottawa by Claude Morin, Quebec's minister of inter-governmental affairs, who had obtained it from a separatist sympathizer working in the ministry of external affairs, proved even more damning. Dated August 30, 1980, and stamped "Ministers' Eyes Only," it had been put together by a group of high-ranking officials under the direction of Michael Kirby, secretary to the Cabinet for federal–provincial relations and Trudeau's self-described "son of a bitch" on the constitutional file. "If the provinces are the pins in this federal game," René Lévesque said mischievously, "they have the right to know where the ball is coming from."[3]

Kirby's sixty-four-page strategy paper was a detailed assessment of where Ottawa and the provinces were positioned to date, but most of the attention went straight to its provocative final paragraph, which read: "The probability of an agreement is not high. Unilateral action is therefore a distinct possibility. *In the event unilateral action becomes necessary, Ministers should understand that the fight in Parliament and the country will be very, very rough.* For as Machiavelli said: 'It should be borne in mind that there is nothing more difficult to arrange, more doubtful of success, and more dangerous to carry through than initiating changes in a state's constitution.'"[4]

The impact was devastating. The small glimmers of optimism earned so laboriously by the travelling village of politicians and civil servants vanished into accusations of betrayal, as though the entire summer's effort had been a publicity stunt rather than a serious exercise to understand the complex issues and come up with real solutions.

"After weeks of discussion on these twelve topics," Lévesque said to his colleagues, stirring the pot with evident pleasure, "after we have been shown certain scenarios that seem desperately prefabricated, after yet another huge advertising campaign paid for out of public funds, after the shocking intentions and the temptation to act unilaterally disclosed in the last few days by the federal prime minister—could all these long weeks of intense discussion be simply a smokescreen to disguise aims that are as centralist as ever and the old desire to offer, not a very necessary increase but a reduction, to their simplest terms, of the powers and freedom of action of the provinces?"[5]

In fact, the Kirby report had urged the prime minister to strive to get an agreement with the provinces. If the conference succeeded, Ottawa would look like a winner. If it failed, Ottawa couldn't be blamed. "The preferred outcome of the September First Ministers' Conference," the report stated, "is clearly to achieve as broad a consensus as possible on as many of the twelve items as possible in order to permit the federal government to proceed to Westminster with the consent of the premiers."[6] Trudeau should be prepared to give ground on the amending formula, provincial control over natural resources, or appointments to the Supreme Court, Kirby recommended, if he wanted to get patriation, a charter of rights, and the economic union.

The confidential briefing that Trudeau was given before going into the conference reiterated the message. "If Canadians receive the impression that the federal government is spoiling for a fight, or that it is unwilling to negotiate seriously with their provincial government representatives," it advised, "then they will be less likely to concede to the federal government the right of unilateral action at the end of the Conference, should it fail to produce a usable consensus."[7]

In other words, unilateral action was primarily to be used as a stick to drive the premiers towards bargaining in good faith, to give as well as to take if they wanted to leave the conference with anything at all. "I mean, why would you go to war if you can solve the problem in peace?" Michael Kirby later recalled. "I used to joke with the press, 'If we were half as good as you guys think we are, we wouldn't be in this shit.' And if I had been really Machiavellian, I would have attributed the quote to Winston Churchill."[8]

Trudeau's anger at the Sunday-night dinner wasn't play-acting. He was genuinely infuriated by the speed with which the premiers had sided with René Lévesque in pursuit of their own interests. Sterling Lyon commended Lévesque and his government for negotiating in good faith. Bill Bennett slammed Trudeau for turning the constitutional process into a personal vendetta against the Quebec premier. Brian Peckford took time out from a nasty dispute over electricity rights on the Newfoundland–Quebec border to declare that he preferred René Lévesque's view of Canada to Pierre Trudeau's—whereupon the federal minister of justice, Jean Chrétien, leaned over to the prime minister and whispered, "Have you got a bag? I think I want to vomit."[9]

"During that time," Angus MacLean of Prince Edward Island recalled, "my respect for Quebec premier René Lévesque increased, and my regard for Trudeau shrank"—which was saying quite a lot, since MacLean had considered Trudeau's 1968 election a national tragedy. "I found Lévesque a reasonable person, not at all stiff-necked or rigid," he went on. "I had an impression that if the federal politicians had had the kind of relationship with him that I did, we would have reached some sort of compromise on the Constitution. Trudeau was particularly antagonistic."[10]

If the September conference began badly, it ended even worse. When the premiers realized they were in danger of losing in the press and the polls with their relentless negativity, all ten signed on to a cut-and-paste document collated in the wee hours of the night by the government of Quebec. Based on the "best efforts" of previous conferences and the summer negotiations, the "Proposal for a Common Stand of the Provinces" agreed to patriation, but only in exchange for an amending formula of the premiers' own devising; a preamble written by them; reform of the Senate and the Supreme Court to increase the provinces' power at the centre; federal equalization payments to the poorer provinces; an extremely modest charter of rights; and a devolution of responsibility over natural resources, offshore resources, fisheries, communications, and family law. Once that was done, but *before* any final petition to the British Parliament, there would be a second round of provincial demands involving culture, social policy, urban and regional affairs, regional development, transportation, international affairs, justice, and the federal spending power.

At ten-thirty on the morning of Friday, September 13, after the premiers had reviewed the proposal over breakfast in Sterling Lyon's suite at the Château Laurier, they presented it to Trudeau at 24 Sussex Drive. In reality, the so-called Château Consensus was acceptable to all of them only because none of them believed it had the slightest chance of being implemented. How could it, since it neglected to address any of the issues that really mattered to the prime minister? In that sense, it wasn't a legitimate counter-offer. It was window dressing designed to absolve the premiers from appearing obdurate and grasping. It was a harmless device to provoke discussion and keep the negotiations going. It was a desperate manoeuvre to sidetrack Trudeau. It was also an inexplicable misreading of the federal strategy, as laid out in black and white in the Kirby report. And it backfired badly.

"Well, now we know there will never be an agreement," Trudeau told them after reading just a couple of pages. "You guys are laughing at me—you're going back to square one. But I'm telling you, gentlemen, I've been warning you since 1976 that we could introduce a resolution in the House of Commons patriating the constitution, and if necessary we'll do this unilaterally. So I'm telling you now, we're going to go it alone. We're going to introduce a resolution, and we'll go to London, and we won't even bother asking a premier to come with us."

"If you do that," Sterling Lyon replied, "you're going to tear the country apart."

"If the country is going to be torn apart because we bring back from Britain our own constitution after 115 years of Confederation and after more than fifty years of fruitless discussions, and because we have asked for a Canadian charter of rights, when most of you already have provincial charters, then the country deserves to be torn up."[11]

The truth was that while Trudeau hadn't orchestrated the failure of the September conference, he didn't mind that it failed. Its collapse did more than reinforce his personal will to act—it gave unilateralism the political high ground. Canadians wanted an end to the feuding, indeed to the entire constitutional debate. They supported the idea of patriation and a charter of rights in overwhelming numbers and in every part of the country. And unlike the premiers, they didn't blame Trudeau in the opinion polls for what had happened in Ottawa.

"By that time," he explained, "it had become obvious that the greed of the provinces was a bottomless pit, and that the price to be paid to the provinces for their consent to patriation with some kind of an entrenched Charter—which had been requested as far back as 1971 in Victoria—was nothing less than acceptance by the federal government of the 'compact' theory, which would transform Canada from a very decentralized, yet balanced, federation into some kind of loose confederation. That is when our government said, 'Enough.'"[12]

Trudeau went back to his caucus and Cabinet to discuss the next move and found them even more "damn the torpedoes, full steam ahead" than he was. He worried about a prolonged parliamentary battle that would distract the government from the economic issues of the day. He resisted arbitrarily grabbing a few more economic powers for Ottawa, as some of his ministers were urging him to do. He cautioned against imposing a comprehensive charter of rights that would impinge unduly on the jurisdiction of the provincial legislatures. In the end, however, he was more than willing to follow the colourful advice of one Liberal backbencher, who yelled, "*Allons-y en* Cadillac! Let's go first-class."

"If that's the way you want it, I'm delighted," Trudeau replied, though not without warning how high the stakes were and how crushing would be the defeat if they lost.[13]

At 8:00 p.m. on Thursday, October 2, 1980, the prime minister delivered a television address in which he recounted the history leading up to the current impasse, repeated the promise he had made to Quebecers during the referendum, and outlined the Proposed Resolution for a Joint

Address to Her Majesty the Queen, which he said he would be tabling in the House of Commons when it reconvened in four days' time. "In accepting that the only agreement could be unanimous agreement," he told Canadians, "we took the ideal of unanimity and made it a tyrant. Unanimity gave each first minister a veto, and that veto was increasingly used to seek the particular good of a particular region or province. So we achieved the good of none; least of all did we achieve the good of all, the common good. We were led by the dictates of unanimity to bargain freedom against fish, fundamental rights against oil, the independence of our country against long-distance telephone rates."[14]

On the one hand, he swept away almost every demand for new powers, federal and provincial alike, and dumped them into a Powers' Package to be dealt with at a later date. On the other hand, he announced his intention to press forward—unilaterally and at once—with a People's Package that would include patriation, a new amending formula, and an entrenched charter of rights, which, not coincidentally, were the prime minister's priorities as well.

"Faced with the problem that we probably weren't going to get Quebec," Michael Kirby explained, "we had to come up with a package that would be extremely difficult for the provinces to reject. We also wanted to be able to say to the people, 'The provinces will not give you your rights unless we give them more powers.' From there, it was very easy to break it into a People's Package, which had all the right ring, and a Powers Package, which was offensive in the communications lingo."[15]

Ottawa's hope was to rush the Resolution through Parliament in two months, send it to Westminster by January, and bring the constitution home in time for Canada Day 1981, the fiftieth anniversary of the Statute of Westminster. To buttress his position, Trudeau quickly secured the support of two Conservative premiers, Bill Davis of Ontario and Richard Hatfield of New Brunswick, as well as that of the leader of the New Democratic Party in the House of Commons, Ed Broadbent. Whatever reservations the three might have harboured about the details, they shared Trudeau's view of the national interest, wanted patriation and a charter, had little fear of a strong central government, and were fed up with what Hatfield called the "pettiness, power-mongering or personal pique" of the opposition.[16] Each also received his own reward. Davis got a commitment that Ottawa wouldn't impose official bilingualism on Ontario. Hatfield got the principle of equalization and official bilingualism for New Brunswick. Broadbent got a clause protecting and expanding the provinces' control over their natural resources.

But dare and prayer weren't enough to give this *coup de force* legitimacy. If Trudeau had hoped he could get a substantial number of other premiers on board, given that the Resolution dealt mostly with motherhood issues, he was quickly disillusioned. Not only did Ottawa's unilateralism pull the rug out from under the other premiers' demands for more power and money, but it also offended their concept of federalism, seemed almost un-Canadian in its disregard for political horse-trading, and might even have been illegal. Indeed, just as the Kirby report had predicted, the process replaced the content as the focus of attack, not least because the content was so hard to oppose politically.[17]

On October 14, six of the premiers responded to an invitation from Sterling Lyon to gather in his suite at the Harbour Castle Hotel in Toronto to consider how they might block the Resolution from ever coming into effect. Davis and Hatfield didn't join them, of course. Allan Blakeney of Saskatchewan and John Buchanan of Nova Scotia decided to hold back in order to try to find a middle ground somewhere between the two camps.[18] The self-styled Group of Six agreed to embark upon a concerted lobbying effort in London, and to launch legal challenges to Trudeau's unilateral action in the courts of Manitoba, Newfoundland, and Quebec.

Ottawa had been eager to avoid a court challenge, even though it assumed it could win on purely legal grounds. Canadians probably didn't have the stomach for a dragged-out constitutional brawl. Margaret Thatcher, while offering her unequivocal support to get the federal government's request through Westminster, wanted it done quickly so that she could get on with her own parliamentary business.[19] And there was a risk that the judges might rule against Ottawa's unilateralism as a breach of constitutional convention, if not of constitutional law. "I too would argue against a reference to the Supreme Court," Trudeau scrawled by hand on a memo sent to him by the justice department in August 1980. "I think that if challenged it would be better to go the referendum route."[20]

Trudeau's determination to do what he had set out to do never faltered, though he was forced to concede more than he wanted and his fast-track timetable kept being extended. His opponents grew stronger over the winter. While the polls continued to show support for patriation and a charter, they also showed that most Canadians preferred a negotiated settlement to unilateral action. The dissenting provinces had enough success wining and dining the power-brokers in London that in January 1981, a British parliamentary committee recommended against passing the Resolution "automatically and unconditionally" unless Ottawa could gather more provincial support, thus casting into doubt the federal government's assumption of a swift, routine assent at Westminster.[21] In February, Saskatchewan and Nova Scotia gave up on making a deal with Trudeau and went over to the Group of Six, which the media immediately rechristened the Gang of Eight. In March, the Progressive Conservative Opposition in Ottawa began a parliamentary filibuster to derail the process, encouraged by the unanimous decision of the Supreme Court of Newfoundland that the federal government's unilateral action was indeed unconstitutional. Even though a majority of judges in both Manitoba and Quebec reached the opposite conclusion, there was enough confusion and contradiction in the three rulings to satisfy everyone and no one.

As a result, Prime Minister Trudeau felt compelled to do what he had previously resisted: he agreed to present the revised Resolution to the House of Commons before the end of April, then immediately refer it to the Supreme Court of Canada. If judged legal, it would be debated in Parliament for two days, put to a vote, and be on its way to London. If not, that would be the beginning of an entirely new battle. "The Supreme Court's judgment respecting patriation of the constitution is unquestionably the most important judicial decision ever rendered in the history of Canadian constitutional law," one prominent lawyer observed. "Its importance with respect to the future orientation of our law, parliamentarianism and federalism cannot be overestimated."[22]

The proceedings began on April 28, 1981, with a verdict expected in June. It didn't come until September 28, creating havoc with the federal government's schedule, and it wasn't as definitive as either Pierre Trudeau or the Gang of Eight had hoped. Yes, said seven of the nine judges, the federal government had the legal right to amend the constitution on its own with a resolution from the House of Commons and the Senate to the British Parliament. However, six of the nine ruled that custom or convention required that Ottawa first obtain "a substantial degree of provincial consent," though not necessarily unanimity. In other words, Ottawa's unilateralism was within the law but outside established tradition and practice—legal but an affront to the principle of federalism.

"We have reached the conclusion," the majority opinion declared, "that the agreement of the provinces of Canada, no views being expressed as to its quantification, is constitutionally required for the passing of the 'Proposed Resolution for a Joint Address to Her Majesty Respecting the Constitution of Canada,' and that passing of this Resolution without such agreement would be unconstitutional in the conventional sense."[23]

But what did "a substantial degree of provincial consent" mean? Five, six, seven, eight? Did Quebec or Ontario have to be one of them? Must there be one from the West and one from the East? The judges refused to say. "Conventions by their nature develop in the political field," they wrote, "and it will be for the political actors, not this Court, to determine the degree of provincial consent required."[24]

Trudeau was puzzled and annoyed. He thought the minority opinion articulated by Chief Justice Boris Laskin in support of the federal government's position was better law, and he said so ten years later when he emerged from retirement to deliver a blistering attack on the ruling, indifferent to the fact that Laskin's successor sat fuming in the audience. ("Why should he be upset?" Trudeau inquired when told of Brian Dickson's reaction. "I appointed him chief justice of the Supreme Court of Canada, didn't I?"[25]) By going beyond the question of unanimity, Trudeau argued, cherry-picking the precedents, blundering into the political arena, and inventing a convention that nine of the ten provinces hadn't claimed for themselves, the judges had "blatantly manipulated the evidence before them so as to arrive at the desired result. They then wrote a judgment which tried to lend a fig-leaf of legality to their preconceived conclusion."[26]

Since the unilateral process had been found legal, why couldn't Trudeau simply disregard a convention he didn't accept, pass his Resolution in the Commons and the Senate, and take it to London to be rubber-stamped? According to the strict interpretation of the law, he could—and very nearly did—but the confusion sown by the Supreme Court gave him pause. If he ignored the convention, he risked losing the legitimacy he had so laboriously tried to establish in the eyes of the Canadian people, the premiers of Ontario and New Brunswick, and the Conservative government in Great Britain.

"In holding that the federal action, though legal, was unconstitutional and illegitimate," he had to admit, "the Court made it effectively impossible for the federal government to proceed to Westminster with any hope of success."[27]

Reluctantly, Pierre Trudeau succumbed to the pressure to make "one final attempt," as he put it, during these few days in Ottawa in early November.[28] Though he felt certain he would never be able to reach a negotiated settlement, the Supreme Court had changed the game in his favour in two ways: first, by declaring that Ottawa wouldn't have to get the consent of every province, and second, by ruling that its unilateral action was technically legal. If Trudeau could make enough concessions to pull three or four premiers away from the Gang of Eight, he might get a deal. If not, he would have demonstrated yet again the intransigence of the provinces to get rid of what the judges themselves had termed this "remaining badge of subservience."

"I didn't really hold out much hope that we would ever be able to sign a deal as long as the Gang of Eight alliance held," he recalled. "Lévesque, I knew, would never agree. But it was important for us to be seen making the effort. And if we tried and failed, I was determined that we would go to London and say: 'We have exhausted all the alternatives. What we are doing is legal, and you must pass what the Canadian Parliament requests.' If the British Parliament balked, we would have the option of a massive demonstration of national will, leading to a unilateral declaration of constitutional independence from Britain."[29]

EIGHT

Deadlock

Pierre Trudeau's marching orders going into the November conference were simple: he would have to take the initiative, demonstrate some flexibility, keep the opponents from getting bogged down in the details, march in lockstep with his two allies, and stay cool. If there was another failure, as he expected there would be, it couldn't be seen as his fault.

"It is essential that some compromise proposal be placed on the table earlier to allow some of the Group of Eight to exercise their independence," the prime minister was advised in the briefing book he was given immediately before the start of the conference. "Otherwise, they will all retreat to their 'united defensive position' and it may be more difficult for them to come forward later during the meeting. The frustration level within the Group of Eight has increased during the past week and lack of trust is emerging. However, this increased frustration could cause some of the eight to be bitter and explosive next week. It is important not to overreact to such developments but rather interpret them as signs that the cohesiveness of the eight might indeed be fragile."[1]

The twelve items that had been on the agenda in September 1980 were now down to three—patriation, an amending formula, a charter of rights—and patriation got settled on Monday, when the premiers, including René Lévesque, agreed to let it proceed without their getting any new powers first. But patriation without an amending formula only raised the age-old question: How were changes to Canada's constitution to be made, if not by the British Parliament? Once again, as it had in the conferences in 1927, 1931, 1935, 1950, 1960, 1964, 1971, 1978, 1979, and 1980, the amending formula proved the major stumbling block. The core of the problem was again the intractable issue of how many provinces would be needed to approve an amendment in the future. All? None? A few? Most? It depends?

The amending formula the federal government placed before the first ministers in November 1981 was more or less the same one that it had tabled in the House of Commons in October 1980, which itself was more or less the same one—with two significant additions—that had been accepted in principle by all eleven first ministers in Victoria in June 1971. Future amendments involving the central institutions and the division of powers would require the approval of the federal Parliament and the legislatures of at least two of the four Atlantic provinces, at least two of the four western provinces, and any province that ever had, in the past, present, or future, more than 25 percent of the country's population.[2]

This represented, as Trudeau portrayed it, a compromise between the rigidity of unanimity and the tyranny of majority rule. It guaranteed the two most populous and politically important provinces, Ontario and Quebec, a new and permanent veto without singling them out for special treatment by name. In effect it gave the West and the East a veto as well. And its regional weighting, which reflected the distribution of seats in the Senate as set forth in the BNA Act, was obviously more democratic than requiring the consent of every province, large and small.

But Trudeau wasn't content to stop there. If the ultimate power to amend the constitution was going to be taken away from the British Parliament, he wanted it to be conferred upon the people of Canada. In the event of the sort of stalemates that had frustrated constitutional reform in the past, the Resolution would allow the federal government to initiate a referendum. Moreover, if Ottawa and the provinces failed to agree on an amending formula now or within the next two years, Canadians would be asked, one time only, to choose between the federal government's option and whatever alternative was put forward by seven or more provinces representing at least 80 percent of the population.

"How were deadlocks broken in the past?" Trudeau explained. "They were broken by the federal government asking Westminster to do something. That is our tradition. That is our law, and that has been our practice. What are we proposing? We propose that when there is a deadlock, the federal government, as traditionally and legally has been the case, asks not Westminster—since we will be independent—but the Canadian people to break the deadlock."[3]

The two referendum proposals were so unexpected that they were widely dismissed as bargaining chips inserted for the express purpose of being bartered in exchange for a deal.[4] But in fact, the sovereignty of the people was especially important to three very powerful federal players—Pierre Trudeau, Michael Pitfield, and Michael Kirby—and it proved the very last thing they were willing to surrender. As a matter of principle, they saw themselves as democrats engaged in a battle against the traditional Canadian elites. As a matter of practicality, they wanted to entrench a tie-breaker into the constitution.

"I hadn't been educated by the Jesuits like Trudeau," Kirby explained, "but I had been trained as a mathematician, so we agreed on the same irrefutable logic: If two governments are elected by the same people to do what each of them believes to be in the public interest, and if those two governments come to hold significantly different views on what that public interest is, which view is right? The only logical answer is to ask the people."[5]

That which had been accepted by all the provinces in 1971, however, was no longer acceptable to eight of them by 1981. Alberta vigorously objected to the inequality of giving only Ontario and Quebec a veto. Though Quebec would have been the beneficiary of a veto, it abandoned the Victoria formula to maintain solidarity with the Gang of Eight. British Columbia insisted on being treated as a region of its own rather than lumped together with the three Prairie provinces. Newfoundland fretted that its boundaries could be changed without its consent. Prince Edward Island worried about its survival as a province. Most premiers wanted unanimity or some other form of protection to prevent any province from being stripped of its powers. As for the referendums, nobody— not even Bill Davis and Richard Hatfield—cared for the idea of handing over his authority to the unpredictable whims of a referendum campaign that could be triggered and conducted by Ottawa alone. Instead of being welcomed as the expression of a more perfect democracy, the referendum proposals were dismissed as inappropriate in a parliamentary system, incompatible with federalism, and a devious device by which Ottawa could sneak around the wishes of the provincial legislatures.

The Gang of Eight showed up at the November conference with its own amending proposal, dubbed the Vancouver formula (though it was in fact the brainchild of the government of Alberta). A few items of common concern, such as the office of the monarchy, the composition of the Supreme Court, and any future changes to the new amending formula itself, would require the consent of Parliament and all ten legislatures.[6] For the rest, Ottawa and seven provinces representing at least 50 percent of Canadians would be sufficient, with the proviso that any province had the right to opt out, with reasonable financial compensation, of any amendment that affected its existing powers and rights.

Though the federal government had resigned itself to accepting Alberta's alternative in September 1980 if it proved to be "the best bet for agreement," Trudeau was quick to reject it now.[7] For one thing, he was extremely reluctant to give up a veto for Quebec or the new referendum mechanisms he had added to the Victoria Charter. For another, he feared that opting out would let the richer provinces kill any new national initiative or, when coupled with financial compensation, would give rise to a "checkerboard" of programs and standards across the country. Handing the provinces the cash to do whatever they want is no way to build a country, he declared; the result would be nothing less than "incremental separatism."

"The Vancouver formula proposed by eight provinces—our objection to it is that it solves the problem of consensus by saying that there cannot be one," Trudeau explained. "It really denies the existence of a national will. It says in reality that if 95 percent of Canadians from nine provinces agree to something, one province can still say, 'Well, that is not the national will.' One province can pick up its marbles and opt out."[8]

"But it's an exaggeration to say there will be no national will," Peter Lougheed responded. "We need only look at the energy situation between 1973 and 1979. We were able to come to agreement."[9]

To most Canadians, the disputes over the amending formula were exasperating bafflegab of interest and importance only to politicians, bureaucrats, scholars, and high-priced lawyers. But the arguments went to the root of the most ancient and essential questions of political theory and practice. Indeed, much of the debate at the time of Confederation was taken up with the question of who should have the final say in the making of a constitution.[10] In a democracy, Trudeau argued, the ultimate power resides with the majority, though the rights of minorities should be protected by Parliament, the courts, a charter, or federalism. Thus he had tried to insert a stirring new preamble that would have affirmed that the *people* of Canada "have chosen to live together" as a national community of free individuals. Not so, replied the Gang of Eight premiers. According to British tradition, as they interpreted it, the people's representatives in Parliament and the legislatures reign supreme, and in a federal system, the central government is created and sustained not by the consent of its citizens but by a compact of the provinces—a shaky claim shot down by the Supreme Court in its September ruling. The premiers' draft of the preamble stated that the *provinces* of Canada "choose to remain freely united," which implied, to the delight of the government of Quebec, that they could also choose to freely separate.[11]

This was the tradition, the very mindset that Pierre Trudeau was trying so hard to displace. Though his privileged background made him an unlikely defender of the people, he was by education and temperament a democrat. An iconoclast who chafed against every kind of authority, a Roman Catholic with a Protestant resistance to unchallenged dogma and blind obedience, he viewed himself as an outsider and an *agent provocateur* even while he was prime minister. He had cut his teeth fighting for democracy against the authoritarian and corrupt politics of Maurice Duplessis, after all, and he didn't trust the elites to represent anybody's interests but their own. If he had his way, this November meeting—eleven men gathered in secret to rearrange the constitution without any direct input from the people—was a necessary but final use of the old machinery of executive federalism, regional barons, and backroom deals.

On Monday morning, as prearranged with Trudeau, Bill Davis announced his willingness to give up Ontario's veto in the Victoria formula if it helped secure a deal, but he seconded the prime minister's objections to the opting-out provision in the Vancouver formula.[12] René Lévesque insisted on having either a veto for Quebec, which was unacceptable to Alberta, or the right to opt out of future amendments with financial compensation, which was unacceptable to Ottawa. On Tuesday morning, the first ministers went round and round in search of common ground. What about a longer list of the items that would require unanimous consent, or a special list for each province, or no list at all? What about the consent of seven provinces representing 60 percent of the population, or eight provinces with no population requirement?

Unable to square the circle, Trudeau returned to the idea of asking the people to decide for them. Failing any other options, why not put the two alternatives to a national referendum in two years' time? "I think that we will have to agree to disagree," he said, "and agree to a deadlock breaker."[13] However, the prime minister and the Gang of Eight quickly fell into squabbling about the conditions and very notion of a referendum.

"A majority of the provinces and a majority of population will be needed," said Premier Blakeney. "You can't simply use a national referendum with a national majority."

But Trudeau argued that a referendum based on a majority of the regions—or more especially, of the provinces—set the bar too high. In other words, while the Resolution's regional formula was fine for future amendments, it wouldn't work in this case. "If we accede to that proposal," he said, "we keep unanimity forever."

"You don't agree with the equality of the provinces?" Lougheed asked him.

"I believe in the equality of people," Trudeau answered.

The dispute flared into a loud and acrimonious quarrel. "At this point," Howard Leeson, Saskatchewan's deputy minister of intergovernmental relations, jotted down in his notes, "Prime Minister Trudeau walked out with obvious disgust on his face."[14]

NINE

Rights and Freedoms

If constitutional reform had meant nothing more than patriation and an amending formula, it's unlikely Pierre Trudeau would have wasted so much time and political capital trying to get them. However basic to Canada's dignity as an independent nation, they were not so essential to his running of the country or to his promise to Quebecers as to be worth the drawn-out angst. Legally, in fact, he could have patriated the BNA Act at any point, and he had long understood that he might have to accept the Gang of Eight's option if cornered. "I find it deplorable," he told the press on Tuesday afternoon, "but I am forced to consider this compromise."[1] What spurred the fight was Trudeau's decision to yoke the federal government's Resolution to a Charter of Rights and Freedoms. As he made clear in his remarks during the televised session on Monday morning, while he was open to discussing its contents and implementation, the Charter itself was not negotiable.

"Given the federal veto, and no proposed amending formula suggests anything else, the federal government has more flexibility with respect to the amending formula than with respect to the Charter: that is to say, the federal government can exercise significant control over the use of the amending formula, even if it is one which the federal government finds deplorable; on the other hand, if a Charter is not obtained this time round, it will be a long time before the chance will come again," Trudeau's advisers counselled in the secret "Sketch of the Negotiating Sequence," which was annexed to his briefing book. "Thus, so long as a veto for Quebec is preserved, a price can be paid through the amending formula for a *quid pro quo* on the Charter."[2]

Patriation, it could be argued, had become Pierre Trudeau's excuse to take advantage of a once-in-a-century opportunity to entrench a bill of rights in the Canadian constitution. The Charter drove him to press ahead to London, come hell or high water. It gave majesty and heart to what might otherwise be seen as a fairly irrelevant and prosaic legalism. It was another foundation stone in the arduous process of building a nation and safeguarding its unity against the forces of dualism and regionalism. Like the Resolution's referendum mechanisms, it was designed to take power from all levels of government and give it to the people of Canada through their supreme law.

"I can think of no better occasion," Trudeau declared in a speech to the Canadian Bar Association on September 4, 1967, in what turned out to be the opening salvo of a fourteen-year campaign, "for seeking to find a solution to the problem of developing a Canadian constitution in Canada—of finally 'patriating' our constitution—than when we have reached agreement on constitutional protection of the basic rights of the citizen."[3]

But the Charter of Rights and Freedoms had become as great an obstacle as the amending formula to any agreement with the Gang of Eight. If the dissidents saw Ottawa's unilateral action and its Victoria formula as an offence to federalism and the equality of the provinces, they viewed the proposed Charter as a shameless raid into areas of exclusive provincial jurisdiction, such as police procedures, affirmative action, labour regulations, and education. "I understand your view on why you want a charter, but why impose it on us?" Peter Lougheed asked.[4]

Sterling Lyon and Allan Blakeney went further in their opposition, with passionate yet highly theoretical denunciations of the very idea of an entrenched charter of rights. They grounded their arguments in the unwritten precedents of British common law, as opposed to the rigid strictures of the French civil code, and the whole debate came back again to the great question of where power should rest. An entrenched charter, they claimed, represented a transfer of decision-making from elected representatives to appointed judges, whether of the left, as Lyon feared, or of the right, in Blakeney's view. Unlike the federal and provincial bills of rights already in place, Trudeau's Charter would be imposed from the top down across the country and prove almost impossible to amend or revoke.

"Prime Minister," Lyon declared at the First Ministers' Conference in September 1980, "you have described the entrenchment of a charter of rights as a mechanism that would give more power to the people. In fact, sir, it takes power from the people and places it in the hands of men, albeit men learned in law, but not necessarily aware of the everyday concerns of Canadians."[5]

Too often, the federal negotiators treated the Gang of Eight's opposition to the Charter as nothing more than a bargaining tactic. That was a mistake. Principle made a deal much more difficult. "I will never agree to an entrenched charter," Lyon repeated shortly before leaving the conference on Wednesday morning.[6] The others weren't quite so dogmatic, if only because they knew how popular the idea was among their constituents, and by November 1981 most of the Gang's members understood its importance to Trudeau. There were even a few murmurs of compromise from some of them during the Tuesday morning session. Nevertheless, none of the Gang was ready to give an inch until there was a final decision on an amending formula. The two items would sink or swim together.

Pierre Trudeau's interest in protecting human rights and democratic freedoms dated back to the 1940s and his days as a student at Harvard, the École libre des sciences politiques in Paris, and the London School of Economics. He reflected on the evils of totalitarianism in Germany and Russia; he studied the classics of French political thought, from Jean-Jacques Rousseau to Emmanuel Mounier; he absorbed the liberalism of John Locke and Thomas Jefferson; and he arrived at a set of values, combining personal liberty with social justice, by which to live his life. At the core was the individual—or more accurately, the person—who freely decides to identify himself or herself with a community, a country, a religion, a language, an ethnic group, or other collectivities for mutual benefit, self-fulfillment, and the greatest happiness of the greatest number.[7]

"I have long believed that freedom is the most important value of a just society," he wrote, "and the exercise of freedom its principal characteristic."[8]

Returning to Quebec in 1949, he applied what he had learned in history books and scholarly texts to taking on the dictatorial regime of Premier Maurice Duplessis. In 1937, Duplessis had passed a law allowing his police to padlock any building suspected of being used to disseminate communist propaganda. In 1946, he had revoked the liquor licence of a Montreal restaurant owner for the sin of bailing out the hundreds of Jehovah's Witnesses who had been arrested and jailed for their religious beliefs. In late 1949, he would send the police to Asbestos to break up an illegal strike with false arrests and billy clubs. As André Burelle noted, no one who hadn't lived under the oppressive atmosphere of *duplessisme* could fully grasp the moral force that drove intellectuals such as Pierre Trudeau to fight for liberty and democracy.[9] Personal experience taught Trudeau how absolute parliamentary supremacy, like any concentration of power, could be translated into despotic abuse if individual rights weren't protected through a system of checks and balances.

Trudeau marched in support of the unions and offered his services as a labour lawyer free of charge across the province. He joined the Canadian Civil Liberties Association and denounced Duplessis's abuses of power in vitriolic essays that prevented him from getting a university position as long as *le chef* was alive. He participated in the founding of two non-partisan movements for the advancement of democracy in the province. In all this activity, he was heavily influenced by the writings and table talk of his mentor, Frank Scott, a brilliant professor of constitutional law at McGill University, a distinguished poet and essayist, a leading socialist thinker, and one of Canada's most respected civil-rights activists. Though no friend of communism, Scott successfully argued against Duplessis's Padlock Act and in favour of freedom of association before the Supreme Court. For the sake of freedom of religion, he helped win the case against the premier himself for violating the rule of law in his persecution of the Jehovah's Witnesses. He went to bat for freedom of expression when *Lady Chatterley's Lover* was banned as obscene. And it was Frank Scott who lent intellectual weight to the constitutional and political case for central planning, national programs, and an entrenched bill of rights to guarantee the freedom of the individual.

"We have a rendezvous with the BNA Act," Scott used to tell his law students, many of whom went on to become major players in Canada's attempts to renew it, and he employed the term "just society" almost thirty years before Trudeau made it famous.[10]

While Trudeau was never a student of Frank Scott's in any formal way, he was undoubtedly a protégé. He attended a lecture on patriation by Scott in 1943, admired his intelligence when they were both minor participants at the federal–provincial constitutional conference in 1950, worked with him on an influential book about the Asbestos strike in 1955, travelled with him to the Arctic in 1956, and looked up to him as a teacher, Renaissance man, and father figure. "It's been [from] my contacts with Frank in his person and his actions that I absorbed much of my constitutional thinking," Trudeau once remarked.[11] And when the battle was over and won in April 1982, the prime minister introduced Frank Scott to Her Majesty the Queen with tears in his eyes and the words "Madam, if we have a charter of rights in this country, we owe it to this one man. Everything I learned about the Constitution, I learned from this man."[12]

A bill of rights was hardly an original idea. France and the United States had each had one since the eighteenth century. In 1948, the United Nations' Universal Declaration of Human Rights was penned by a Canadian, John Humphrey, a colleague of Frank Scott's at McGill's faculty of law. In 1960, Prime Minister Diefenbaker introduced the Canadian Bill of Rights with great pride and fanfare. Saskatchewan passed a bill of rights as early as 1947, and Ontario, Alberta, and Quebec passed human rights codes in 1962, 1971, and 1975, respectively. In 1976, Canada signed the U.N.'s International Covenant on Civil and Political Rights. Nevertheless, because these were applicable only within certain jurisdictions and vulnerable to being altered or revoked at any moment by a simple vote, they never had the overriding authority of an entrenched constitutional amendment. Trudeau wanted to fix that once and for all, and not just in Quebec but across Canada, where the record of justice and tolerance wasn't always a happy one. Aboriginal Canadians, Chinese Canadians, and Black Canadians had been the victims of egregious discrimination. Japanese Canadians had been dragged off to internment camps during the Second World War. Communists, real or imagined, had been persecuted in Ontario. The freedom of the press had been violated in Alberta. Women hadn't even been recognized as "persons" until 1929.

"More recently," a federal briefing document noted, "laws have been adopted restricting residents of one province from acquiring property (PEI and Saskatchewan) or seeking employment in another province (Quebec and Newfoundland), restraining public assemblies (Montreal street bylaw), limiting the use of English (in Quebec) and restricting freedom of speech and association (Quebec referendum).

Beyond these laws, we have also witnessed illustrations of police practices that call into question how effectively some of our legal rights are protected."[13] It might also have mentioned Trudeau's own override of the Canadian Bill of Rights in October 1970, when a cell of Marxist terrorists kidnapped a British diplomat and killed a Quebec Cabinet minister in Montreal.

Perhaps no single piece of legislation in Canadian history has been studied and debated more thoroughly than the Charter of Rights and Freedoms. It was constructed upon the early drafts in the 1940s, Diefenbaker's Bill of Rights in the 1950s, and the provincial charters in the 1960s. A bare-bones version was accepted by the first ministers at the doomed Victoria conference in 1971, and in 1978, the federal government proposed an entrenched charter that would apply to Ottawa and any province that chose to opt in. The travelling road show of ministers and officials examined various texts during the summer of 1980. The first ministers argued about the pros and cons of a charter during their disastrous September conference. The federal Cabinet spent almost thirty hours over two and a half weeks going through a draft in minute detail before presenting it for Parliament's consideration in early October. (Some of the arguments got so emotional that three ministers were reported to have broken down in tears.[14]) In November, a joint committee of the House of Commons and the Senate began televised hearings; during the course of 267 hours over fifty-six days, 914 individuals, 294 groups, and 104 witnesses made known their views, the overwhelming majority of which were on how to improve the Charter, not kill it. The government responded to the committee's report in February 1981 by agreeing to a host of amendments, dealing with everything from the rights of the disabled to the rights of aboriginals, and these were incorporated into a fifth, unamendable version of the Resolution, which was adopted by Parliament on April 23–24, 1981, but still required a final vote.

Not only had the process made the Charter of Rights and Freedoms stronger and more comprehensive than that first proposed in October

1980, but it also gave a surprising depth and breadth to the popular support for patriation. Far more than federal strategists had ever imagined, the Charter became the banner that rallied the Liberal caucus, the federal Cabinet, and most of the country to persevere through the grimmest days of the battle for constitutional reform.

"Polling commissioned by the federal government showed this patriation initiative needed a grinding dynamic that had popular legitimacy and popular momentum," said Hugh Segal, a key adviser to Premier Bill Davis and close friend of Michael Kirby's. "They coalesced all the previous discussion of rights and freedoms into a single Charter, and when they tested it, they found not only was it popular among traditional Liberal markets, but it was popular among francophones, it was popular in the West, it was popular everywhere. They believed the country needed this kind of rebalancing, but the fact that it was attractive did not go lost upon them—or upon Ontario."[15]

The result was the Charter that Trudeau placed before the premiers in November 1981. It enshrined the four fundamental freedoms—of conscience and religion; of thought, belief, opinion, and expression; of peaceful assembly; and of association. Democratic rights included the right to vote and the right to regular parliamentary elections. Equality rights ensured equality before and under the law to every Canadian, regardless of race, national or ethnic origin, colour, religion, sex, age, or mental or physical disability. Legal rights, which were of particular concern to police associations and the provincial ministries of justice, dealt with such technical issues as search and seizure, detention and arrest, cruel and unusual punishment, criminal proceedings, and self-incrimination. Mobility rights, the most important remnant of Ottawa's aborted attempt to strengthen the economic union, permitted every citizen to live and work in any province. In addition, there were general guarantees recognizing aboriginal rights, preserving Canada's multicultural heritage, and promoting equality of opportunity through economic development, essential services, and the principle of equalization.

Pierre Trudeau consulting with Jean Chrétien during a break.

"In the grand tradition of the 1789 Declaration of the Rights of Man and the Citizen and the 1791 Bill of Rights of the United States of America," Trudeau proclaimed, "it implicitly established the primacy of the individual over the state and all government institutions, and in so doing, recognized that all sovereignty resides in the people. In this respect, the Canadian Charter was a new beginning for the Canadian nation: it sought to strengthen the country's unity by basing the sovereignty of the Canadian people on a set of values common to all, and in particular on the notion of equality among all Canadians."[16]

Though the Charter carried the debate way beyond Quebec's issues, no sections were more contentious—or of greater importance to Pierre Trudeau—than the two on language rights. The first enshrined the Official Languages Act of 1969, which put English and French on an equal footing in all the institutions and services of Parliament and the government of Canada. Linguistic equality was also to be entrenched, at the request of Premier Richard Hatfield, in the province of New

Brunswick, a third of whose citizens were francophones (though in order to get Bill Davis's support for the Resolution, Trudeau backed away from imposing it on Ontario).[17] The second section went even further by guaranteeing, wherever the numbers were sufficient, primary and secondary school education in English or French to any child of Canadian citizens who had either of the official languages as their mother tongue or had received their primary-school education in English or French in Canada, as well as to children (and their siblings) who had begun their schooling in either language.[18]

No matter what happened this Wednesday in November 1981, Pierre Trudeau wasn't going to give up on the Charter because he wasn't going to give up on minority-language rights, and he wasn't going to give up on minority-language rights because he wasn't going to give up on the survival of French Canada. That was the promise he had made to francophones inside and outside Quebec. That was his reply to the separatists. That was his life's work. "It's the essence of my existence," he told B.C.'s Bill Bennett during a private meeting at 24 Sussex Drive six weeks before the November conference.[19]

Language rights were individual rights, Trudeau insisted, not collective rights, and certainly not rights belonging to any government claiming to be acting on behalf of a particular group. But why, Premier Blakeney of Saskatchewan once asked him, should language be included in a charter of rights at all, since speaking English or French was not in itself a human right? "I suggested that he was embedding them in the charter because it was easier to argue for a charter than it was to argue for free-standing language rights," Blakeney remembered. "He readily agreed. Since he clearly wanted the language rights provisions, he had decided to wrap them in a charter. From that, I concluded that the language rights provisions were part of Mr. Trudeau's bottom line."[20]

Language and education had been the sparks of political and social conflagration since the first decades following the Conquest. They were the instruments by which the Roman Catholic Church secured the survival of the *Canadiens* for two hundred years. They were among the most difficult issues to be solved in the negotiations leading up to Confederation.[21] When the government of Quebec replaced the Church as the guardian of the flock in the 1960s, French replaced the Communion wafer as the sacred benediction on the tongue. Every schoolchild was taught to genuflect before the agonies of anti-French legislation as if they were the Stations of the Cross—Royal Proclamation of 1763, Act of Union of 1840, New Brunswick Common Schools Act of 1871, Manitoba School Act of 1890, Ontario's Regulation 17 of 1912—and René Lévesque defined Quebecers not by history, religion, or even citizenship, but by their use of French. "Everything else depends on this one essential element," he wrote, "and follows from it or leads infallibly back to it."[22]

To which many anglophones in suburban Montreal and Orange Ontario, Loyalists down east, and cowboys out west replied, "If the English language was good enough for Jesus Christ, it damn well ought to be good enough for those bloody frogs," or sentiments to that effect.[23] French to them was the language of popery, of Napoleon, and of the conquered *habitants*. It had no place in the glory that was the British Empire in North America or the future that was the American Dream. When John Diefenbaker soared to oratorical heights with his vision of One Canada or railed against "hyphenated" Canadians, he was elevating no language other than English and no culture other than British. And when Pierre Trudeau introduced the Official Languages Act in 1969, he barely survived the political backlash from those English-speaking Canadians who felt that French was being rammed down their throats.

The choice, to Trudeau, was clear: either English Canadians had to accept the fair demands of their French-speaking compatriots for equality or they faced the very real prospect of dismemberment. History gave the union two predominant language groups; the BNA Act authorized the federal government to protect the use of French and English;

and justice required an end to the discriminatory practices that had kept French Canadians at a disadvantage and confined to Quebec.[24] Combating separatism meant compelling federal institutions, from the highest courts to the local post office, to communicate with Canada's francophone citizens in their own tongue. It meant providing franco-phones with schools, media outlets, and government services wherever the numbers were sufficient. It meant enabling more francophones to attain high-level, high-profile positions in business and the bureaucracy, in academe and the arts, for both the precedent and the power of it. It meant appointing francophones as senior Cabinet ministers, gover-nors general, commissioners of the RCMP, and chiefs of defence staff. Ultimately, it meant making francophones feel secure, in both a real and a psychological sense, about their future place in Canada.

"I believe that the bargain of Confederation is that French-speaking Canadians can move, live, and work anywhere in Canada," Trudeau said, "and send their kids to school and deal with the federal govern-ment in their language."[25]

Pierre Trudeau had no illusions about the risks he was taking with the minority-language education clause. The Charter would be crossing the Rubicon into provincial jurisdiction on an especially volatile issue in every region of the country. By going that far, he was exposing his unilateral action to attacks from the provinces, the courts, the *indépen-dantistes*, and Westminster. But Trudeau dreamed of restoring the Confederation bargain, of doing what Laurier and St. Laurent hadn't been able to do, of righting the historic wrongs done to French-speaking Canadians outside Quebec, and he couldn't accomplish that without protecting the rights of English-speaking Canadians inside Quebec as well. That wasn't, in his opinion, a power grab by the federal govern-ment. It was a matter of making the courts, rather than the politicians in Ottawa or Quebec or any particular province, the guardians of minority-language rights for all time.

"If certain language and educational rights were written into the

Constitution," Trudeau believed, "along with other basic liberties, in such a way that *no* government—federal or provincial—could legislate against them, French Canadians would cease to feel confined to their Quebec ghetto, and the spirit of separatism would be laid to rest forever." [26]

TEN

Cat Among the Pigeons

René Lévesque was in a particularly sour mood that Wednesday morning, November 4, 1981. He seemed like seven dwarfs rolled into one: grumpy, angry, edgy, mopey, distracted, and sullen one moment and cynical the next. He smelled danger in the air. His instincts told him, as did his advisers, that some or all of the other members of the Gang of Eight were about to buckle under the tremendous pressure they were feeling not to end the day in failure. "We were already getting signals that two or three of our allies were becoming shaky," he recalled, "and that secret transactions were taking place in the wings."[1]

On the night of the Supreme Court's ruling in September, for example, Saskatchewan's attorney general, Roy Romanow, had met with his federal and Ontario counterparts, Jean Chrétien and Roy McMurtry, at Chrétien's house in Ottawa. Romanow was supposed to show up with the bottle of Scotch he had lost in a wager about what the judges would say, but he arrived empty-handed—the liquor stores having already closed—so the three veteran politicians, all close buddies despite their different party affiliations, had to share a few beers instead. Their chit-chat naturally drifted into free-wheeling speculation about whether a compromise was any more likely and, if so, what it might look like. No conclusions were reached, beyond a resolve to keep pushing for a negotiated settlement. Innocent enough, except that when the media got wind of the meeting, Romanow thoughtlessly denied having discussed anything of substance. At a ministerial conference in Montreal on October 3, 1981, he was forced to apologize for misleading his colleagues and received a sharp rebuke from Claude Morin, Quebec's veteran minister of intergovernmental affairs.

All through October and to the eve of the November conference, Morin fuelled Lévesque's suspicions with rumours and reports. Ottawa was talking to British Columbia. Ontario was conspiring with Saskatchewan. Saskatchewan was on the phone to Nova Scotia. Ottawa was trying to tempt Nova Scotia and Newfoundland with side deals on offshore resources. And those suspicions grew stronger once the first ministers arrived in Ottawa. On Monday morning, *The Globe and Mail* carried a front-page story claiming that Saskatchewan and B.C. were "prepared to move away from the basic position of the so-called gang of eight."[2] On Tuesday afternoon, Bill Bennett, stirred to action by his new role as chair of the Annual Premiers' Conference, persuaded the rest of the Gang—with Quebec and Manitoba's grudging acquiescence—to propose a few new concessions to Trudeau and Davis. On Wednesday morning, during the Gang of Eight's daily breakfast meeting at the Château Laurier, Allan Blakeney informed his colleagues of his intention to put forward some suggestions of his own when the session opened. "They're getting ready to screw us," Lévesque said to his advisers on his way out of breakfast. "It's now every man for himself and too bad for the others."[3]

The *indépendantiste* hardliners in Lévesque's Cabinet, caucus, and party, not least his powerful finance minister, Jacques Parizeau, had begged him not to return to the negotiating table after the failure of the Yes vote in May 1980. As they saw it, the federalists won the referendum only by spreading fear, lies, and tens of millions of dollars of illegal advertising across the province. To engage in any further constitutional talks, they argued, would be to recognize the legitimacy of the No side's tactics and humiliate a proud Quebec. At best, they said, the process would be a waste of time. At worst, it would be a trap. The deck was stacked against Quebec ten to one; the other premiers were never going to give the province what the Parti Québécois wanted, and Trudeau was a slippery bastard who would stoop to any dirty trick to trounce the nationalists. In the end, the gains weren't likely to be worth the risks. Even a success would be a setback for the ultimate goal of independence.

"What else could we do with the gas that remained in our tank?" asked Claude Charron, the young, effervescent Government House Leader with hair like a clown's wig, one of a small coterie of loyalists whom Lévesque had brought with him to the November conference, along with his moderate (and unilingual) minister of justice, Marc-André Bédard; his most senior bureaucrat, Louis Bernard; and the formidable Claude Morin. Though Parizeau turned up in Ottawa uninvited, he was deliberately kept out of the inner circle. "When Parizeau made strategy," Charron said, "he made it in stone. His problem: he was never wrong, never compromised. Moreover, he was paranoid."[4]

Grief-stricken after the loss of the referendum and rarely engaged by the details of constitution-making, Lévesque succumbed once again to the advice of Claude Morin, who now sat like a tall, impassive, bald-headed abbot between Lévesque and Trudeau, stroking his sideburns and sucking on his unlit pipe. "Giving us a 'no' vote meant sending us to Ottawa with a terrible handicap," the intergovernmental minister admitted.[5]

Morin was one of the most intriguing characters in the long history of Canada's constitutional negotiations. With university degrees from Laval and Columbia, the former professor of economics and political science was a survivor of three ideologically different regimes and almost twenty years of political turmoil. Appointed by Jean Lesage in 1963 to be the first deputy minister of the new ministry of federal–provincial relations and reappointed by Daniel Johnson and Robert Bourassa, he quit the public service in 1971 to return to teaching, only to re-emerge as a candidate for the Parti Québécois two years later. With the election of the Parti Québécois in 1976, he became Lévesque's chief constitutional adviser. Morin was front and centre when Lesage pushed for special status, when Johnson demanded equality or independence, when Bourassa walked away from the Victoria Charter, and when Lévesque fought the referendum on an ambiguous question that had Morin's fingerprints all over it. Given the general weakness of the Quebec delegation, Morin was the heavyweight, a role he relished.[6]

Claude Morin had begun his career with a vision that Canada could rearrange itself into a government of two equal majorities, one based in English Canada, the other based in French Quebec. When that proved unachievable, he moved towards breaking up the country and then

Claude Morin and René Lévesque.

putting the pieces back together again as an economic association of two independent nations. In both cases, the result was to be attained gradually, step by step, without drama or trauma or penalty, in part to avoid any social or financial crises, and in part to lead Quebecers by the hand into very deep waters. More than any other single person, Claude Morin was identified with the incremental strategy that would see Quebec sever its relations with Canada just as Canada had severed its relations with Great Britain—a few powers here, a few powers there, until there were no bonds left worth keeping. As such, he became the lightning rod for all those who wanted complete and immediate independence. They accused him of being too cautious, too conflicted, too clever by half. Their suspicions turned to shock and fury in 1992, when it was revealed that Morin had been a paid informant of the Royal Canadian Mounted Police until shortly after he entered the Cabinet in November 1976.[7]

Amid the ruins of the referendum, Morin had persuaded Lévesque that the ball was now in Ottawa's court. Since it was Trudeau who had made the promise to renew the federation, Quebec had to do nothing but wait to see what he offered. If it was acceptable, well and good, Quebecers would get powers or privileges somewhere between sovereignty-association and the status quo, and the PQ would enjoy a lift in the polls. If it was unacceptable—a far more plausible scenario and an even better one for the cause—Quebecers would feel tricked by the federalists and, in their disappointment, take a second look at independence.

"In voting No in the referendum," Lévesque told reporters a few days after his government's resounding setback, "the citizens of Quebec clearly indicated that they wanted to give renewed federalism another chance. The government has no right to run away from this decision and will therefore participate faithfully in every effort at constitutional reform."[8]

Quebec's strategy was made easier by the instructions Trudeau gave his staff on the day following the referendum. "Now," he had said, evoking Napoleon at Austerlitz, "we have to attack everywhere."[9]

His bellicose tone at the meeting with the premiers in early June, his unnecessary rush to negotiate the twelve items on his agenda during the summer, and his surprising demand for new federal powers over the economic union—all played into Lévesque's hand. Though each of the provinces had its own issues with Ottawa, from oil pricing and freight rates to budget cuts, most of the premiers were alarmed by the prime minister's threat to proceed unilaterally to Westminster if he couldn't get their agreement by September 1980. It stoked everything they disliked in the man—his bullying, his taunting, and his arrogance.

Throughout the summer negotiations in 1980, Quebec worked at re-establishing amicable relations with the other provinces after the wounds of the referendum campaign. By being open—or at least appearing to be open—to a new deal, the Parti Québécois couldn't be charged with ignoring the will of the majority of Quebecers or singled out yet again as the spoilsport of Confederation. Claude Morin would benefit from gaining whatever bits of knowledge or influence he could at the meetings. Building a fresh rapport with the other delegates might demonstrate to the premiers, to Canadians, and to the people of the province that a sovereign Quebec would be able to negotiate an association with the rest of Canada someday. And if Ottawa had to be stopped, there would be strength in numbers.

"What do we Quebecers expect from the resumption of negotiations?" Morin asked. "First, that they firmly, openly and clearly take account of what might be regarded as a common denominator among Quebecers: that, for us, Quebec is a distinct society that wishes to be recognized as such, that it is free to decide on its future, and that it is determined to keep in and for Quebec—and to acquire when they are lacking—the cultural, economic and linguistic tools through which it can affirm itself and develop according to its own aspirations and needs. Next, we expect these negotiations to lead to clarification in the sharing of powers and a significant decrease in federal–provincial duplication of services. Finally, we expect these negotiations to confirm that, within the federal system, the central government regards the provinces not as regional administrative entities to be kept under constant surveillance, but as major responsible partners in whom confidence can and must be shown."[10]

Slyly, methodically, Morin insinuated himself into the other provincial camps, aligning with them in their concerns, sympathizing with their indignation, and speaking up with them whenever there were items or ideas that didn't adversely impact the goals of the Parti Québécois. "If we showed ourselves too enthusiastic, too 'activist,' too in charge," he later explained, "the others, always a bit suspicious, might detect, in the putting together of common positions, some diabolical *péquiste* strategy, perfidiously designed less to help the provinces than to promote the interests of Quebec alone and those of a single political option, sovereignty-association."[11]

His stealth worked. By the time the first ministers met in Ottawa on September 8, 1980, as we have seen, Quebec had managed to convince most of the other provinces that it might indeed sign a deal in exchange for a few new powers and a couple of face-saving gestures. In believing this, Pierre Trudeau thought, the anglophone premiers were either incredibly naive or unconscionably self-serving. They clearly didn't know the separatists as well as he did. The Parti Québécois government was interested only in stopping the patriation process, or at least delaying it until Trudeau was out of the picture.

"You know," Jean Chrétien had remarked to Claude Charron during the summer negotiations, "if you were to make a deal on the Constitution now, you could get a lot for Quebec and the people would be pleased."

"Jean," replied Charron, whose assignment from Lévesque was to make sure Claude Morin stayed on the nationalist straight and narrow, "don't waste your time. You know we are separatists. Independence is the first article of our party program. So how can we sign up for a new Confederation?"[12]

Not only would passage of the federal government's Resolution deprive Lévesque of a tool he and other Quebec premiers had used so effectively to gain more for their province, but it was also far from the special status and devolution of responsibilities that Quebec governments of all stripes had been demanding for more than a quarter of a century. On the contrary, it tilted in the opposite direction, towards the rights of individuals and more interference in provincial affairs. Trudeau had deftly defined "renewed federalism" not in the PQ's terms but in terms of his own vision, values, and priorities—which he then equated with the vision, values, and priorities of all Canadian people, including Quebecers. "Mr. Trudeau is making a grave mistake," Lévesque warned, "if he tries to profit from the referendum results to impose a centralist vision of Canada that Quebec has always repudiated and fought."[13]

From the First Ministers' Conference in September 1980 to this make-or-break one in November 1981, Lévesque's objective was to build and maintain a common front with as many of the other premiers as possible to stop Ottawa from taking advantage of the confusion and squabbling inside the Parti Québécois, the weakness of the Quebec government in the polls, and his own demoralization. Not that he wasn't leery of common fronts. Indeed, in this very same room on the fifth floor of the Government Conference Centre in December 1976, the nine English-speaking premiers, infuriated by Lévesque's frank talk about independence, broke a pact they had made with Quebec to fight Trudeau's plan to cut Ottawa's fiscal transfers to the provinces. "It's an illusion to count on a concerted action by the provinces," he warned his Cabinet ministers as late as August 1980.[14] But perhaps it might work out better this time, he hoped, a hope based on what he had witnessed at the First Ministers' Conference in September. Almost every premier—and not one Liberal in the whole bunch—had a bone to pick with the federal government, hated Trudeau's guts, resented Ottawa's withdrawal of its earlier concessions, and feared what unilateral action might mean for the fate of their provinces down the road.

What other options did Quebec really have? It couldn't win by boycotting the process. It couldn't win by holding another referendum. It couldn't try to exercise a veto on what was still a mere proposal. It couldn't get away with a unilateral declaration of independence. It couldn't know what the Supreme Court might decide or what the British Parliament might do. And with an election on the horizon, the Parti Québécois was too low in the opinion polls to risk losing the soft nationalists who only wanted a new deal with Canada. In truth, Lévesque's best defence was his only defence. "Ottawa undertook to reduce the powers of the provinces, in particular Quebec's," said Claude Morin. "From that perspective there was only one thing for us to do: block Ottawa. And to accomplish that, there was only a single means: an alliance for that purpose with as many provinces as possible."[15]

As a result, Quebec was especially active in patching together the Group of Six in October 1980. It challenged the legality of Ottawa's Resolution in the Quebec Court of Appeal in March 1981. It initiated a sophisticated campaign to win over British MPs and opinion-makers at the dining table of Gilles Loiselle, Quebec's gregarious, epicurean agent general in Great Britain. At the same time, Lévesque went on the offensive, launching a publicity campaign across the province, organizing a massive protest rally in the Montreal Forum, and passing a resolution of his own in the National Assembly.

As loud and as often as Lévesque protested that Quebecers had been duped by Trudeau's "vague, but very touching words" in the referendum, however, he could only get so far by fixating on what wasn't being offered. He had to attack the Resolution directly. But patriation, the Charter, and equalization were hard to oppose in and of themselves. Few Quebecers wanted to preserve the remaining links to British colonialism; Ottawa's proposed Charter had been modelled to a certain extent on Quebec's; and as a have-not province, Quebec stood to gain from equalization payments. So Lévesque's argument was reduced to just three basic points: Trudeau's unilateralism was a violation of the law and spirit of Confederation, mobility rights threatened the province's ability to manage its own economy, and education rights for its English-speaking minority would undermine its efforts to protect and strengthen the French language.[16]

"We are the only representatives of our race on a continent where everyone else is and remains forever destined to speak another language and live another culture," Lévesque argued. "It is for this reason that Quebec insisted from the beginning that, at the very least, it have, for itself alone, a democratic Parliament with sovereign powers in the areas which at that time were felt to be essential to maintaining and developing its national identity. It goes without saying that these powers are still essential, particularly in the spheres of language policy and education. There can be no question of taking these powers away from our National Assembly in any way, nor can they be to the slightest degree subject to outside decisions."[17]

Defending provincial autonomy against a rich, expansionist federal government, which also happened to be in the hands of the Anglo majority, was the time-honoured custom of Quebec premiers from Honoré Mercier to Maurice Duplessis. It was especially potent when mixed with the issues of language and culture. Language was called "mother tongue" for profound psychological reasons, after all, and culture was part and parcel of everyone's personal identity. ("Language, guardian of faith," the Church had declared.) With the rise of Quebec nationalism during the 1960s, moreover, the fight had shifted from protecting the French language and French-Canadian culture across the country to promoting them inside the "homeland."

Increasingly, the nationalists gave up on French Power in Ottawa and the francophone communities outside Quebec and turned their attention to containing English wherever it reared its ugly head in the province—in the head offices and department stores of downtown Montreal, on commercial billboards, around the campus of McGill University. At the same time—and even more explosively—plunging birthrates and soaring immigration frightened old-stock French-speaking Quebecers into believing that their cultural survival was under a new demographic threat. Not only were the immigrants bringing alien traditions to the province, but the overwhelming majority of them were choosing to integrate into the anglophone minority, because they saw English as the language of the North American economy, of global technology and Hollywood, of prosperity and opportunity.[18]

As a result, bilingualism and multiculturalism came to be portrayed as a federalist trick to promote English in Quebec rather than a sincere effort to protect the French-speaking minority in Canada. Year by year, the political pressure grew to make daily life as French in the province as it was English in the rest of Canada. "*Québec en français*," chanted the protesters. Robert Bourassa took the first tentative steps with Bill 22 in 1974; René Lévesque completed the job with the more draconian Bill 101 in 1977. French became Quebec's official language.[19] French was to be the language of work and advertising. French-language schooling was compulsory in the public system for any child whose father or mother hadn't received a primary-school education in English *in Quebec*. (Of great significance, as we will see, Lévesque fought successfully to include a "Canada clause" that would extend minority-language education rights to anglophone citizens from *any province* that signed a reciprocal agreement to guarantee the same rights to its francophone communities.[20])

"We weren't told to 'Speak white!' anymore," Lévesque explained, "but we were still obliged to do so in many cases, right here in our own home. One day, if we wanted it badly enough, French would be at home everywhere in Quebec and, as in any normal country, we could finally toss aside the crutches of legislation that have always seemed to me to be deeply humiliating. But for the time being, the prosthesis remained necessary."[21]

Bill 101 was, of course, in direct opposition to what Pierre Trudeau was trying to do across Canada in the face of stiff resistance. Quebec nationalists were writing off the significant French-speaking minorities in New Brunswick, Ontario, and Manitoba as a lost cause just when Ottawa was fighting to assure them government services in their own tongue and guarantee their schooling forever. Why should English Canadians, many of whom were being won over by Trudeau's appeals for justice, now tolerate the rights—even the existence—of the French-speaking minority if the government of Quebec wasn't going to tolerate the rights of the English-speaking minority? If an attack on the French language in Manitoba in 1890 was such a grievous injustice, why was an attack on the English language in Quebec any less so?[22] If the language learned at the breast was so precious to the development of an individual and the flourishing of a people, as Quebec's poets and intellectuals had claimed when pleading the case for French, why, then, were these same poets and intellectuals ready to suppress the mother tongue of others?

Like Lévesque's decision to raise a statue of Maurice Duplessis in front of the National Assembly, the PQ's discrimination against the English language revealed, in Pierre Trudeau's eyes, the "true colours" of Quebec nationalism: intolerant, regressive, even totalitarian. "An independent Quebec will not only seek independence," he said, "but also the creation of a monolithic society, dominated by a single language."[23]

Bill 101 proved extremely popular among French-speaking Quebecers, despite the fact that it impinged on their freedom of choice as much as that of immigrants. French, they believed, unlike English, had to be artificially nurtured and safeguarded in North America or else it would disappear. The regulations that were forced upon the public and private sectors—as well as the exodus of young anglophones who felt pushed out of the province by those regulations—helped franco-phones move up the social and economic ladder. A spat over whether French-speaking controllers should be allowed to direct air traffic with French-speaking pilots in French over the skies of Quebec blew up into a major political firestorm in Ottawa, which, in the words of one Trudeau adviser, "also revealed the ugly side of majoritarian democracy."[24] French Montreal took on an increasingly French personality. There was even a whiff of sweet revenge in the air, as if the shame of two hundred years of subjugation had finally been cast off and self-determination already achieved. As for the Anglos who remained, their complaints were dismissed as nothing more than the sour grapes of an isolated and privileged minority who still enjoyed more rights, influence, and public services than the francophone minorities of any other province. Even Pierre Trudeau didn't dare to take on Bill 101 by challenging it in the courts or disallowing it, as Ottawa was permitted to do by the BNA Act.

Now, René Lévesque proclaimed when the federal government tabled its People's Package in October 1980, the prime minister was trying to do through the constitution what he hadn't been able to do politically—and do it in a way that would deny the people of Quebec any opportunity to object. "Under the pretext of giving citizens a new charter of rights," he said, "the Ottawa project is, in fact, an unprecedented attack on the powers of the National Assembly of Quebec, designed to limit and restrict it, especially with regard to the language of education."[25]

All through the winter and into the spring of 1981, Lévesque and Morin were at the forefront of the battle against the Resolution. "Quebec provided the glue which kept the opposing provinces together," Roy Romanow, Saskatchewan's attorney general, later confirmed. "Although the Quebec government was not in a strong political position, judged by its numerous by-election losses, it displayed a cunningness towards federal–provincial relations, which created the maximum level of uncertainty and, in fact, began to place the federal government on the defensive in both Canada and London."[26]

While the Resolution was buffeted by three contradictory court decisions, the slap on the wrist by a British parliamentary committee, the remarkably effective lobbying efforts of the provincial and aboriginal delegations in London, the transformation of the Group of Six into the Gang of Eight, the stalling tactics of the Official Opposition in the House of Commons, and the federal government's own reluctant reference to the Supreme Court, Quebec helped keep the dissident premiers united in their opposition. Yet hidden beneath the common front's string of successes were growing tensions and fraying nerves.

Even Ottawa's leading opponent in English Canada was beginning to have second thoughts about the Gang of Eight's strategy. "It was clear that most Canadians wanted patriation," Peter Lougheed noted, "and believed that the premiers could not even agree among ourselves on something as fundamental as an amending formula."[27] Indeed, he feared his group was at risk of winning a lot of battles but losing the war. If the Supreme Court ruled in Ottawa's favour, Trudeau's Resolution would be rushed to London, and no one—not the people, the press, or the British parliamentarians—was likely to stand in its way if there wasn't a viable alternative. Mere opposition was no longer enough. There had to be a counter-proposal, something so reasonable that rejecting it would blow up in the federal government's face.

"Our accord has got to be palatable to Trudeau," B.C.'s minister of intergovernmental relations, Garde Gardom, told Claude Morin. "Otherwise, it won't work and we'll be back to square one."[28] Gardom's words sent chills down Morin's spine, and he never forgot them in the months ahead. The government of Quebec still believed that it wasn't up to the provinces to propose anything. Trudeau had made an offer; the Gang had rejected it.

On April 13, 1981, less than a year after its referendum setback, the Parti Québécois surprised almost everyone by winning another majority in the provincial election. *"Faut rester forts au Québec"* was its campaign slogan. "We must remain strong in Quebec." Though the PQ's victory had been achieved by a record of decent government, a dislike of Claude Ryan, and a commitment not to hold another referendum in the immediate future, it gave René Lévesque a vitality and bargaining power not seen since May 1980. Quebec may have needed the common front just as much as ever to stop Trudeau's Resolution, but it didn't like feeling cornered.

"For René Lévesque," wrote Martine Tremblay, one of his senior staff advisers, "whose room to manoeuvre was already very narrow, the challenge was to get the maximum for Quebec all the while knowing that he had to avoid provoking a rupture in the common front, not least because the Supreme Court hadn't yet ruled."[29]

On April 15, 1981, two days after his comeback at the polls and the very day the Quebec Court of Appeal came down on the side of the federal government, Lévesque went to Ottawa to meet with the rest of the Gang of Eight. Since the premiers' officials had been doing the spadework at seven meetings over the past two months, everything was supposed to be in place for a quick, pre-authorized agreement. There would be no Charter, no minority-language education clause, and no mobility rights. In return, Quebec went along with immediate patriation, greater provincial control over natural resources, and the principle of equalization, subject to the condition that Ottawa resume negotiations over the next three years to redistribute powers and reform the central institutions by means of the new amending formula.

But what new amending formula? None of the seven anglophone premiers was prepared to give Quebec or any other province a veto unless everyone got one. Instead, they reaffirmed their support for the formula Alberta had put forward in Vancouver in July 1980: at least seven provinces representing more than 50 percent of the population on matters affecting provincial rights and powers, with the right to opt out. Okay, said Lévesque, but only if Ottawa was forced to pay reasonable financial compensation to any province that chose to exercise the opting-out provision.

Saskatchewan and British Columbia resisted. Trudeau, they assumed, would never buy it, and they didn't particularly like it either: it would encourage a patchwork of programs across the country and allow a couple of the wealthier provinces to thumb their noses at the national interest. To help swallow the bitter pill, they wanted to make opting out conditional on the approval of two-thirds of the legislature of the province wishing to exercise that right, and they thought, before arriving in Ottawa, that they had received Quebec's consent. But Lévesque, who wanted to make the process easier rather than more difficult, objected at the very last minute. Since few Quebec elections produced overwhelming majorities, he argued, the opposition parties would in effect be empowered to decide. What was supposed to lead to a public show of unity, prearranged by secret negotiations, turned into the ugly midnight confrontation between Lévesque and the other seven premiers. The heated discussion went back and forth in Sterling Lyon's suite at the Château Laurier until two-thirty in the morning.

Lévesque eventually got his way, though it left him no choice but to add his signature to those of the others in the full-page advertisement that soon appeared in newspapers across the country, complete with the text of the Gang of Eight's constitutional accord and a maple leaf. "There," he said, pretending to bop Bill Bennett on the head with a bundle of papers in a fit of pique during the elaborately staged ceremony televised live from the Government Conference Centre, "I've signed your damn ad."[30]

Lévesque had paid a very high price to hold the common front together. For the first time, a government of Quebec was prepared to formally concede patriation before getting a new division of powers. Moreover, by accepting the Vancouver formula, Lévesque had put his signature to recognizing "the constitutional equality of provinces as equal partners in Confederation" and had declared his willingness to exchange Quebec's historic claim to a veto for the right to opt out with financial compensation.[31]

A veto was of enormous psychological value in the minds of Quebecers. As founding partners of Confederation, they saw it as a sacred birthright, and as the ultimate defence against abuse and aggression by Canada's English-speaking majority. Pierre Trudeau himself argued on behalf of its entrenchment in the constitution in his defence of the Victoria formula. But was it a genuine weapon or merely a symbolic one? Yes, the government of Quebec had been able to sink two constitutional deals all by itself, but it couldn't prevent Ottawa from exercising its spending power in the province. And a veto alone was of no value in winning new powers or special status.

"A veto can be an obstacle to development as much as an instrument of defence," Lévesque explained in his memoirs. "If Quebec had it, Ontario and perhaps other provinces would surely ask for it, too. And, as in Victoria in 1971, it would be possible to block change and in protecting oneself paralyze others, leaving everyone way ahead ... or behind. On the other hand, the right to opt out, which we had learned to use in the Sixties—the best example being the creation of the Caisse de dépôt—is in my view a much superior weapon, at one and the same time more flexible and more dynamic. 'You wish to take this or that path we are not ready to follow? Very well, my friends, go ahead. But without us.' From stage to stage, I repeat, we could create something very like a country in that fashion."[32]

There it was—exactly the "incremental separatism" that Pierre Trudeau had warned against. Indeed, he quickly dismissed the so-called April Accord as "a victory for those who want to move Canada toward disintegration."[33] It proved to him that Quebec wasn't negotiating in good faith, and had signed the accord only because it knew for certain that he could never accept it. The wonder was that any of the anglophone premiers imagined Trudeau might actually consider it, given the lack of a charter and language rights.

The April Accord was a fatal gamble for René Lévesque. It would be scrutinized and debated for months, years, even decades to come. Though the Supreme Court was later to rule that Quebec had never had a veto in law, Lévesque let slip a unique opportunity to entrench one in the constitution when he rejected the Resolution's amending formula. More dangerously, if the other Gang of Eight members ever came to view the accord as a basis for further compromise, Quebec had no fallback position.

"The truth—and the problem—is that the Accord of April 16 was, for us, a defence mechanism and, for them, a negotiating tool," Morin recalled. "It contained the maximum concessions that Quebec, given the gravity of the situation, could accept with any decency, and, at the same time, the maximum dissent that the anglophone provinces allowed themselves when faced with the 'national government of Canada.'"[34]

"Aren't these admissions of bad faith in negotiations," Trudeau later asked, "and wouldn't it have been more forthright for the Quebec government to have declared from the start—at the first meeting in June 1980—that it had no intention of accepting any federal reform that would not fit in with sovereignty-association?"[35]

Rather than demonstrating the solidarity of the Gang of Eight, the April Accord exposed the underlying strains. It revealed that the eight premiers, divided as they were by different purposes and pressures, could actually agree on very little beyond their opposition to Trudeau's unilateral Resolution.[36] It signalled the distrust that was developing between Quebec and its allies. The English-speaking premiers wanted to get Lévesque's signature in a highly public ceremony because they wanted to make it harder for Quebec to renege, as it had done in 1966 and 1971. For his part, Lévesque wanted to pin them down to what he later described as "a genuine contract which could not unilaterally be modified without consulting, or at the very least informing in advance, the other provinces which had co-signed the Agreement."[37]

Nobody disputed that. The dispute, when it erupted so suddenly and spectacularly on this Wednesday morning in November, was about who first broke that "contract" and whether Quebec would ever have accepted any modification to it.

The fuse was lit when Allan Blakeney, asking to speak following the prime minister's opening statement, presented an elaborate compromise proposal for the first ministers to consider. While everybody else took it for what it was—just another cul de sac—Lévesque saw it as a double-cross. Its length and complexity were proof to him that Blakeney had been preparing to abandon the Gang of Eight for weeks, if not months. "It is not something that could have been done in one day," he fumed, "so I must conclude that Saskatchewan had it in its hip pocket all the time."[38] It unleashed all the grievances and tensions between the two men that had been accumulating ever since the premier of Saskatchewan intervened on behalf of the No side in the 1980 referendum, an anger that was only fuelled when Bill Bennett announced that British Columbia was ready to support minority-language education rights as a sop to Pierre Trudeau.

"Blakeney had drawn up a 'new' formula whose sole originality was that it purely and simply eliminated the opting-out clause," Lévesque remembered. "Since this treachery was backed by a thick document, it was certainly not the fruit of nocturnal inspiration. On top of this, as I realized shortly after, our chairman, Bill Bennett, was not standing exactly square on his feet. I had given him the text of the statement we had prepared for the public meeting, but he had simply mislaid it—'So sorry!'—and didn't seem to be in any great hurry to find it again. Whereupon I had only to pick out around the table several other pairs of averted eyes to conclude that the 'Gang of Eight' had decidedly had its day."[39]

"You're overreacting to this," Roy Romanow protested when confronted by an irate Claude Morin during the brief coffee break. "The Gang still exists. We were only looking for a new approach to force Trudeau to modify his position."[40]

But Morin didn't want a new approach. "Your province confused the guaranteed failure of the federal plan with the failure of the conference," he later explained in a letter to Romanow. "But don't you admit that, on the contrary, it would have been a success if Ottawa's *coup de force* had been completely blocked?"[41]

Trudeau saw an opening, his best chance, the last card. For two days he had tried to split the Gang of Eight, to pull enough provinces out of the common front to give him the number he needed to satisfy the Supreme Court's constitutional convention. Now he seized the moment.

"Rather than break up in disarray and continue our fight on the doorstep of the British Parliament," Trudeau asked the premiers, "why don't we get patriation first—nobody can object to that—then give ourselves two years to solve our problems over the amending formula and the Charter, and, failing that, consult the people in a referendum? There, that's a new offer. The thrust of it is to do with the Charter what we did with the amending formula. I believe we have to have an end to this, a binding process."[42]

Was it premeditated or spontaneous, accidental or calculated, a sincere offer to secure a deal or merely a tactical ploy to break the Gang of Eight? It was a testament to Trudeau's skill as a negotiator—and as an actor—that no one around the table knew for sure. According to his memoirs, he had been toying with the idea in the event the British Parliament did indeed reject a resolution from Ottawa that had little or no provincial support. In his speech to the House of Commons on March 31, 1981, he had raised the possibility of a national referendum, "if that is the only way in which we can get the people of Canada to affirm their loyalty to Canada over and above their regional loyalties." On September 24, 1981, he had hinted at it again during a meeting with Premier Bill Bennett at 24 Sussex Drive. In the wake of the Supreme Court's decision, he had instructed his principal secretary, Tom Axworthy, to prepare for a referendum or an election in 1982, in case the federal government needed to reinforce the legitimacy of its position with a mandate from the people. On the eve of the conference's opening, he had alerted his ally Bill Davis that he was prepared to play this card if and when all the other efforts to break the Gang of Eight failed. Or as he put it to his friend Gérard Pelletier, "I'm going to propose a referendum to the provinces, and if they're stupid enough to accept, I'm going to win it."[43]

Lévesque alone rose to the bait. "Don't assume you'd win," he snapped.

"Surely a great democrat like yourself won't be against a referendum?" Trudeau taunted.

Then, to Trudeau's astonishment, Lévesque took the hook. "That is *not* a non-starter for me," he said. "In spite of our recent experience, I think that we should consult with the people. It's not the end of the world."

"I think that you're wrong," Peter Lougheed jumped in. "It's very divisive."[44] And suddenly the unity of the Gang of Eight was fractured.

Why did Lévesque break from his allies without so much as a sideways glance? In April and again at the Gang's strategy meeting on Sunday, he had pledged along with the other premiers that none of them would take a new initiative without giving everyone else due warning. What made him change his mind? "It seems," he explained to the conference and later to the press, "an honourable way out."

It was also an act of desperation. If the Gang was on the verge of breaking up, as he was by now convinced, a direct appeal to the people through a referendum seemed the safest way for Quebec to prevent or at least hinder the federal government from going to London. Moreover, it was the first offer Lévesque had heard all week that didn't infringe on the powers of Quebec. Anything might happen over the next two years to throw a spanner in the works; Trudeau was likely to retire or be defeated, and Lévesque had as good a chance—maybe, he hoped, a better chance—of winning a referendum by persuading Quebecers that the package was a heinous assault on the powers of the National Assembly and far from what Trudeau had promised them in May 1980.

"I was trying to weigh the pros and cons," Lévesque recalled. "Our common front was a dead issue. For the time being, then, we didn't have much to lose, and two years down the road … who could tell? Besides, if the whole population had a chance to vote on such a fundamental subject, wouldn't that be democratically more respectable than all this intriguing that ended up poisoning the atmosphere?"[45]

Trudeau's sarcastic jibe was unwarranted: René Lévesque was indeed a great democrat. He had built his separatist party election by election when more radical voices had claimed that the rules of parliamentary democracy and the manipulations of the federalists would make victory impossible. He had resisted the arguments of the hardliners that the Parti Québécois win in 1976 was enough to declare independence, without any need to go back to the people for assent. He had kept showing up at First Ministers' Conferences, if only to pick up a "few crumbs of autonomy" before independence took place.[46] He had accepted the results of the 1980 referendum, even though he felt Ottawa had lied and cheated its way to triumph. From that time until as late as October 1981, he had consistently argued that the federal government had no mandate to proceed with its constitutional reforms unilaterally and should submit them to a referendum. On Monday morning and again on Tuesday afternoon, he'd demanded that Trudeau call an election before taking another step. So how could he now refuse?

"We knew that the other provinces, including Alberta, weren't in favour of a referendum because they were sure to lose it," Claude Morin recalled, "mostly because of the Charter that the constitution would contain. For us, we had signs that Quebecers would reject the federal proposals if there was a referendum."[47]

Finally, at the psychological level, Lévesque had been goaded by Trudeau's contemptuous, macho dare. Worn down and fed up after two days of deadlock and brinkmanship, increasingly paranoid and isolated, he suddenly saw a chance to replay the referendum and inflict on Pierre Trudeau the defeat he himself had suffered. He was itching for a comeback match, one last fight against his old nemesis, and that was tempting enough to make him change his plans and stay on for the afternoon session.

"He thought, Trudeau's bluffing," was Claude Charron's interpretation. "And like a good poker player, he said to himself, Okay, let's go to the people, you son of a bitch, you'll find me there!"[48]

Charron wasn't alone within the province's delegation in supposing that Trudeau himself was either in a tight fix or had made a terrible mistake in proposing it. Only later on did the realization take hold that

Library and Archives Canada/e010768034

Trudeau to the press corps: "And the cat is among the pigeons."

grabbing Trudeau's offer, for real or as a counter-bluff, had been a negotiating blunder and a public-relations disaster. It wreaked havoc with the
Gang of Eight. It startled the ministers and senior officials left behind in
Quebec, as well as the francophone media. And it played straight into
the federal government's hands.[49]

"I have great news," Trudeau announced to the press on emerging
from the conference room when the meeting adjourned at twelve o'clock
for lunch. He hadn't looked so happy since the conference began. "If
we can agree to a charter, all of us, in full or in part, well and good. If
we haven't, we will put the whole question of a charter to the people
of Canada. 'Do you want this charter or do you not want this charter?'
and the people of Canada will decide. Mr. Lévesque agreed with that—
so we have a new alliance between the government of Quebec and the
Canadian government. And the cat is among the pigeons."[50]

PART 2
Wednesday
Afternoon
November 4,
1981

ELEVEN

High Noon

"We'll fight them and we'll win!" Peter Lougheed growled as he strode away from the morning session. Though the premier of Alberta hated the idea of a referendum, his competitive instinct was to take up Pierre Trudeau's challenge and wallop him. Lougheed was certain that the people of his province were on his side. Trudeau hadn't won a seat there since 1968, and the federal government was at the nadir of public opinion following its recent attempt to make off with a chunk of Alberta's lucrative oil-and-gas revenues. And Albertans would never accept the inequality of provinces explicit in the Victoria Charter. "Trudeau couldn't have won with us opposed," he insisted. "Sure, Albertans liked the idea of patriation and the Charter, but they liked our government too. If we said it was wrong, they would have gone along with us."[1]

The problem was, neither Lougheed nor anyone else knew the conditions under which the two referendums would be held. Would a Yes vote require a national majority alone? Or a national majority plus a majority in each region? Or a majority in every province? What would happen in the event of a No vote? Would a referendum be on the whole of the Charter or on each part separately? Would the Charter apply in the parts of the country that voted Yes and not in the ones that voted No? Although Peter Lougheed was convinced that he could defeat Trudeau in a showdown in Alberta, no matter what the polls were showing, he couldn't tell how most other Canadians or even most other westerners might vote. Nor was he willing to risk a scenario that would force Albertans to live with a constitution they had resoundingly opposed.

If the gunslinger from the East wanted a shootout, Lougheed would be ready and waiting for him at the O.K. Corral. He suited the part, with his handsome features and the physique of an aging athlete. Short, tough, laconic, he was a Marlboro Man who had traded his horse, his

Library and Archives Canada/e010768033

John Buchanan (left), Bill Bennett (third from left), and Peter Lougheed (fourth from left).

Stetson, and his home on the range for law school, a Harvard MBA, and a corner office downtown. Despite the rock-hard stubbornness with which he presented his arguments, as though the least sign of compromise would expose a chink in his armour, there was a kindness around his blue eyes and a boyishness in his tight smile that suggested a shy, sensitive, slightly insecure but fundamentally decent soul protected by a steely resolve—very much like Pierre Trudeau, in fact, which is what made them such well-matched protagonists. They battled hard, but they battled honest, and their battle only made them stronger. "Don't mistake our reluctance to have a referendum as not being able to fight one," Lougheed warned the prime minister.[2]

Averse to losing and with wills of steel, both men brought to the table opposing visions of the country. Trudeau was a national politician with no experience and little interest in provincial government. Having grown up in Quebec, where provincial autonomy was an excuse for corruption, isolation, and ethnic nationalism, he associated the provinces with parish-pump politicians whose narrow interests prevented them from seeing the grandeur and potential of Canada. Lougheed was a provincial CEO who lacked experience on the national stage, spoke no French, and never dared risk failure by running for the leadership of the federal Progressive Conservatives. He saw the world through the eyes of Albertans and viewed Alberta mostly through the prism of its natural resources—a perspective that earned him the honour of being voted, in one poll, the most selfish premier in Canada, ahead of René Lévesque.[3]

While the great debate between Trudeau and Lévesque sprang from the question of who spoke for Quebec, the essential question for Trudeau and Lougheed was "Who speaks for Canada?"

"We all do," Lougheed replied, for he saw the federation as a partnership of eleven sovereign governments.[4] In other words, Ottawa could only speak for all Canadians in areas of federal jurisdiction. "Trudeau believed," or so Lougheed alleged, "that Canada would be a much more efficient, a much more successful country if the national government in Ottawa had almost all the powers. I disagreed with him strongly, but that is what he believed. In addition to that, he was concerned that developments, instead of moving towards stronger central government, had been swinging the other way; that Alberta had been a focal point for the shift. Trudeau felt the best strategy was to go right at the strength, weaken the Alberta government by weakening Alberta's control of its resources."[5]

That was an extreme interpretation of Trudeau's motives. The prime minister's purpose was to restore the balance that had been lost with the devolution of revenues and authority since the mid-1960s. Certainly the premiers were powerful players with important responsibilities under the BNA Act, but, he argued, their role was limited to looking after the needs and desires of their own citizens. The federal Parliament— and the federal Parliament alone—had been ordained by the founding fathers to look after the needs and desires of all Canadians. The will of the whole was more than just the sum of its parts, and whenever the national interest conflicted with individual, municipal, provincial, or regional interests, the good of the nation had to prevail.

"That is the enemy within," Trudeau declaimed in the House of Commons in the midst of the Quebec referendum campaign, "when loyalties are no longer to the whole but there is a conflict in loyalties; when we seek protection of our wealth, our rights or our language not in the whole country but in a region or a province. That is how we come to shut doors in each other's face, because we feel we will not get our fair share in every part of the country."[6]

Like most Albertans, Lougheed felt his province had not received its fair share from Confederation. And he did not accept the tacit assumption that the good of the nation was synonymous with the good of Central Canada. Why was a discount price on Alberta's natural resources deemed in the national interest, for example, when there was no discount price on Ontario's cars or Quebec's paper? Why should there be an export tax on western oil and gas but no export tax on eastern hydro power? Why should he be smeared as an enemy of Canada just because he stood up for the rights and prosperity of his province?

On the surface, the premier projected the patrician self-confidence that came from being the grandson of Sir James Lougheed, a prominent lawyer in the early days of Alberta, one of the province's wealthiest citizens, and an influential senator in Robert Borden's Conservative government in Ottawa. Beneath, however, lurked the disgrace of a fortune lost to death duties and the Great Depression, as well as a resolve to restore the family's name and position. It was as though Lougheed harboured—even personified—the same memories of paradise lost and hard times, the same slighted feelings and chip-on-the-shoulder resentments, the same paranoia and hostility as every other Albertan who had suffered from the boom-and-bust cycles of a one-crop, resource-based economy.

"My experience in a complex way was quite typical of what happened to most westerners," Lougheed said. "Our destiny was formed by outside forces—the railways, the pipelines, the banks, and, above all, the federal government—acting on matters of direct importance to us but without consultation. Not all of these forces were negative all of the time. But our overall feeling was that the west had not had a fair deal in the Canadian federation."[7]

The list of grievances was long and not without cause. The tariffs that nurtured eastern industry hurt western farmers. Large, remote corporations decided on freight rates, wheat prices, and grain elevators to their own advantage. Western Canada was under-represented in the management of important national institutions, such as the Bank of Canada, the Canadian Broadcasting Corporation, and Air Canada. Alberta was in effect a colony of Central Canada until 1905, and the federal government retained ownership of the province's natural resources until 1930. Even the prosperity that followed the discovery of an oil bonanza at Leduc in 1947 couldn't alleviate Albertans' sense of alienation. Far from the boardrooms and backrooms of power, they still felt like the abused stepchildren of Confederation. Yet British Columbia, even farther from the centre, and Saskatchewan, created at the same time with even greater economic handicaps, didn't share the same degree of brooding, ornery anger.

The difference was rooted in Alberta's political culture. Its largest wave of white settlers hadn't been French *habitants* or Loyalist refugees, like the founders of Quebec and Ontario. Nor did it receive either the dialectical mix of Tory traditionalists and working-class radicals who put the British in British Columbia or the hodgepodge of British, French, Eastern European, Scandinavian, and Russian immigrants who flooded into Saskatchewan. Instead, Alberta was marked by the influx of farmers and ranchers who migrated north from the United States in search of cheap land and wide-open spaces. Making up a quarter of the population by the time the province was formed, they brought with them from the American West a unique ideology of frontier individualism mixed with democratic populism, agrarian protest, and fundamentalist religion. A mishmash of left and right, the province's political culture remained profoundly hostile to central authority, whether the federal government in Ottawa, the banks and railway companies in Montreal, or the High Church Establishment in Toronto.[8]

Alberta's "initial bias," as one prominent historian termed it, was evident in its voting history.[9] After first rewarding the federal Liberals for answering the people's call for provincial status, Albertans sent eight Progressives, two Labour, two United Farmers of Alberta (UFA), and no Liberals to Ottawa in 1921. At the same time, they tossed the provincial Liberals out of power in Edmonton in favour of the UFA. In 1935, in the wake of the UFA's inability to deal with the devastating effects of the Depression, the liberal strains that survived in the province's few urban areas were overwhelmed by the rural, evangelical, populist appeal of Social Credit, a right-wing British movement based on the unorthodox theory of stimulating the economy by putting cash directly into the pockets of ordinary people.[10] Led at first by a high school principal turned radio preacher named "Bible Bill" Aberhart, Social Credit evolved after his death in 1943 into a more conventional laissez-faire government under Ernest Manning and Harry Strom. In 1971, Lougheed's Progressive Conservatives basically picked up the tried-and-true message of private enterprise, individual freedom, fiscal prudence, provincial rights, and bashing the bastards back east, and gave it a more youthful, urban, secular, activist, outward-looking spin under a new brand.

The Lougheed government reflected the coming of age of a less populist managerial class, and it happened to coincide with an unprecedented bonanza in oil and gas, especially after the Organization of Petroleum Exporting Countries (OPEC) cartel caused prices to more than quadruple in 1973 and more than double again in 1979. Alberta boomed at the expense of Central Canada's manufacturing base. Wealth, employment, and head offices shifted from Toronto and Montreal to Calgary. While Ottawa began running annual deficits and piling up debt, Edmonton enjoyed huge surpluses and squirreled away billions of dollars in its rainy-day Heritage Savings Trust Fund.[11] It moved to take charge of the provincial economy and build a competent bureaucracy. It invested heavily in education, medical research, infrastructure, and diversification, to the point of owning its own energy company and buying a western-based airline. It opened overseas offices and initiated the annual Western Economic Conference.

The quick and dramatic change was in many ways Alberta's equivalent of Quebec's Quiet Revolution, with religion pushed out of the foreground of politics and energy substituting for language. And just as Quebec had done a decade earlier, Alberta launched a fierce battle against the centralist views, policies, and actions of the federal government—with the important distinction that it was fighting not for more power and money, but only for that to which it was entitled by the BNA Act. No matter how intense the wars with Ottawa became, separatism never took hold in Alberta to the degree it did in Quebec.

"The only way there can be a fair deal for the citizens of the outlying parts of Canada," Lougheed declared at the First Ministers' Conference in 1978, "is for the elected provincial governments of these parts to be sufficiently strong to offset the political power in the House of Commons of the populated centres. That strength can only flow from the provinces' jurisdiction over the management of their own economic destinies and the development of the natural resources owned by the provinces."[12]

What might have seemed a theoretical debate ignited into a major conflict when the federal government opened an almost reckless second front within three weeks of tabling its constitutional Resolution in the House of Commons. On October 28, 1980, with oil-and-gas prices at record highs, Ottawa introduced the National Energy Program (NEP), which was designed to ensure a self-sufficient energy supply, made-in-Canada pricing, more Canadian ownership in the energy sector, and enough revenues flowing into the national coffers to cover the equalization transfers that were due to the less advantaged provinces. Trudeau saw it not only as a necessary and urgent response to a world crisis, but also as the federal system working at its best. "In effect," he explained, "for most of the period from 1961 to 1973, the producers in Alberta had been subsidized by consumers in other provinces, and this had enabled the oil industry to establish itself in a way that led to Alberta's later prosperity. So my argument was that now that prices were going sky-high, the shoe should be on the other foot and we would share in the opposite direction."[13]

To Albertans, however, the NEP was nothing more than a shameless money grab that would stifle production, distort the market economy, cripple their province, and quickly kill the goose that was laying the golden eggs. Lougheed fought back, "turning down the taps" on oil production and taking Ottawa to the Supreme Court. In the end, after wringing out a few important concessions on pricing and ownership, he toasted Trudeau's compromise offer with a glass of champagne on September 1, 1981, just two months before the first ministers were to meet in Ottawa for this ultimate round of constitutional negotiations.[14]

The energy battle ensured that natural resources would be the lens through which Alberta would view the battles over the constitution. So did the timing. The OPEC crises and the subsequent quarrels between Ottawa and Edmonton over oil prices and export taxes happened to coincide with the intense round of constitutional negotiations following the collapse of the Victoria Charter in 1971, the election of the Parti Québécois in 1976, and the Quebec referendum in 1980. The NEP, coming as it did on the heels of the federal government's Resolution, inflamed Lougheed's rage and lent credibility to his claims about Trudeau's centralist designs. The details were bad enough, but the unilateralism really shook him and got his government involved.[15]

"It is my belief that the prime minister's plan to unilaterally change Canada's constitution over the opposition of the majority of the provinces," Lougheed said in a speech to the Edmonton Chamber of Commerce on November 19, 1980, "is closely linked to resource development and western Canadian development ... If the country proceeds as intended by the prime minister, we will have a very different kind of Canada. It will be a much different federal state—if a federal state at all. In my judgement, it will be primarily a unitary state, with provinces other than Ontario and Quebec being in a second-class position."[16]

On the contrary, Trudeau shot back—it was Lougheed who wanted to destroy Macdonald's vision of Canadian federalism by interpreting the constitution as a "compact" of provinces with Ottawa as their creation. Ottawa, he repeated, was not trying to grab power for itself. Indeed, the Supreme Court was to rule in September 1981 that the Resolution would "preserve a federal state without disturbing the distribution or balance of power."[17] Ottawa's concession on natural resources to gain the support of the federal NDP represented the first transfer of jurisdiction in favour of the provinces in Canadian history. Moreover, the federal government's proposed amending formula was a voluntary surrender of its legal right to act unilaterally.

But the Victoria formula was no comfort to Peter Lougheed. If the federal government was allowed to change the constitution with the support of seven provinces representing at least 50 percent of the population, what would prevent it from conspiring to rob Alberta of its resources, or to eliminate a province altogether in the name of the national good? Even if the four western provinces were to gain a kind of regional veto, Lougheed could never accept the possibility that two or three NDP governments in British Columbia, Saskatchewan, or Manitoba could gang up on a Conservative government in Alberta. As a matter of principle, too, he was never going to accept vetoes for Ontario and Quebec alone (even though the formula would also give Alberta a veto if it ever represented more than 25 percent of the population). Granting the two most privileged and pampered members of the country even more power and prestige touched a sore spot with Albertans.

Soon after being elected in 1971, Lougheed officially withdrew the agreement the previous Social Credit government had given to the Victoria Charter. At first, to advance its view of the federation and protect its interests, Alberta went back to what Ottawa and the provinces had tentatively accepted in 1964: the unanimous consent of all provinces for a new amending formula. When that got nowhere, it went back even further in time and suggested a variation on an alternative that had been proposed at a federal–provincial constitutional conference in 1936: Ottawa and seven provinces representing a majority of the population, with an opting-out provision for amendments affecting provincial rights and powers.

Alberta advanced this alternative at the ministerial meetings in Vancouver during the summer of 1980. Picked up by the Gang of Eight in their April Accord and garnished with financial compensation for the provinces that opt out, it was on the table at the November confer-ence as the Vancouver formula, though everyone knew it was in fact Lougheed's. "Darn right it was," he later boasted, though he was savvy enough to realize at the time that it might be an easier sell in Ottawa and Toronto if it wasn't identified with him.[18] It was his ball, he was the quarterback, and he became heavily invested politically and personally in its success. The Vancouver formula represented nothing less than the ascendancy of his province—and of himself—as the leading defender of provincial autonomy and cooperative federalism in English Canada. It was a sweet moment, long overdue, and Lougheed was determined not to be hoodwinked by those slick, selfish, sanctimonious politicians and bureaucrats back east ever again.

The Alberta premier busied himself forging alliances in Atlantic Canada. He visited each of its capitals to drum up support on the constitutional and energy issues. He supported Newfoundland and Nova Scotia in their claims to offshore resources. He scared the daylights out of Prince Edward Island by describing a scenario in which the small island province would be eradicated under the federal formula. At the Annual Premiers' Conferences, he reminded Brian Peckford, Angus MacLean, and John Buchanan that they, like him, were Progressive Conservatives who would pay a heavy political price in their provinces for siding with the Liberals in Ottawa. Alberta even extended more than $2 billion of financial credit to them, as well as to Quebec, on especially favourable terms.

"It was amazing to me that they all came on board if you look at history, equalization, and the degree of their reliance on federal transfers," Lougheed reflected. "Some people have tried to make a lot of our loans to them, but I don't. They could have got that money from other places at slightly higher rates. Basically we had the same view of the federal system."[19]

At the same time, Alberta came to dominate the weaker economies and leaders of Manitoba, Saskatchewan, and British Columbia. During the 1970s, it was instrumental in transforming an economic council of the three Prairie provinces into an annual meeting of all four western premiers and making it a coherent and powerful lobbying force, whatever the differences in party affiliation and ideological orientation.

Sterling Lyon, Peter Lougheed, and Brian Peckford.

Library and Archives Canada/e010768038

"Its strength is underrated," Lougheed said, "but it had a lot to do when it came to the constitution with our strength in forming the Group of Eight."[20]

While Lougheed led the charge on the amending formula, he let Sterling Lyon take on the Charter of Rights and Freedoms. Trudeau once dismissed the Manitoba premier as Lougheed's dummy, but there were underlying differences between the two westerners that would prove pivotal.[21] Lougheed was a rational, well-mannered, technocratic Tory who fought Pierre Trudeau as a politician without despising him as a person. Lyon was an abrasive, neo-conservative ideologue whose nickname, "Red," had nothing to do with his political orientation and everything to do with the colour of his hair and his fiery debating style. The type of short, freckled fellow who walks down the street looking for a fight, Lyon had fallen under the spell of Ronald Reagan and Margaret Thatcher—not least because it helped him solidify his rural base against the Manitoba New Democrats—to the point that his tirades against government intervention in the private sector caused Peter Lougheed and Bill Davis, not to mention Pierre Trudeau and Allan Blakeney, to roll their eyes. He, in turn, tended to look upon his fellow Tory premiers as weak-kneed wets.

Though Lougheed shared Lyon's concern that an entrenched charter would pass power to unelected judges, weaken provincial authority, and prove impossible to amend, the very first act he introduced as premier had been the Alberta Bill of Rights. Moreover, he was shrewd enough to reason that the Gang of Eight would probably have to give Trudeau some sort of charter if it wanted to block his unilateral patriation and amending formula. "I have been very silent properly on the whole question of the charter of rights," he admitted at the end of the conference. "It's useful to hold a few things in reserve."[22]

With Bill Davis so quickly and completely "in Trudeau's lap," as Lougheed put it, Alberta also stepped forward to take Quebec's side in combating Ottawa. Politics has seldom seen stranger bedfellows than the stiff conservative from Calgary and the slovenly social democrat from the Gaspé. Circumstances made them as tight as Butch Cassidy and the Sundance Kid. They had a common enemy in Pierre Trudeau and the federal government. They respected each other's courage and needed each other's strength. And even though Lougheed had campaigned during the Quebec referendum on behalf of the No side, all was forgiven when he argued that Trudeau should have fulfilled his promise to Quebecers by means of a greater devolution of powers to the provinces rather than the so-called People's Package.

Lougheed was Lévesque's sole line of communication to the Gang of Eight and the one premier he trusted to be with him to the very end. Calling him "the most remarkable man on the Prairies in his time," Lévesque concluded that the Albertan was "so passionately concerned

Claude Morin, Peter Lougheed, and René Lévesque.

about sovereignty in his own way that, even though opposing us, he can understand our position."[23]

"Likeable isn't the right word," Lougheed said of the Quebec premier. "He was shrewd, affable, and naturally friendly. He saw me as an ally, and we worked closely together to stop Trudeau's unilateral action. But dealing with a separatist who had just tried to take Quebec out of Canada was always front and centre in my mind, and it made me uneasy about where we were at and where we would end up."[24]

Unlike Lévesque, Lougheed wasn't out to derail the Trudeau train to patriation. He merely wanted to reroute it down another track by forcing the federal government back to the table to negotiate a better deal, which meant in Alberta's case the Vancouver amending formula and the protection of the province's natural resources. That was a very important difference with a very important consequence, but as long as the enemy of his enemy was his friend, Lougheed and Lévesque needed each other inside the common front. Though distracted for most of the year by its campaign against the National Energy Program, the government of Alberta did what it could to support Quebec's initiatives in London and in the courts. It also passed a resolution in the legislature, seventy votes to one, urging the resumption of the constitutional discussions as soon as possible. Nevertheless, the inherent fault line became harder and harder to avoid after Saskatchewan and Nova Scotia joined the Group of Six, after the courts in Manitoba and Quebec ruled that the federal government's Resolution was legal, and after the Parti Québécois was returned to office with a majority in April 1981.

By that point, Alberta had moved to the forefront of those arguing that the dissident provinces needed to come up with a positive alternative to impress the Canadian people and the British parliamentarians. As Lougheed understood it, the April Accord was a negotiating manoeuvre that "did not irrevocably tie any of the signing governments to any constitutional position—amending formula or otherwise—if Mr. Trudeau abandoned his unilateral process and agreed to modify his position and truly attempt to negotiate a consensus."[25] Whether from innocent hope or self-serving convenience, wishful thinking or blind ignorance, he clung to the belief that Lévesque was of the same mind. "There was some unease or suspicion raised by remarks made by Claude Morin in particular during the period from April to November that Quebec would never sign on," he said. "But René was very skilful throughout it all in not giving us that impression."[26]

Failure was never Lougheed's ambition. Jogging past the Supreme Court on Wellington Street each morning in that first week of November 1981, he used to bow his head in its direction in gratitude for giving the Gang of Eight another chance to win. Westminster, he figured, would never rubber-stamp a resolution that had been judged unconstitutional by the highest court in the country, and he was made comfortable in his assessment by British contacts in high places.[27] Now it was just a matter of playing hardball to get a deal that would be good for Canada in general and for Alberta in particular. If we just keep hanging tight together, Lougheed told his fellow dissidents during a pre-conference strategy session in Premier Bennett's suite on the fourth floor of the Château Laurier on Sunday evening, Ottawa will be forced to back down.

As far as he was concerned, "it was clear from our discussions on November, 1, 1981, that each of the eight governments wanted to see the constitutional matter resolved in Canada through negotiation, and that we were all going to try to do our best to bring about this important result."[28] Indeed, his officials hadn't warned Lougheed until that weekend to prepare for the possibility that Lévesque might never go beyond the April Accord. If so, Alberta would face a terrible dilemma. As the prime minister's briefing book stated, Lougheed was "angry and worried" that Ottawa seemed to be helping Quebec to separate, and reportedly felt that "the Premiers must not isolate Quebec in any way in these upcoming constitutional discussions."[29]

With nothing else to offer, the Gang of Eight decided to reaffirm its support for that dead duck, the April Accord. But why would both sides waste their time and raise the public's expectations just to repeat what they had been saying to no avail for more than a year? "Clearly," Lougheed observed, "it was anticipated that change was not only possible, but likely."[30] When it came, however, it shouldn't come as a surprise. The eight premiers therefore agreed that if any of them was going to propose or accept something other than the accord in the days ahead, he would first notify the group, which was planning to meet at least once a day at breakfast. "Obviously implicit," Lougheed added in hindsight, "was that if the federal government responded affirmatively to everything we asked for, we would go along with a new Canadian constitution."[31]

Thus when British Columbia wanted to try adding a very limited charter to the April Accord on Tuesday afternoon, Bill Bennett first asked permission of his colleagues. Lougheed went along with the idea just to "smoke out" whether Trudeau really wanted to find a compromise or was just stringing everyone along to orchestrate another failure.[32] And thus, when Allan Blakeney wanted to present a comprehensive proposal to try to break the impasse on Wednesday morning, he gave his colleagues a heads-up at their breakfast meeting. Though Lougheed worried that it might be interpreted as a sign of weakness and division, he didn't want to undermine his friend and assumed—correctly—that it wasn't going to be accepted anyway.

Then, towards the end of the morning session, just as the eight seemed ready to regroup into a solid phalanx, René Lévesque seized upon Pierre Trudeau's offer to go to the people on the amending formula and the Charter of Rights and Freedoms. "That was very disruptive," Lougheed recalled, understating how stunned he had been. "Trudeau's concept was very offensive to me. 'My referendum is an election' was how I put it to him. So I was never in favour of a referendum, even if I was ready to fight him in one."[33]

As an Albertan, Peter Lougheed might have been expected to embrace the challenge of a referendum, as he seemed to do when leaving the meeting at noon. The populist impulse that the American migrants had brought with them favoured all manner of direct democracy, from town hall meetings and recall mechanisms to plebiscites and referendums. That impulse was fortified by the province's alienation from the central government, a feeling that extended even to the MPs it sent to Ottawa. (One day, the story goes, a bunch of jubilant Calgarians escorted their freshly elected candidate to the airport for his first trip to the nation's capital. As the plane was taking off with him aboard, one of them turned to another and said, "Goddamn son of a bitch, he's sold us out.") But Lougheed was a classic Progressive Conservative, not a Prairie populist and certainly not a radical. He believed in the supremacy of Parliament, the free will of elected representatives, and the legitimacy of the party system. He believed in executive federalism, elite accommodation, brokerage politics, and negotiated compromises. And though plebiscites might have their place on secondary provincial matters, he felt that constitutions were best left to governments.

René Lévesque had split from the Gang of Eight on the one issue where none of the other premiers could follow. They all had in their briefcases the same polling results that the federal government had, showing 90 percent in every province in favour of patriation and over 80 percent in favour of the Charter. Who among them would choose to come out, side by side with the separatists from Quebec, in favour of maintaining Canada's colonial status or opposed to human rights and fundamental freedoms? Even if they tried to turn the debate into a protest vote against Pierre Trudeau, what were their chances of winning against the civil liberties associations, the women's rights alliances, the disabled and other single-issue lobbies, the aboriginal and multicultural organizations? Did they really want to campaign against the sovereignty of the people, the values of a just society, the honour of the nation? The very possibility of losing to the federal government in their own provinces was enough to put the fear of God into the hearts of the Anglo premiers.

"As in the Marienbad game," Trudeau recalled, "I knew I could lose, but would not. Several of the most influential provinces (including Quebec) had already adopted their own charters, and it would ill befit them to campaign in a referendum against Canada having one. As for the amending formula, the one the provinces were postulating was that all provinces were equal, whereas in ours all Canadians would be equal."[34]

The polls aside, the victory of the No side in the Quebec referendum had made Trudeau more confident than ever that the provincial elites did not speak for the majority of their people when speaking about Canada. If he could win in Quebec against an *indépendantiste* government led by a formidable foe like René Lévesque, the odds were good, he believed, that he could win in Alberta against Peter Lougheed.[35] In turn, that reinforced his deep faith in democracy and the will of the people—the result not only of his intensive study of political theory, but also of the unusually strong and direct bond he had forged with the Canadian electorate since 1968. Unlike most prime ministers, he hadn't ascended to the leadership of his party and his country primarily through the manipulations of political insiders, backroom boys, and business networks. Instead, he had been lifted up on an unexpected surge of grassroots excitement and media frenzy, themselves the result of the social, cultural, generational, and national transformations of the late 1960s. Even after Trudeau had to turn himself into a more conventional politician to secure his power in 1972, 1974, and 1980, a cult of personality lingered around him.

When it came to constitutional reform, it was natural for him to turn to the people of Canada to override the obstacles and bestow their blessing on the package he wanted to take to London. He called it the People's Package because it took power from both levels of government and gave it to the citizens. He introduced an amending formula by which the people could break future deadlocks when their governments couldn't agree. He invited Canadians to tell the Joint Committee of the House of Commons and the Senate how to strengthen the Charter of Rights and Freedoms. He fought a losing battle to get the phrase "we the people" into a constitutional preamble.

"My faith in Canada is, indeed, based on my faith in the people," he declared. "Throughout my years in office, that faith proved justified over and over again, whenever the going was tough and the reforms we were trying to introduce were being opposed by the multinational corporations, by the provincial premiers, or by a superpower. I invariably found that if our cause was right, all we had to do to win was talk over the heads of our adversaries directly to the people of this land."[36]

Peter Lougheed returned to the conference room at two-thirty on Wednesday afternoon, determined to see the rules for referendums on the amending formula and the Charter set down in writing. He was no happier when the federal officials produced a document, 800-15/020, which they had typed up over lunch. (If it seemed improvised and rushed, that's because it was. Only a very few had known that Trudeau was going to throw down the gauntlet, and none of them had expected Lévesque to pick it up.) This document dealt only with the first of the two issues; another was in the process of being drawn up for consideration later in the day. In essence, it affirmed that a referendum to decide between the federal and provincial amending formulas would be based on regional approval—majorities in Ontario, Quebec, the West, and the East—just as the Resolution had laid out for future amendments. If both options failed to win support in all four regions, constitutional amendments would require unanimity. "Any referendum that ignores the views of the provinces and deals with regions," Lougheed fumed, "is fundamentally opposed to our view of Canada. It's not a nation of regions; it's a nation of provinces."[37]

Lévesque, who may in fact have been looking for a way to pull back from his disruptive acceptance of Trudeau's referendum challenge, wasn't happy either. According to parliamentary procedure, the slightest change to the Resolution now before the House of Commons would require the consent of every MP or else the whole thing would have to be withdrawn, rewritten, and introduced all over again. To avoid such a debacle, 800-15/020 proposed that the Resolution be passed by the Parliament of Canada and sent on to London as it was. Only then would the choice between the Victoria and Vancouver formulas be put to the people. Ottawa, Lévesque protested, was trying to fix the game.

"Trudeau had in effect said that his referendum would take place *after* patriation and *after* the changes that he wanted to insert into the Constitution," Claude Morin later explained. "That changed everything. In other words, it would no longer be a referendum of the kind we had had in Quebec, but would be a referendum of ratification, once the federal project was a *fait accompli*! For that reason, we immediately rejected it."[38]

"Well, by all means, let's define what a charter is and what is an accord," Trudeau challenged the first ministers, "but what do we do at the end of the day? I'll tell the press we'll put in a referendum on both."[39]

Lougheed, Blakeney, Bennett, and their three Atlantic allies returned to railing against the idea of a referendum. Referendums are anathema to a federation, they argued, ignoring the fact that they have worked in Australia, Switzerland, and the United States. Newfoundland was the only province to join the federation as the result of a referendum; Quebec was the only province to try to get out of it by means of one. The extraordinary plebiscite conducted by the federal government in 1942, asking permission to impose military conscription to help fight the war, triggered a crisis of national unity by pitting Quebecers (who voted 72 percent No) against other Canadians (who supported the measure in numbers ranging from almost 70 percent in New Brunswick to 84 percent in Ontario).

When Gerry Mercier, Manitoba's attorney general, expressed concern that a referendum on the Charter of Rights and Freedoms would explode into a fiery debate about the funding of Roman Catholic schools in his province, Trudeau pleaded with the anglophone premiers to join him in defending minority-language rights so as not to hand the Parti Québécois "a first-class tool to fight for independence." That set Lévesque off into a long and emotional digression about Quebec's exemplary treatment of its Anglo minority since Confederation, the precarious position of the French language in North America, and the benefits of sovereignty-association. "I hope we can sell this idea again in the future," he concluded.[40] Richard Hatfield then launched into a rambling but articulate defence of the Charter. Lougheed followed by tearing it apart. Trudeau returned to attacking Blakeney and Lougheed for supporting the idea of opting out with financial compensation. So it went, late into the afternoon.

"Well, we've tried everything, screw it," Trudeau finally said in exasperation. "I think we should be prepared to meet the television cameras at five and tell them we couldn't agree."[41]

TWELVE

Bland Works

Bill Davis wasn't a man who angered easily. Silver-haired, avuncular, pleasant in appearance, even-tempered, prone to speaking softly when not calmly puffing on his pipe, he was the personification of decent, middle-class, traditional Ontario. His office may have been situated among the bank towers, media headquarters, and university campuses of downtown Toronto, but his home was in Brampton, a leafy village turned bedroom community on the northwest fringes of the metropolis. And since Davis was also one of the two premiers who had from the very start supported patriation, the Charter, and even the threat of unilateral federal action, it made quite an impact when he began to scold Pierre Trudeau for giving up too quickly.

Davis wasn't surprised by Trudeau's referendum challenge. He and the prime minister had discussed it the previous Sunday afternoon during a two-hour meeting in the sunroom at 24 Sussex Drive to coordinate their positions going into the conference. Their strategic objective was to divide the Gang of Eight and lure to their side as many provinces as it took to satisfy the Supreme Court's ruling. On day one, they would show reasonableness and flexibility, if only to impress the millions of Canadians watching the opening session on television. On day two, they would toss out a compromise or two. If nothing broke by day three, Trudeau said he was going to suggest a national referendum on the amending formula and the Charter. Davis replied that he thought it a terrible idea, provocative, upsetting to everyone, and likely to turn into a vote on what Canadians really thought of the prime minister and his government. "A national referendum will not produce the kind of result that you and I want, in my view," he said.[1] Trudeau agreed to keep it as a last resort.

For Bill Davis, the referendum was not—and should never have been—a serious option. He saw it only as a tool with which to try to pry apart the Gang of Eight and open the possibility of a negotiated settlement. Trudeau, however, having succeeded in drawing René Lévesque away from the others, now seemed intent on using a referendum to ram his Resolution through Westminster. "We've been had," Roy McMurtry whispered into Davis's ear. "That son of a bitch doesn't want to compromise."[2]

Bill Davis's immediate and unequivocal support of the federal government's Resolution in October 1980 had required his placing a great deal of confidence in the prime minister. There were details Ontario didn't like in the package, such as the deadlock-breaking referendum provisions that Ottawa had tacked on to the Victoria formula, and the probability of further alterations along the way to accommodate side deals with other premiers, the House of Commons, and a variety of interest groups.[3] Nevertheless, presented as he was with a choice between unilateral action and perpetual impasse, Davis didn't hesitate. He had made a promise to Quebec during the referendum campaign—not to Lévesque or the PQ government, but to Quebecers—and he intended to keep that promise. The fear of failure pushed him past every doubt and criticism. "To do nothing at this point," Davis explained, "not to seek patriation and reform, would be to admit a victory to those who say this nation is unworkable."[4]

"Something dramatic was necessary to free the process from the quagmire into which it had fallen," said Hugh Segal, one of the premier's closest political advisers. "The fight between Pierre Trudeau and René Lévesque could not be solved by consensual negotiation in the typical Canadian fashion. It had to be solved mano-a-mano, which is quite un-Canadian."[5]

Davis's decision surprised and upset many powerful people, including members of his own Cabinet and caucus, eight of the other premiers (five of whom were fellow Conservatives), the leader of Her Majesty's Loyal Opposition in Ottawa, and the thirty-eight federal Progressive Conservative MPs from Ontario. He wasn't a politician known for dramatic gestures, hasty decisions, and take-it-or-leave-it ultimatums. By temperament and philosophy, he preferred piecemeal changes, pragmatic compromises, and polite manners. "Bland works," he famously declared.

Nor were he and Pierre Trudeau kindred spirits or partisan allies. Trudeau was a cosmopolitan, intellectual Grit; Davis was a suburban, pragmatic Tory. Their differences were exemplified by how they had dressed for their Sunday meeting: Davis wore a tweed jacket, grey trousers, and loafers; Trudeau wore a designer sweater, jeans, and clogs. "Friendship might be too strong a word," Davis later said of his relationship with the prime minister, "but we had a fair degree of mutual respect. We were always able to talk to one another. He consulted me on some things. I made certain recommendations. We had our differences on some of the economic issues, but I knew what his real interests were, and they were the same as mine—except the extent of French-language rights in Ontario."[6]

Trudeau, of course, was unequivocally in favour of making Ontario an officially bilingual province under section 133 of the BNA Act, which protected the use of English and French in the legislatures and courts of Quebec and Manitoba. Doing so would strengthen the position of Ontario's half a million francophones and send a conciliatory signal to French-speaking Quebecers. But Davis saw it as more symbol than substance, and worse, given the periodic outbreaks of old-fashioned bigotry in Ontario, as a symbol that would blow up in both their faces. Quietly, steadily, cautiously, Ontario had been moving on French-language education, French-language government services, and bilingualism in the courts without waving a red flag in front of the British traditionalists and anti-Quebec reactionaries who still existed in large numbers in the province. Going any further, Davis feared, even if it only meant translating legislative proceedings and provincial statutes, would unleash a backlash of anger, fear, and mistrust. And he knew his people well. When the *Toronto Star* inaccurately reported that Trudeau was going to impose official bilingualism on Ontario, the hostile response came thundering down the phone lines at Queen's Park loud and clear.

"Ontario has always taken the view that the future of French–English understanding in this country lies in the schools," Davis warned Ottawa the day before Trudeau was to unveil the Resolution, "lies in educating a generation of Canadians who are able to understand each other and communicate effectively in either of the two major languages. Forcing bilingualism on any provincial government by constitutional means would evoke the kind of bad feeling and resentment which will set the cause of French–English relations back many decades. I would not be part of that, nor would the government I lead."[7]

Trudeau had indeed come close to imposing section 133 on Ontario. He was under pressure to do so, particularly from members of his Quebec caucus. He could seldom resist pushing Davis to accept it, even during their Sunday meeting at 24 Sussex.[8] In the end, however, he understood the political realities of the province and deferred to Davis's judgment. Ontario's support for the federal government's Resolution was absolutely essential. Unilateral patriation and the Charter would have gone nowhere in Canada and the United Kingdom, Trudeau later admitted, if Bill Davis hadn't agreed to back them from the beginning.[9] Besides, as Claude Morin made clear during the November conference, if Ontario did reverse its position on official bilingualism, "it would change absolutely nothing" as far as Quebec was concerned.[10]

"It is hard to imagine a politician who worries less, plans less, conspires as little as Bill Davis," Hugh Segal and Nate Nurgitz, a Tory senator from Manitoba, observed in their joint memoir of the constitutional exercise. "It is not so much a sense of selflessness as a belief that opportunities either appear or they do not. It may be a throwback to the small-town days of Brampton, but he is a politician who believes in living a day at a time, and not necessarily the entire day before it's absolutely necessary. He believes that an opportunity missed will most probably come again, but an opportunity improperly seized or executed can make things considerably worse."[11]

From the premier's personal style, wrote Segal and Nurgitz, flowed the province's strategy. "The purpose was not to manipulate the events as the Liberals proposed, but to prepare options for the moment when compromise and progress would be possible. The Ontario strategy was to keep channels open, sustain political momentum behind the proposal, build goodwill and ensure that when the opportunity came, it would not be botched. Building that goodwill as part of a gang of nine or ten was tactically irrelevant. Building that goodwill with the government of Canada facilitated an opportunity for compromise when the time came."[12]

There was nothing sudden or simple about Davis's decision. It was the result of ten years of ruminating on the constitution following the collapse of the Victoria Charter in 1971. As a freshly elected premier of Canada's largest province, representing more than a third of all Canadians, Davis had gone to the federal–provincial conference in Victoria full of optimism and goodwill. This was politics at the highest level. He was proud of the part he played in getting the tentative agreement, and he felt that its amending formula and charter of rights were as good as— maybe even better than—any of the ones subsequently proposed. Robert Bourassa's unexpected reversal was a crushing disappointment that marked him forever. More significantly, it shattered the view Ontario had long held of itself as the genial intermediary between Ottawa and Quebec, an honest broker between the national interest and provincial autonomy.

In August 1976, Roy McMurtry, the smart, congenial lawyer who had played varsity football with Davis and joined his Cabinet as attorney general in 1975, attended a constitutional conference in Edmonton. Bourassa was on the eve of going to the polls, the separatists were on the rise in Quebec, and Trudeau was under a great deal of pressure to come up with an alternative to the failed Victoria agreement. At dinner one evening, a member of Bourassa's team thanked McMurtry for all his efforts, then added, "But frankly, Roy, we don't want a settlement. We're going into an election, and as long as these issues are unresolved, we have something we can use to beat up the federal government."

"That had a big impact on me," McMurtry recalled. "As an Anglo-Canadian, I felt it was humiliating that our constitution could only be amended by the Parliament of Great Britain. That was certainly true for new Canadians as well. But it didn't seem to bother the political class in Quebec, despite the British Conquest and all that. They weren't irritated by this last vestige of colonialism. They only saw it as a lever with which to get more powers, and they didn't want to lose that leverage. That's when I decided that Quebec would never agree to anything. No matter what party was in power in the province, it would always find some reason or excuse to say no."[13]

With the defeat of the Yes forces in the 1980 referendum, Bill Davis shared Trudeau's conviction that the time to reform the British North America Act was long past. Patriating the constitution and entrenching a charter of rights, as he saw it, were not a power play by the federal government. They were essential to national sovereignty and national unity. The amending formula that had been acceptable in 1971 should still be acceptable in 1981. And what was so wrong with a charter that protected individual freedoms and safeguarded minority-language rights?

Of utmost importance, in Davis's opinion, was to deliver something positive to the people of Quebec before its next provincial election.

"Lévesque could have signed something that gave him part of what he wanted," he said, "but no one was going to do that, so my feeling, like Trudeau's, was that it was important to get it done in any event, even without Quebec's signature. Someday it would be supported in Quebec, but there was no chance of that while Lévesque was there."[14]

Defending Ottawa's centralist vision lost Bill Davis the mantle of being the chief spokesman of the English-Canadian provinces on the issue of provincial rights, and Peter Lougheed was quick to pick it up. By most criteria, the two premiers should have been close allies. They were guys' guys who had excelled at football and loved nothing better than to spend the weekend watching a professional game on television. They were modern, moderate, liberal-minded Progressive Conservatives. They had a constitutional duty to defend the interests of their provinces against the rapacious, capricious bullying of the federal government. They were old friends, a year apart in age, honest, forthright, and adept. Davis had even persuaded his government to invest more than $100 million in Syncrude in 1975 to help develop the Alberta oil sands. He had offered his personal support if Lougheed had wanted to run for the leadership of the federal PCs in 1976. Lougheed's distinguished grandfather had even been born near Brampton.

But perhaps they were too similar in some ways, like brothers engaged in an intense sibling rivalry. Lougheed was the hot-headed one, always competing for respect and the keys to the family car; less experienced and therefore less secure; more sensitive and therefore more chippy; aggressive and defensive at the same time; driven, blunt, and not fully comfortable in his own skin. Davis, for his part, was the plump and dutiful son, now sitting at Dad's right-hand side in his three-piece suit with the smile of the cat who had just swallowed the canary; self-satisfied in his unruffled confidence, amiably offering advice as if from the height of better instincts and disinterested wisdom; the rosy-faced

Bill Davis and Peter Lougheed.

favourite who cloaked his huge ambition in magnanimity, modesty, and statesmanlike sentiments, which René Lévesque derisively described as Davis's "habitual 'noble father' patter."[15]

More than by personality or psychology, the two premiers—like their provinces—were deeply divided by history and economics. Lougheed interpreted Ontario's grandiloquent perorations about national unity as a cynical, self-serving manoeuvre to steal Alberta's oil-and-gas revenues, no different from what Davis had done by begging Ottawa for cheaper energy when the oil-and-gas bonanza of the 1970s allowed Alberta to thumb its nose at the Upper Canadian old boys. Davis had even supported the federal government's thwarted attempts to strengthen the economic union, as he believed had been the intent of the founding fathers. "To reassert that heritage is not a subtle Ontario strategy to dominate markets and natural resources," he declared. "It is to reassert a political and human ideal that was sound in its vision when first conceived over a hundred years ago."[16]

It helped, admittedly, that this position made life easier for Davis's minority government in the Ontario legislature, where his party had been outnumbered by Liberals and New Democrats since 1975. On energy issues, besieged by two opposition parties who viewed Peter Lougheed as a greedy blue-eyed sheik, Davis couldn't appear to be, as he ironically understated it, "totally unsympathetic to the concerns of the Ontario consumer."[17] On constitutional issues, he had a vision of the country not unlike Pierre Trudeau's. "I actually don't think the federal government is just a 'travel agency' for the provinces," Davis once told a private meeting of his advisers. "I think this is one country, and we do have some national obligations to each other that only the federal government can discharge."[18]

The province's political culture, even its conservatism, differed from the laissez-faire, anti-establishment individualism dominant in Alberta. It was an iteration of the eighteenth-century British Toryism of the Loyalist refugees—which was characterized by a respect for the Crown, deference towards authority, and a vision of society as a collective, organic, orderly whole—blended with the reform-minded liberalism of the working-class immigrants who flooded into Upper Canada in the nineteenth century. Among the results was that very successful political hybrid, the Progressive Conservative, or Red Tory, who mixed fiscal prudence with state intervention, traditional institutions with contemporary values, personal liberty with social justice. Thus Davis was ready to support an American-style bill of rights, but only if Trudeau didn't tamper with the monarchy.

What's more, the majority of Ontarians didn't share the knee-jerk fear of a strong central government that possessed the people of western Canada. On the contrary, they tended to identify their interest with the national interest, as though Canada were still the empire of the St. Lawrence, with the Atlantic provinces vassal states and the western provinces hinterland colonies. As the inhabitants of the biggest, wealthiest, and most populous province, Ontarians had a self-confidence bordering on smugness and a sense of entitlement bordering on arrogance. Though English-speaking Montreal had been the nation's commercial, financial, and cultural metropolis for nearly one hundred years, Toronto was now the hub of banking and manufacturing, of head offices and investment dealers, of high society and the arts, as well as the provincial capital. Even the national capital was just a medium-sized city in Eastern Ontario. According to the polls, in fact, Ontario was the only province in which most people, like their premier, saw themselves as citizens of their country first, ahead of their region or province.[19]

"As a Conservative in the Ontario tradition," Davis said, "I am unrepentant in my belief that Canada must have a strong national government that can speak and act for all Canadians. Sir John A. Macdonald, as the key father of Confederation, struck to turn the vision of such a government into a reality."[20]

That belief took particular hold among the massive number of immigrants who flooded into Ontario during the 1950s and 1960s. Their first loyalty was to Canada—and in many cases, the federal Liberal Party—for welcoming them to the land of freedom and opportunity. Thus while Ontarians had been electing Progressive Conservative governments at the provincial level since 1943, they voted overwhelmingly for Trudeau in 1968, 1974, and 1980. They liked his patriotic vision of Canada. They liked his Canada-first energy policy. They liked his made-in-Canada constitutional package. And so, in March 1981, during the heat of the battle with the Gang of Eight, they finally gave Bill Davis his first majority in a decade.

"We had a problem with our core voters during the election," he recalled. "They weren't disagreeing with patriation or the Charter, but they didn't like Trudeau or our association with him. So I gave a speech at the Empire Club in which I laid out our position and said, 'If you want to say I'm in bed with Trudeau, so be it, but ultimately this is about

Canada's becoming a sovereign nation.' Not only did we get our core back, but we also got thousands of votes from new Canadians who had moved to Canada from countries where there was no charter. Even the *Toronto Star* supported me editorially for the very first time."[21]

It was no coincidence that the only other province to support Ottawa's constitutional package was New Brunswick. More than Nova Scotia, Prince Edward Island, or Newfoundland, it most closely resembled Ontario, despite the fact that one was a have-not, resource-based hinterland subsidized by federal cheques and the other was a wealthy, industrialized powerhouse at the heart of the Canadian economy. Both had been founded by Loyalist refugees but had a large French-speaking minority. Both bordered on Quebec and had, it could be argued, the most to lose from its secession. Both were led by middle-of-the-road Red Tories, who shared many of the same backroom strategists, an attachment to the British monarchy, and a strong vision of a united Canada.[22]

More to the point, of all the premiers at the Ottawa showdown in November 1981, Bill Davis and Richard Hatfield were the only ones who had been at the Victoria conference ten years earlier and every first ministers' constitutional meeting since then. They had had enough of the feuding and blackmail. They had intervened in the Quebec referendum campaign on behalf of the No side and felt obliged to make good the renewal Trudeau had promised. Hatfield had even represented his province at the ministerial negotiations during the summer of 1980, the only premier to do so. "I don't trust my ministers," he explained with a laugh.[23] Mostly, he relished being where the action was.

While Bill Davis was low-key, reflective, and discreet, with the cautious nature and sound judgment of a small-town lawyer, Richard Hatfield was impetuous and colourful, a social and intellectual gadfly with an unpredictable intuition, a quick intelligence, and an irresistible sense of play. He was tall, fair-haired, good-looking in an aging, heavy-set preppy sort of way, and his fashionable wardrobe and jet-set lifestyle almost gave the impression that Fredericton was the cosmopolitan

Richard Hatfield and Pierre Trudeau.

capital and Toronto the provincial backwater. After the end of one
conference in Ottawa, when Hatfield announced he was heading home,
Davis cracked, "Via San Francisco or Marrakech?"[24]

Unlike Davis, Hatfield seemed exhilarated by the sheer panache of
Trudeau's initiative, and relations between the two allies chilled when
he publicly accused Davis of abetting the separatists by not allowing
the federal government to impose section 133 on Ontario. Hatfield
studied the history and politics of Quebec in detail. He liked to hang
out with nationalist artists and thinkers in Montreal bistros. Caught
up in the energy and excitement of the province in the early 1970s, he
even became a member of the Parti Québécois while serving as premier
of New Brunswick. But he drew the line at independence. Instead, he

embraced Trudeau's vision of a pluralistic Canada with guaranteed individual rights and sought to make his province officially bilingual. Though a more practical thinker than the prime minister, driven more by political realitics than erudite principles, he, too, wanted to correct the historic injustices suffered by the Acadian francophones. After categorically denouncing Ottawa's threat of unilateral action during the summer of 1980, he signed on when it became clear that the Resolution was the only way to get patriation, the Charter, the entrenchment of language rights in New Brunswick, and a constitutional guarantee of equalization payments. Trudeau later said that the minority-language education clause in the Charter had been made possible by Hatfield's efforts.[25]

Despite their alliance, Hatfield couldn't get past the prime minister's introversion, his cold logic, his evident contempt for the premiers, or his blindness towards the progressive aspect of French-Canadian nationalism, whether in Quebec or Acadia. For his part, Trudeau couldn't identify with the premier's emotional flightiness, his philosophical contradictions, or his notorious indiscretions. Hatfield loved people, loved stories, and loved gossiping, particularly over a few vodkas late into the night in hotel bars or nightclubs with journalists and politicos. Such was his reputation that at a federal–provincial conference in 1976, when the premiers were handed a confidential federal document, Hatfield tossed his copy over his shoulder without looking at it and yelled to his officials, "Here, leak this."[26] In keeping with his maverick reputation, Hatfield refused to join Trudeau and Davis at their Sunday afternoon strategy session, preferring to conduct his own private discussions with federal officials. Nevertheless, once committed, he never broke ranks.

While the differences between the premiers of Ontario and New Brunswick kept them from being chums even when they were joined at the hip to Trudeau, Bill Davis was nevertheless closer to Richard Hatfield than either was to Joe Clark, the Alberta-born leader of the federal Progressive Conservatives. It was easy for Clark to dismiss Hatfield as "Disco Dick" or "King Flake," but Davis's decision to support the

Liberals' Resolution triggered a crisis within the Tory caucus in Ottawa. How could the federal PCs *not* support patriation when the Conservative premier of Ontario, the province with the largest number of seats in the House of Commons, backed it, as did a majority of Canadians? How could the party of John Diefenbaker say no to an entrenched bill of rights? And yet how could Her Majesty's Loyal Opposition simply roll over and submit to Trudeau's unilateral package without alienating the forty-nine MPs who represented the party's western base—most of whom were already furious at Clark for having botched their first chance at power in almost two decades? Let Bill Davis do what he would, but Joe Clark wasn't prepared to abandon all hope of a breakthrough among the anti-Liberal forces in Quebec or to toss away the many efforts the national party had made to rebuild itself by catering to the provinces.

Clark's solution, ingenious and disingenuous at the same time, was to support patriation and the Charter in general terms but vehemently oppose the process and the details. He queried the federal government's haste to drive the Resolution through Parliament by Christmas 1980 without subjecting it to closer examination or an opinion from the Supreme Court of Canada. He berated Trudeau's high-handed disregard for the united opposition of eight provinces. He scorned the prime minister's contemptuous insistence that the MPs at Westminster should merely "hold their noses and vote" if they didn't like the smell of whatever Ottawa sent to London. And he made those arguments seem reasonable enough, even among Canadians who were strongly in favour of Trudeau's package.

Clark was an easy figure to ridicule and dismiss. Almost adolescent in his appearance, with his chipmunk cheeks and physical awkwardness, he tried to compensate for his lightweight mien by an earnestness of manner and gravity of tone far beyond his middle years. Worse, he was caught in an almost impossible position between Peter Lougheed and Bill Davis, two Conservative heavyweights who were at loggerheads over energy prices and annoyed at his equivocation.[27] Yet Joe Clark was a skilled parliamentarian with a terrier-like persistence who aimed higher than Lougheed to become a national politician, achieved what Davis never did by learning a passable French to woo Quebec, and strove to transform a rump of dyed-in-the-wool malcontents into a modern, moderate, multicultural party. His success in keeping his caucus united, given the conflicts and the circumstances, was truly impressive. He also had a surprising ability to unsettle—and even unseat—Pierre Trudeau.

On March 23, 1981, frustrated by almost six months of delays and Clark's obstructionist tactics, the prime minister rose in the House of Commons with a few questions of his own. "Let me ask those who want to see the defeat of this motion what their victory cry will be. Will it be 'Praise God, we have defeated the charter of fundamental rights and freedoms'? Is that the course that they really want to see followed? What will be the boast of those who have defeated patriation? Will they say, 'We were there, we were sitting in Parliament when we prevented Canada from taking its final step toward sovereignty'? Tell me what the provincial governments will say. What will their shout of triumph be? Will they say, 'We were successful through the courts, through Westminster, in keeping Canada a colony a little while longer. Hooray! We managed to delay one year, five or ten, the coming of age of this country'?"[28]

His rhetoric fell on deaf ears. Even after achieving a number of amendments to the draft Charter, the Tories launched a two-week filibuster that helped push the federal government to the Supreme Court in April 1981. In retrospect, Trudeau paid tribute to the leader of the Official Opposition as the man who had "singlehandedly" prevented the unilateral patriation of the constitution.[29] Perhaps, but with the law on the government's side, Joe Clark never had the power to block the Resolution, which by November 1981 was back before Parliament awaiting the outcome of this final, all-important meeting. Nor did he have a voice at the negotiating table.

In the days and weeks following the Supreme Court's decision, Bill Davis stuck to Ottawa's side in public. The Resolution was legal; the next stop was London. In private, however, he joined his voice to the chorus that was urging Trudeau to meet with the premiers for one last round of talks. "Pierre," he said, "I will not help you unless you try once more."[30] Even if that last round failed, as Trudeau expected it would, Davis was careful to avoid committing Ontario to going along with the federal government to Westminster. He would cross that bridge if and when he came to it. In the meantime, he explored the elements of a deal with Allan Blakeney and Bill Bennett, who had succeeded Sterling Lyon in August as chair of the Annual Premiers' Conference. At the same time, Hugh Segal stayed in constant communication with his pal Michael Kirby, while Roy McMurtry dealt with Jean Chrétien in Ottawa and Roy Romanow in Saskatoon.

The affable, heavy-lidded Torontonian, the tough-edged populist from industrial Shawinigan, and the good-looking, smooth-talking son of Ukrainian immigrants were the best of friends. Despite their different backgrounds and party affiliations, the three ministers had formed a tight bond based on laughter, storytelling, sports, and a shared view of moderate, pragmatic politics. They crossed the country together in the summer of 1980, hung out together during a conference at Cambridge University in July 1981, and got together for a beer at Chrétien's home on the night of the Supreme Court's ruling in September.

"People, of course, shape events," McMurtry later reflected. "However, the process is somewhat complicated by the fact that it is often difficult to sort out the extent to which people shape events or events shape people." In a footnote he added, "For example, while revisionists or hagiographers may portray the final meeting of early November 1981 as proceeding according to some omni-percipient master plan of the Prime Minister's, it was apparent to this participant that, like many court cases, the final outcome depended as much on chance remarks and accidents of timing as on any grand design."[31]

Several days before the start of the conference, McMurtry and Chrétien had breakfast together. A breakthrough was possible, they felt, and both were eager to avoid a debacle like the one that had taken place in September 1980. "I urged him," McMurtry recalled, "to bring whatever modest influence he had with the prime minister to prevent him from getting into this argumentative mood every time somebody wants to take a position contrary to him."

"You know, Roy," Chrétien replied, "he'd rather win an argument than anything else in life. You know, you can win a lot of goddamn arguments but still lose the war."[32]

On Monday, the federal side's coordinated strategy unfolded much as the prime minister's briefing book had outlined. Trudeau repeated his willingness to give up the Victoria formula if Canadians preferred another one in a national referendum. Davis volunteered to give up Ontario's veto, a major concession designed to satisfy Alberta's insistence on the equality of the provinces. Trudeau offered to reconsider the timing and substance of his Charter. Hatfield suggested splitting the Charter into two parts and putting off the more controversial issues of legal rights and equality rights for three years of further negotiations, at the end of which any six provinces could prevent those rights from being entrenched. Though Trudeau indicated that he might be willing to go along with Hatfield's suggestion if that was the only way to get an agreement, he also insisted upon the immediate entrenchment of fundamental freedoms, democratic rights, and the language provisions—all of which the Gang of Eight was still refusing to accept.

By Tuesday morning, however, the first division appeared between the prime minister and the premier of Ontario, and it seemed to grow wider with each passing hour. When Davis ventured to suggest exchanging the Vancouver amending formula for a modified charter, Trudeau immediately shot the idea down. "That was partially his negotiating technique and partially his nature," Davis thought. "He was a very single-minded person who never lost focus on what he wanted to achieve, and here were people trying to water down the Charter."[33]

The hint of discord among the three allies bewildered the Gang of Eight. There was also some confusion about whether Davis had suggested swapping the Gang's formula for *a* charter or *the* Charter. "I don't think any of us knew what was going on," Allan Blakeney remembered. "We couldn't quite figure out whether Davis and Hatfield were setting out positions that distanced themselves from the federal government—unlikely but possible—or signalling that the federal government was open to their position. But obviously somebody was loosening this thing up."[34]

On Tuesday afternoon, when the eight dissidents opted to meet privately in Bill Bennett's suite at the Château Laurier rather than return to the conference room after lunch, Davis shuttled between the two camps, happy to be back playing Ontario's old role as the honest broker of Confederation. "All I was trying to do was keep the thing alive, keep them from walking out," he remembered. "They were reaching a point where they wanted to see a reasonable, constructive solution. There was a lot of walking back and forth."[35]

While Davis's intuition was telling him that a negotiated settlement was possible, especially with Saskatchewan and British Columbia, Trudeau still clung to his perfect Charter and didn't believe that the Gang was any nearer to giving it to him. Holding court in the Government Conference Centre while waiting for Davis to return, he was already speculating about what he could do if the conference failed and Britain refused to pass the Resolution. Perhaps Canada should resign from the Commonwealth. Perhaps it might move to expel Great Britain. The Ontario and New Brunswick delegates present were horrified. "Tell you what, Pierre," Premier Hatfield deadpanned, "I'll take care of Liz [the Queen] if you'll resign."[36]

At one point, Roy McMurtry found himself alone with the prime minister. He used the rare occasion to reintroduce an old idea that had been gaining fresh steam over the past few weeks. What about inserting into the Charter a "notwithstanding" clause—*non obstante*, as it was technically called—that would allow the legislatures to override specific provisions when and if they wished? Not only would such a clause respect the principle of parliamentary supremacy, but it would also act as a safety valve for those premiers who feared that appointed judges would usurp the power of elected politicians to ban child pornography, for example, or to introduce affirmative-action programs.

Though unique to Canadian jurisprudence, it wasn't a radical idea. (Indeed, its case was helped by the confusion about its origins. Because it wasn't identified with any one side, it could be claimed by both.) A "notwithstanding" provision was in Diefenbaker's Bill of Rights, as well as in the human rights legislation of Alberta, Saskatchewan, and Quebec. It had been suggested by Saskatchewan at constitutional meetings in the late 1970s. It had been resurrected during the ministerial discussions in the summer of 1980, floated by Peter Lougheed at the disastrous First Ministers' Conference in September, and proposed for legal and non-discrimination rights in the Château Consensus.[37] It had been put forward in an academic paper by Paul Weiler, a Harvard law professor and former chair of the British Columbia Labour Relations Board, who brought it to the attention of his friends in Victoria, who then passed it along to their contacts in Toronto and Ottawa.[38] It was presented as an option in the briefing book federal officials had prepared for the prime minister going into the November conference, but only if absolutely necessary for a deal, only with a "sunset" clause that would compel the legislature to renew the override every five years, and only if it didn't apply to fundamental freedoms, democratic rights, language rights, and mobility rights.[39]

Allan Blakeney revived the idea on Monday afternoon and again on Tuesday morning, and Lougheed declared that he was prepared to look at entrenchment if there was a *non obstante* provision. By then, too, Bill Davis and Roy McMurtry, both of whom had initially resisted the idea of a notwithstanding clause, saw it as the bridge to a deal. "It was something you would rather not have, because you could guess as to who might use it," Davis said. "But my approach was that it may be a way to break the deadlock."[40]

McMurtry now urged the prime minister to take it seriously. "There has to be a graceful exit for those people who want to have a better balance between the courts and Parliament," he told Trudeau. "Besides, given the Charter's popularity, no government will dare use it, except maybe Quebec."[41]

Trudeau wasn't buying. A notwithstanding clause would defeat his very purpose, which was to protect the rights and freedoms of individuals from the caprices of government. If rights were so fundamental, how could he accept a scenario in which they could be taken away by the vote of a legislature? Didn't the proposed Charter already permit "such reasonable limits prescribed by law as can be demonstrably justified in a free and democratic society"?[42] And it was surely cold comfort for Pierre Trudeau to be told that no one but the government of Quebec would likely invoke it.

"I saw the charter as an expression of my long-held view that the subject of law must be the individual human being; the law must permit the individual to fulfil himself or herself to the utmost," he later explained. "Therefore the individual has certain basic rights that cannot be taken away by any government. So maintaining an unweakened charter was important to me in this basic philosophical sense. Besides, in another dimension, the charter was defining a system of values such as liberty, equality, and the rights of association that Canadians from coast to coast could share."[43]

When Lougheed, Bennett, and Buchanan arrived with the Gang of Eight's tentative proposal around five o'clock on Tuesday, Trudeau was outraged by their emasculation of the Charter. Democratic rights entrenched, but fundamental rights optional. Language rights entrenched, but minority education rights left to the discretion of each province. The rest to be left to further study and negotiation. "You must be joking," the prime minister said scornfully after taking one look at the piece of paper, and he proceeded to tear a strip off the emissaries for being dupes of the separatists.[44] His reaction to the Gang's suggestions was so heated and dismissive that the three premiers went back to the hotel shaken by the half-hour confrontation, and Bill Davis found himself berated for being their accomplice. If we have to compromise, Trudeau argued, we want the very best deal, and he insisted that the Gang of Eight wasn't going to give up anything substantial until it was broken into pieces. At 6:00 p.m., the two allies went off in very different directions.

"Davis was beginning to say to us that we were going to have to make some compromises," Michael Kirby remembered, "which we knew, of course. But we weren't going to accept anything until we knew we had broken the log-jam. I mean, why should we make compromises in advance of knowing we had a deal? If we had to go along, we wanted to go with the best package, our package, because it was more saleable."[45]

By chance, Bill Davis and his team found themselves seated beside Allan Blakeney and his officials at Mamma Teresa, an informal and convivial Italian restaurant removed from the hubbub of the hotels and the conference centre. They chatted about the impasse as much as the noise and public nature of the room allowed. The main message to Saskatchewan was that Trudeau required a charter or everything was back to square one. "The Ontario people passed on to us," Howard Leeson, Saskatchewan's deputy minister of intergovernmental affairs, wrote in his follow-up notes, "that they thought a *non obstante* in the charter had much more chance of being accepted by Trudeau than any other arrangement with the charter." While Blakeney got a lift back to his hotel with Davis, McMurtry and Leeson walked to the Four Seasons to fine-tune the proposal Saskatchewan wanted to present on Wednesday morning. Unfortunately, the Ontario suite was hot and stuffy, McMurtry arrived droopy from dinner and only grew droopier, and the best Leeson could get by midnight was lukewarm support and a desire to prolong the talks. "I was very angry at the reaction of Ontario," he recalled. "They were unconcerned with new efforts and patronizing to say the least."[46]

Davis found the random encounter helpful, nonetheless. "It further encouraged me in what Allan really believed and wanted to do," he said. "He would have loved to have been with Hatfield and myself—I knew him so well—but he had a gentleman to the west who was fairly adamant on some issues and not necessarily any friends to the east. But my instincts told me he was very anxious to see this come to a positive conclusion."[47]

Trudeau's instincts were telling him the opposite. At eight o'clock, while Davis and Blakeney were dining at Mamma Teresa, the prime minister reported on the day's events at a special four-hour meeting of his Cabinet on Parliament Hill. As much as he disliked the Gang of Eight's Vancouver formula, he told his ministers, he might have to accept it in return for the Charter, but only the full Charter. If not, he was ready to take the Resolution to London and the Canadian people. "I was willing to talk about a referendum strategy as a strategic threat when negotiating with the provinces," Chrétien remembered, "but I never wanted or expected to use it. Now I realized that Trudeau was prepared to use it as more than a fallback position."[48]

On Wednesday morning, over breakfast at 24 Sussex, Trudeau told Bill Davis and Richard Hatfield that he was going to try to break the Gang by offering to hold a national referendum. Davis repeated the cautions he had expressed on Sunday about its divisiveness and risks. "I never understood whether it was a question of a vote in each province or a national vote," he later admitted. "If province by province, it was guaranteed to fail in Quebec and Alberta, and maybe three or four other provinces, so what was the gain?"[49] But he was prepared to go along with the idea for the moment as a tactical ploy.

Hatfield, however, was horrified. He had already been quoted in the press as saying that referendums were just an escape hatch for weak politicians. "I'm going to have to swallow myself a second time," he moaned.

"Don't worry," Trudeau reassured him. "Lévesque will never accept."[50]

If Lévesque's surprising acceptance fractured the solidarity of the Gang of Eight, it also shook loose the federal side. Bill Davis and Roy McMurtry now feared—rightly or wrongly didn't matter—that the referendum was for Trudeau no longer a tactic but a real, perhaps even a desirable, option. A failed conference would give him the excuse he needed to get his Resolution through Westminster and to legitimize it, if need be, with an appeal to the people.

"I didn't knock it down immediately because it gave something else for people to talk about," Davis recalled. "As long as people were talking, there was still some hope. I took it seriously from the standpoint that the prime minister might decide to do it, but I was never a believer that it was the right route to go, and I think he recognized that a referendum might just as likely fail. He was getting impatient. I don't think he ever felt, as I felt, that one more crack would maybe do it. That doesn't mean he didn't want to do it; he just felt it wasn't going to happen."[51]

So Bill Davis decided to strike out on his own. "There's always time to go to the cameras," he said, jumping in when Trudeau seemed on the verge of giving up at four-thirty. Perhaps, he suggested, it was time to take another coffee break to try to come up with something more constructive.

No one goes into politics, rises to the leadership of a party, fights to become premier of a province, and wins four consecutive elections in ten years without being fiercely competitive. Beneath his somewhat passive civility, Davis was a tough, behind-the-scenes politician, determined to do whatever he thought was the right thing. In September 1980, that meant signing the Château Consensus. In October 1980, it meant supporting unilateral action. In November 1981, it meant getting a negotiated deal. And now he sensed a feeling in the room to get the thing over and done with. During the coffee break, before going off to speak with Trudeau, Hatfield, and Blakeney, he dispatched the members of his team to seek out their federal counterparts and give them a clear and simple message from Ontario: "If you guys can't find a way to compromise, then don't count on us to be with you at Westminster."[52] He himself would think about the notwithstanding clause and attempt to get Pierre Trudeau to concede something on minority-language education.

"The feds were stunned," Hugh Segal remembered. "They just expected Ontario to sit there and accept everything."[53]

THIRTEEN

Last In, First Out

Allan Blakeney watched Pierre Trudeau and René Lévesque stick pins into each other over the referendum issue during the Wednesday afternoon session, and he was bewildered, distressed, and appalled. He again felt, as he had so often since his election as premier of Saskatchewan in 1971, that he was being dragged into the middle of a long and savage family dispute, relegated to being a bit player in a drama with only two protagonists, and forced to choose one side or the other when neither reflected his own agenda or even cared to hear it. Saskatchewan was the only province where Canadians of British or French heritage constituted a minority. Multiculturalism was of more concern there than the old Central Canadian duality. Oil and potash were more essential than official languages and francophone education. And on a personal note, Trudeau struck Blakeney as an arrogant, patrician intellectual who seemed to feel he could ignore the rubes in western Canada or the fuddy-duddies in Atlantic Canada in the pursuit of his goal to annihilate the separatists.

"Since some others and I wanted no part of a referendum," Blakeney remembered, "either for adoption of the changes or as part of a new amending formula, I found these dogfights unhelpful. I still did not understand the way politics in Quebec was conducted. I was reasonably sure that the protagonists did not mean what they said, but that gave me little help on what they did mean."[1]

Like Bill Davis, Blakeney feared that Trudeau and Lévesque were sufficiently bold, dogmatic, and reckless to plunge the nation into a protracted and divisive fight over patriation and the Charter. Since it would be difficult for any provincial premier other than Davis or Hatfield to defend Trudeau's amending formula, his inclusion of language rights, or even his national vision, Blakeney foresaw the campaign degenerating into battles between region and region, rural and urban, English and French—and he realized that it was a campaign he himself could very well lose. That had to be avoided, at almost any cost, he felt, by negotiating a last-minute compromise.

Nobody else was better positioned to do so, for Allan Blakeney was at the centre of an intricate web of partisan divisions and personal relationships, the only premier with good lines of communications to both sides. Through Davis, he could get to Trudeau and Hatfield. Through Lougheed, he could get to Lévesque and the rest of the Gang of Eight. As well, Saskatchewan's personable attorney general and deputy premier, Roy Romanow, and his skilled team of constitutional experts had laboured long and effectively to keep open the lines to their counterparts in Ottawa, Toronto, Victoria, and—until everything went seriously awry—Quebec City. If Blakeney had little leverage to persuade Alberta, Quebec, and Manitoba to abandon their positions, he still retained some hope of getting Ottawa and the other provinces to come together on a middle ground.

Being in the middle may have been ultimately rewarding, but it hadn't been a comfortable position to occupy for the past year. In trying to be friends with all, Blakeney more often found himself friends with none. The adversaries saw the battle for patriation and the Charter as a struggle between right and wrong, not a quest for peace at any price.

"Anyone who tries to build a bridge between two warring camps," Blakeney admitted, "is likely to be shot at from both sides."[2] But he was a man of the middle—a child of Loyalist parentage from Nova Scotia who became a socialist after studying on a Rhodes Scholarship in post-war Oxford; either a Red Tory or a Liberal-in-a-hurry, depending on your perspective; a New Democrat in name and conviction, yet not unlike Bill Davis in style and politics; cautious, methodical, and practical.

On the one hand, given Saskatchewan's abundance of oil, gas, potash, and uranium, Premier Blakeney shared Peter Lougheed's determination to safeguard and enhance provincial control over natural resources. He was under enormous pressure from his Cabinet and caucus to maintain solidarity with the western premiers, and he didn't want to disappoint Lougheed, whom he liked and perhaps also feared. He went along with the game of holding patriation and the Charter hostage for more power and money to the provinces. He vigorously opposed Ottawa's unilateralism, which he saw as an arbitrary and aggressive violation of federalist principles. And in tandem with Sterling Lyon, with whom he normally clashed on a host of ideological and governmental issues, he led the intellectual crusade against the Charter.

Though Blakeney shared Lyon's view that power should remain in the hands of elected parliamentarians, he came at it from the opposite end of the political spectrum. Instead of fearing the impact of Liberal-appointed, liberal-oriented courts, the NDP premier looked upon judges as conservative toadies of the Establishment, often fresh from serving the well-heeled clients of the biggest law firms, the very type of reactionaries who had struck down Franklin Roosevelt's New Deal legislation and R.B. Bennett's social reforms in the 1930s. The U.S. Bill of Rights hadn't spared American citizens of Japanese origin from the persecution that Japanese Canadians had suffered during the Second World War, he noted, nor did he think that such charters, designed as they were to protect individuals from their governments, were of any use in shielding individuals from the abuse of corporations or guaranteeing the right to food, shelter, or medical care. Indeed, they were just as likely to stand in the way of affirmative-action programs to help women, aboriginals, or seniors.

"I freely acknowledge," he explained, "that a charter can be something that unifies all citizens around values set out in a document phrased in inspirational language. And this is no small benefit. But it carries with it the belief that somehow a constitution or charter protects freedom. Only citizens and vigilant citizens protect freedoms. A charter may or may not assist them to do so."[3]

What gave emotion and reason to his arguments were two significant rulings the Supreme Court of Canada had recently made against his government, one involving the province's authority to tax its oil companies, the other its power to regulate its potash industry. In both instances, Blakeney suspected that the federal government had encouraged private corporations to go to court with the sole intent of undermining provincial autonomy. "Alberta and Saskatchewan didn't own their resources when they became provinces in 1905," he explained. "The federal government held on to them until 1930. With the Canadian Industrial Gas & Oil and Central Canada Potash cases, then with the National Energy Program, there seemed to be a feeling in Ottawa that our resources were still under its control."[4]

On the other hand, Saskatchewan was not Alberta, Allan Blakeney was not Peter Lougheed, and the New Democrats were not the Progressive Conservatives. Though Saskatchewan was granted provincial status in the same year as Alberta, it attracted more Europeans than Americans; its political and religious leaders were closer to Christian socialism than to end-of-the-world fundamentalism; and the severity of the Great Depression, compounded by a prolonged drought, fostered a spirit of collective cooperation rather than frontier individualism. Thus when Alberta went to the right in 1935 with Social Credit, Saskatchewan went to the left in 1944 with the Co-operative Commonwealth Federation (CCF), an alliance of farmers, trade unionists, and intellectuals, and the forerunner of the New Democratic Party.[5]

The CCF's founding manifesto, passed at a convention in Regina in 1933 and co-authored by Trudeau's future mentor, Frank Scott, demanded national solutions to national problems. The class struggle bestrode the divisions of regions, ethnicities, and language. The banks and corporations had become increasingly centralized, and in the absence of federal legislation, they were adept at playing weak or bankrupt provinces against each other. Industrial growth and social justice required national planning, national regulations, national standards, and national programs. "What is chiefly needed today," the Regina Manifesto declared, "is the placing in the hands of the national government of more power to control national economic development." Among the policies it advocated were the reform of the BNA Act, the abolition of the decentralist Judicial Committee of the Privy Council as Canada's highest court, and an entrenched bill of rights.

By the time the CCF modernized itself into the NDP in 1961, it had shifted away from doctrinaire socialism. Not only was state ownership a tough sell in a liberal, capitalist society increasingly dependent on the United States for investment and exports, but central planning didn't find much political favour in a diverse, fractious federation. The federal New Democrats suffered wherever Ottawa was seen as more the problem than the solution, most especially in Quebec and the western provinces. And when the party's provincial wings became the Official Opposition in Ontario in 1943 and formed the governments of Saskatchewan in 1944, of Manitoba in 1969, and of British Columbia in 1972, many New Democrats discovered new virtues in giving the provinces more power and money. They simply had to point to the example set by the Saskatchewan government when it introduced the first public health-care program in North America in 1962 to show how the provinces could serve as laboratories for economic and social innovation.

"It was a different perspective," Romanow explained. "In Saskatchewan, we believed that you'd get your equality programs by door-to-door campaigning. At the federal level, where they thought they'd never be elected, they had to use the courts and charters and so forth."[6]

Like every other national party, the NDP was forced to internalize the stresses and strains of Canada's federal system in its policies and its politics. Just as Trudeau's constitutional package pitted the federal Liberals against the Quebec Liberals and the federal Tories against the Ontario Tories, it also set the federal NDP against the NDP government in Saskatchewan. The day before unveiling his Resolution on October 2, 1980, Trudeau secured the support of Ed Broadbent, the national party leader, who represented an industrial riding near Toronto. Broadbent's support, which he announced without giving any advance notice to Allan Blakeney, was a coup for the federal side. It lifted the constitution above Liberal partisanship in the House of Commons, eased its passage through Parliament, and brought into the fold thirty-two more MPs, twenty-six of whom represented western Canada. Many of them went unwillingly, but Broadbent, a former political science professor with a taste for rumpled corduroy suits and Cuban cigars, believed in the social-democratic credo that the will of the people should prevail. If the majority of Canadians wanted patriation and a bill of rights, if language rights and equalization were in the national interest, and if the provinces could never come to an agreement with Ottawa, then Broadbent thought it acceptable for the national government to proceed unilaterally. Tellingly, he was joined by two legendary New Democrats and former federal leaders, T.C. Douglas and David Lewis, as well as Dave Barrett, the leader of the party in British Columbia.[7]

To appease his western caucus and placate Allan Blakeney, Broadbent insisted that the People's Package include a constitutional amendment confirming the provinces' right to own and manage their natural resources, to levy indirect taxes on those resources, and to share power with Ottawa with respect to interprovincial trade in natural resources. Those had been on the list of items to be negotiated at a later date in exchange for the strengthening of the economic union, but Trudeau readily agreed to Broadbent's changes—with more yet to come—in order to be able to point to some support in the West and perhaps lure Saskatchewan on board.[8] (Indeed, in anticipation of the pending fights over constitutional renewal and energy pricing, he had recently offered Broadbent and a few western New Democrats senior positions in the Liberal Cabinet.[9]) Yet Broadbent's significant gain made little impact. Saskatchewan's antipathy towards Trudeau and the federal Liberals was so great that Roy Romanow threatened to mobilize the party's provincial machine to hinder the re-election of any NDP MP who voted in favour of the Resolution.[10]

"That was unquestionably the most intense period of my political life," Broadbent recalled. "It was a really trying time, very raucous, with plenty of emotional highs and emotional lows. My leadership in the caucus was on the line. There were heated debates at our councils and conventions. And though I don't remember any personal acrimony between Allan Blakeney and myself, there were obviously serious tensions at the staff level. At one point I could see the party splitting in two, with a permanent rift between the East and the West, even if the differences weren't that substantive. Fortunately, Tommy Douglas and Dave Barrett, who could hardly be called easterners, were on my side. Their support helped maintain cohesiveness, as did David Lewis's. After one private meeting in which Allan Blakeney argued against and I argued for, David actually wept. His heart was broken to see the party so divided."[11]

Blakeney was in a bind. With Broadbent carrying the CCF/NDP's centralist legacy like a torch held high, the Saskatchewan premier was in danger of looking like a fussy provincial standing in the way of national independence and national unity for his own parochial interests and pedantic concerns. He was annoyed at Broadbent for presuming to negotiate natural resource rights on Saskatchewan's behalf, and he was puzzled as to why Broadbent had accepted so little without putting up more of a fight. As one Saskatchewan official put it, "Broadbent was a fool to think it was all about resources and resource rents. He insulted us in that way, because it was grander than that."[12]

What's more, Blakeney didn't believe that Broadbent was any more principled or patriotic in supporting Trudeau's Resolution than Blakeney himself was in opposing it. What could be more principled than standing up for provincial rights against federal unilateralism, he argued, or protecting social programs from the right-wing opinions of undemocratic judges, the "handmaidens" of the economic elites? Hadn't Blakeney campaigned on behalf of federalism during the Quebec referendum at Ottawa's behest? Didn't he have a bigger view of the country and of the national interest than Peter Lougheed? And though it was high time that Canada took full and proper control of its constitution, Blakeney believed that should be done according to the traditions of the country—that is, by consensus rather than by confrontation, by negotiation rather than by ultimatum.

"He was not a fervent decentralist but a pragmatic provincialist, one who understood that New Democrats had to use the governments that they controlled now," observed Roy Romanow and two of his closest advisers in the account they later wrote of the constitutional wars. "This made more sense than adding powers to the federal level, in the hope that the New Democratic Party would someday form the government of Canada. Furthermore, Blakeney was a federalist who believed that the interests of the people were served through regional governments, elected by people with a common regional perspective."[13]

With his party divided along ideological and regional lines, his officials arguing about which path to take, and he himself torn between each side of the debate, Blakeney decided to stand squarely in the middle. At the premiers' meeting in Toronto on October 14, 1980, he declined to join the Group of Six in categorically opposing the federal government's

Resolution. Instead, he announced his intention to keep "fighting for change."

"What Blakeney is doing to stall for time," Michael Kirby stated in a confidential report to Trudeau on October 17, 1980, "is insisting that every detail of every amendment be worked out before he comes on board publicly. Frankly, this worries me. I suspect his real plan may be to keep stalling and then find a pretext for backing off at the last minute."

"To hell to them!" Trudeau scribbled in the margin.[14]

In secret talks with Trudeau and Chrétien, then in a public presentation to the Special Joint Committee of the Senate and the House of Commons on December 19, 1980, Blakeney laid out his government's position. While Saskatchewan might be able to live with some version of Ottawa's amending formula, he said, it could not accept the new referendum provisions, unless they were modified to give the provinces an equal right to initiate a deadlock-breaking appeal to the people.[15] As to the Charter, Blakeney continued to oppose it as a transfer of power from the provincial legislatures to the courts, though he was willing to go along with minority-language rights and even pressed for aboriginal rights.[16] Finally, on natural resources, Blakeney wanted to augment the concession Broadbent had received on *interprovincial* exports to increase provincial control over the production and pricing of *international* exports, since most of his province's resources were sold to the United States.

For a while, Blakeney's fence-sitting looked like a very clever strategy. As Ottawa's position weakened over the winter, as its Resolution crawled at a snail's pace through Parliament and three provincial courts, as a majority of Canadians grew weary of the whole damn business and pleaded for a negotiated settlement, as MPs in Britain made threats about delaying or even defeating patriation and the Charter for their own political reasons, Trudeau began to see Saskatchewan as more and more crucial to his success. It was a province west of Ontario; it had an NDP government; it had friends inside the Labour Party in London. Even though Blakeney could never match Lougheed's clout with the predominantly Conservative members of the Gang of Eight, he had the credibility to make a strong case for a compromise, and if Saskatchewan moved, there was a chance that it might bring along Nova Scotia or British Columbia as well. Conversely, if Saskatchewan decided to come out against the Resolution and join the Group of Six, there were fears that Ed Broadbent would no longer be able to guarantee the support of all or even some of the western MPs in the federal NDP caucus.

"It seems to me that you and the government are faced with a historic decision," Michael Kirby advised Trudeau in a secret memorandum dated January 16, 1981. "At stake is not only the capacity of the government to press its constitutional proposals through Parliament and to persuade the Parliament of the United Kingdom to do the same, but the capacity of the constitutional proposals themselves to become accepted and eventually revered by the people of Canada. I feel certain that these things can all be accomplished much more readily if there is real support from the NDP in Parliament (including necessarily its western members) and from Premier Blakeney, whose reaction will influence NDP supporters in every western province ... It would be sad to look back, five or ten years from now, and realize that if only there had been a little more generosity, at the right moment, it might have guaranteed the successful achievement of an historically unparalleled political endeavour, and the successful achievement of a goal long sought after by you and your predecessors."[17]

Though Trudeau held firm in his opinion that Ottawa should not abandon the principle of giving the people of Canada the power to break a constitutional deadlock, Jean Chrétien and many of his senior officials in the justice department had come round to the notion of dropping the referendum provisions if that would help expedite a deal with Saskatchewan. Still feeling badly burned by the quarrels and nastiness of the previous year's campaign in Quebec, Chrétien abhorred the idea of fighting another referendum. Once, when Michael Pitfield began lecturing a group of ministers and officials during a meeting in the

Prime Minister's Office in his ponderous, academic way about Jeffersonian democrats versus Hamiltonian elites, Chrétien humiliated the patrician Clerk of the Privy Council by asking, "Tell me, Michael, which of those teams is playing against the Montreal Expos tonight?"[18] Everyone burst out laughing, but Pitfield and Michael Kirby knew that Jean Chrétien was their most effective rival for the ear of the prime minister.

According to a memo prepared by Chrétien's chief political adviser, Eddie Goldenberg, there would be half a dozen major benefits to giving up the referendum provisions in exchange for bringing Blakeney onside. The support of a western province would increase the legitimacy of the federal government's unilateral action, strengthen Ottawa's case in the courts and in London, reduce the intensity of the opposition to the Resolution among the Gang of Eight and in Parliament, undercut the perception that the referendum mechanism was simply a tool by which Ottawa could circumvent the provincial legislatures and take over provincial resources, and give Trudeau the appearance of conciliation at no real practical cost. "What is central to our objective is not an amending formula with a referendum," Goldenberg argued.[19]

With so little rapport or trust existing between Pierre Trudeau and Allan Blakeney, the negotiations fell to Jean Chrétien and Roy Romanow, who had co-chaired the four-city ministerial negotiations that took place during the summer of 1980, which some wits dubbed "The Tuque and Uke Show." Gregarious, media-savvy politicians who shared a love of baseball, a competitive and ambitious nature, and an eye on the prize they were later to win, Chrétien and Romanow usually operated on the belief that a bird in the hand was worth two in the bush. Though Romanow was in unison with Blakeney's hang-tough strategy, he was increasingly eager not to let ideology, ego, or even consistency get in the way of a workable solution that would satisfy his province and avoid yet another failure.

At one point, Chrétien read a newspaper article in which Romanow claimed there were only three items standing in the way of Saskatchewan's consent. He immediately picked up the phone. "I can't deliver three," he told his friend, "but I can deliver two. Do you think your premier will accept two?"

"Yes," Romanow replied, "I think he will."

So Chrétien, as he remembered it, hurried over to see Trudeau with the latest development.

"You don't have a deal and you will never have a deal" was Trudeau's reaction. "Blakeney will never sign."

"If you're so certain," Chrétien countered, "let's offer to meet all three of Romanow's conditions. I'll bet you a dollar. You have nothing to lose."

He made the offer to Romanow, Saskatchewan came back with more conditions, and Trudeau won the dollar. He knew, the prime minister later explained to Romanow, that Blakeney would never desert Lougheed.[20]

Romanow himself admitted as much when he and his officials met with federal negotiators on January 23, 1981. The NDP government, he remarked in a particularly forceful manner, would surely lose the next election in Saskatchewan if Blakeney came out in support of the Resolution. And yet he insisted, with equal forcefulness, that Saskatchewan had no wish to align itself with the Group of Six or to fuel the fires of western separatism.[21]

This meeting, held over three days in two hotels in Toronto, was the last-ditch, all-out effort by both sides to reach an accommodation. With Chrétien hospitalized from exhaustion, Trudeau instructed his powerful minister of energy, Marc Lalonde, en route from Edmonton to Montreal, to stop off in Toronto on Friday evening to brief Romanow at the highest political level on the federal government's final offer. Time was of the essence. The joint committee was getting ready to report on its proposed amendments, the Manitoba court was about to rule on the constitutionality of the Resolution, and Saskatchewan had to get off the fence.

The negotiations were now down to only two "bottom line" issues: the referendum procedure in Ottawa's amending formula and the international dimension of Saskatchewan's natural resources proposal.[22] Hour after hour, well into each evening, the two delegations, led by Michael Kirby and Howard Leeson, argued back and forth, poring over the fine print and bickering about the legal technicalities. Was "assuring" the same as "protecting and promoting"? Was "regulating" better than "in relation to"? Was "economic well-being" worse than "economic viability"? Saskatchewan still preferred no referendum clause at all, but if there had to be one, the "two orders of government" should have an equal right to conduct a referendum or prevent one. ("There's nothing worse than putting a bunch of New Democrats in front of words," Jean Chrétien once observed. "They will spend hours nitpicking over the details."[23]) Though Ottawa wouldn't budge from its determination to give the people the power to break constitutional deadlocks or from its reluctance to give the provinces the right to initiate a national referendum on their own, it did offer seven provinces representing 50 percent of the population the power to stop a vote on a particular amendment. On Saturday morning, the two parties called in J.J. Robinette, the venerable Toronto lawyer, to arbitrate on the wording of a compromise that would give Saskatchewan the authority it wanted to regulate the international export of its natural resources without infringing on Ottawa's jurisdiction over foreign affairs. It was a good compromise, Robinette concluded, fair to both sides.

Romanow briefed Blakeney on the progress, though in his opinion it wasn't enough for Saskatchewan. To his great surprise, Blakeney replied, "Roy, I really want to do this."[24]

What had been a slim hope on Thursday afternoon, with Saskatchewan hardening its position the more Ottawa softened, emerged by Saturday afternoon as a draft agreement on two amendments to the Resolution, a draft letter from Trudeau to Blakeney outlining the agreement, and a draft letter from Blakeney to Trudeau accepting it. One set of documents was sent to the prime minister at his weekend retreat at Harrington Lake and another was flown to Premier Blakeney, who was on vacation in Hawaii. All that was needed were their signatures.

At 6:00 p.m., Pierre Trudeau and Michael Pitfield went over the deal with Fred Gibson and Frank Carter, two of the federal officials who had participated in the Toronto talks. They were joined by Jean Chrétien, eager to know what he had missed while out of action. He had no problem with the two amendments, Chrétien said, but he adamantly opposed a condition that would give Saskatchewan a veto on any further amendments to the Resolution. The demand was reasonable enough. How could Blakeney support the Resolution if he didn't know what was in it? But Chrétien did not want to hamstring any changes that the joint committee, Parliament, the other provinces, or even the federal government might want to make in the weeks to come.

"The Prime Minister noted these difficulties," Frank Carter wrote in his private report of the meeting, "but said he had always taken it for granted that when Premiers 'embarked with us' a kind of alliance was then forged. Premier Davis had thus been given a veto concerning Section 133. The federal government itself had agreed to certain changes respecting the Senate only if those changes were acceptable to Mr. Broadbent. The new agreement with Saskatchewan was in this vein. He recognized that Mr. Blakeney was a 'désagréable' negotiator, but the Prime Minister would like nevertheless to push through to the end of the process, hoping that Mr. Blakeney would subsequently accept any of the changes which the government really wanted to make."[25]

With that, and a few minor changes to the wording of the letters, Trudeau signed.

The next morning, Sunday, January 25, 1981, Roy Romanow and Howard Leeson fought their way through a fierce snowstorm to travel from Toronto to Honolulu, while Fred Gibson, who had left Ottawa at 6:25 a.m., reached the Ilikai Hotel in Waikiki bearing Trudeau's offer twenty-one hours later. After being briefed by Romanow and Leeson on

Monday morning, Blakeney accepted the texts regarding the amending formula and natural resources, but he added a number of handwritten revisions. Not only did he still want to see and approve the other proposed amendments to the Resolution, but he also wanted a "full and complete" debate in Parliament and a positive ruling in the courts about the legality of the federal government's unilateral action. If and when those terms were met, he was ready to support the "substance" of the Resolution; by design or neglect, he didn't promise to commit to it publicly.

Gibson reported the revisions back to Kirby, who felt confident that they could be resolved or clarified to everyone's satisfaction during the phone call between the prime minister and the premier scheduled for later that day, at 5:30 p.m. Hawaii time (10:30 p.m. in the nation's capital). As fate would have it, Trudeau's limousine broke down on the highway from Montreal to Ottawa, and the call was postponed until Tuesday morning. In the meantime, after speaking by phone with Ed Broadbent about Native rights and other issues, Blakeney had been pacing back and forth on the balcony of his hotel, debating the issues aloud with himself, as was his habit. Suddenly an old, unsettled point of contention came back to him. Would the Senate be able to veto future constitutional amendments or merely delay them? It might have seemed like a secondary and rather technical issue, but the CCF/NDP had been calling for the abolition of the Upper House ever since the Regina Manifesto. Blakeney was not about to give a bunch of appointed senators the right to entrench their own powers and privileges. His thoughts became fixated on the defeat by the British House of Lords of Gladstone's Second Home Rule Bill in 1893.

"I don't think I can do this," he told Romanow after stepping back inside.[26]

A subsequent flurry of exchanges between Ottawa and Honolulu eventually ascertained that the federal government had indeed promised to let the senators keep their full veto as a necessary concession for getting the Resolution through Parliament. Otherwise, Trudeau was warned in a memo on January 19, 1981, "the likelihood of approval of the draft Resolution in the Senate will be, at best, marginal."[27] If forced to choose between the Senate and Saskatchewan, the federal government had no choice but to go with the Senate. Though Kirby thought he had made that clear to the Saskatchewan officials in Toronto, Blakeney began to suspect that he would never be able to pin Ottawa down on a final package, that the Resolution would always remain a moving target, and that it was better to wait and see how it all played out.

"I don't think the feds deceived us," said John Whyte, who was the Saskatchewan government's legal adviser at the Toronto negotiations. "Al's his own lawyer, and he's a damn good lawyer, but I wasn't invited to go to Hawaii to make sure he understood the precise nature of what we had agreed to in the Four Seasons. It was a complete deal. However, I remember seeing some members of his Cabinet hanging around the hotel and wondering to myself, What the hell are they doing here? Looking back, I think they were shadowing Romanow to give him a message to take to Al. Blakeney wanted to sign, he wanted patriation badly, he understood the consequences of failure, but Cabinet solidarity prevailed. It was vicious in there."[28]

When the prime minister and the premier finally spoke at 11:00 a.m. Tuesday (4:00 p.m. in Ottawa), the call was short and brusque. In fact, the two men never got further than the first item on the five-point agenda, the senators' veto. Blakeney declared that it was, for him, a matter of principle. Trudeau explained his dilemma and offered to "fight the Senate together." The premier said no deal.

In hindsight, Blakeney felt that he had been "deluding" himself since October into believing he could ever reach an agreement with Ottawa.[29] But it was the politics of allying with the federal Liberals against Lougheed and the other western premiers that made it virtually impossible for the Saskatchewan government to have supported the Resolution in any form. Making common cause with Conservatives in other provinces enabled the NDP government to deflect the attacks of the Conservative Opposition in Saskatchewan, while siding with the arch-demon Trudeau would have hurt the New Democrats going into the next election. "I was never going to be number three with Ontario and New Brunswick," he later admitted. "Unless I could get six there, it wasn't going to happen. The politics of western Canada made anything else impossible. Trudeau had stolen our oil; he was anathema, and the animosity was visceral."[30]

"For a man of intelligence and principle Blakeney disappointed me," Jean Chrétien concluded. "Although he understood every nuance of Ottawa's position and a deal would have helped him make peace with the federal NDP caucus, he never stopped looking over his shoulder. But all his wariness didn't help his career; he was defeated in the next election anyway, so he should have done what he knew to be right in the first place."[31]

On February 19, 1981, two days after the federal government tabled its latest amendments to the Resolution in the House of Commons, with no middle ground in sight and Trudeau pushing ahead to London, Allan Blakeney came out against it, joining four western MPs from the NDP's federal caucus who broke ranks with Ed Broadbent over issues ranging from aboriginal rights to the Senate veto. A few weeks later, Saskatchewan formally joined the Gang of Eight, though not as a particularly comfortable member. Blakeney was the lone New Democrat among five Conservatives, one Social Credit, and an *indépendantiste*. He was the only one of them who argued that patriation didn't require unanimity as a matter of law. He was prepared to accept the Victoria formula, including its veto for Ontario and Quebec, if the federal government dropped the referendum mechanisms. He didn't make the Charter or minority-language education rights a deal-breaker for Saskatchewan, despite his own intellectual and political reservations. Nor did he care for the Gang's amending formula, fearing, as Trudeau did, that it would create a "checkerboard" of national social programs, which was why he pushed—unsuccessfully—to remove financial compensation from the April Accord and require a two-thirds vote of the legislature of any province that wanted to opt out.

"Some things we simply had to swallow," Romanow explained, "even though we didn't think that giving the provinces the cash to do things their own way is any way to build a country. And though we had heard Trudeau say often enough that he needed minority-language education, I guess it hadn't sunk in. Remember, while trying to keep a national vision, we were still worried about resources and resource revenues."[32]

In Saskatchewan's eyes, the April Accord was nothing more than a bargaining tool to get a better deal. "Mr. Blakeney and his representatives made it completely clear then—both publicly and privately—that Saskatchewan's involvement with the other seven provinces did not commit him or his government to any constitutional position if new negotiations developed," Peter Lougheed remembered, "and that his and his government's involvement was solely on the basis of changing the process of constitutional action."[33]

Claude Morin had heard that argument often enough from Romanow, but why, he asked, would the premier of Saskatchewan have gone before the cameras and signed the accord with such great ceremony if Blakeney hadn't believed it to be a firm and important intergovernmental entente? "Or else the accord was simply a negotiating tactic," Morin later wrote to Romanow, "in which case the television special was a trick and misled the public about the significance of the genuine offer by the eight provinces. I find it difficult to believe that your premier would have participated in such a manipulation of public opinion."[34]

Blakeney destabilized the Gang of Eight as much as he strengthened it. Lévesque harboured a lingering animosity towards him for intervening on the No side in the 1980 referendum, and Saskatchewan arrived with a proactive, well-prepared, and highly intelligent team of constitutional advisers who had a strong bias towards negotiation and compromise.

"Last in, first out" was the word in the Quebec delegation, while Claude Charron dismissed the premier as "the Trojan horse Blakeney with his wheat salesman's smile."[35]

Relations between Saskatchewan and Quebec only worsened following the April Accord. The Parti Québécois election victory reinvigorated René Lévesque and resurrected his dream of sovereignty-association or special status. There were reports in the press that the PQ was preparing for another referendum, this one aimed at defending Quebec's language laws against Ottawa's proposed Charter. While Blakeney and Romanow had been encouraged by Quebec's participation in the constitutional process after the 1980 referendum, it now looked to them as if Trudeau and Chrétien had been right all along: Lévesque was prepared to destroy Canada in his personal and political crusade to destroy Pierre Trudeau; Quebec could no longer be trusted to negotiate in good faith. More likely than not, the anglophone premiers of the Gang of Eight would have to abandon their efforts to accommodate the *indépendantistes* if they wanted a deal.

On June 21, 1981, just a few weeks after the signing ceremony, during a meeting of ministers and officials in Winnipeg to prepare a response to the eagerly awaited Supreme Court decision, Claude Morin dropped a comment that profoundly unsettled Roy Romanow. "If we win, we win. If we lose, we win," he said. "If we win in the U.K., we win. If we lose in the U.K., we win. We win all ways!" It took a moment for the penny to drop with the others that "we" meant the separatists in Quebec. If the Supreme Court and Westminster stopped Trudeau, fine. If they didn't stop him, then the Parti Québécois would have a stick with which it presumed it could beat Canada to death. "But, Claude," Romanow replied after a long pause, "what about us, *les Anglais*, what do we win?" The chair, fearing a brawl, quickly adjourned the meeting for lunch.[36]

"That was a major blunder on Morin's part," said Howard Leeson. "He ought to have kept quiet, but he was so full of himself. It was quite clear to us that things had changed for them. Whereas they had been in a weak position after the referendum, they were re-energized after the election. They didn't even want to go back to the negotiating table, whichever way the Supreme Court went. They saw it as a trap. When it became clear that there would not be an agreement with Quebec under any circumstances, that reshaped the views of Saskatchewan and, I think, the views of others."[37]

Two significant events occurred in September that caused Allan Blakeney to further reassess his position. The first was Lougheed's signing of a revenue-sharing energy agreement with Trudeau. It relieved a major source of tension between Ottawa and the western provinces and removed an obstacle that had stood in the way of a constitutional deal. The second was the Supreme Court decision, which gave Ottawa the legal right to proceed on its own to London, even while it agreed with Saskatchewan's opinion that there existed a constitutional convention somewhere between unanimity and unilateralism. Blakeney didn't know how the federal government was going to manage to bulldoze its way past the Gang of Eight and through the British Parliament, but he had no doubt that it would try. Trudeau had come too far to turn back now, and the prime minister wasn't the kind of man to step away from a fight.

What were Blakeney's options at this point? He could stick with the Gang of Eight, come hell or high water. He could gulp hard, swallow his pride, override his Cabinet, and join Trudeau's side. Or he could try to come up with a last-minute compromise that would be acceptable at least to the "bendables"—that is, British Columbia, Nova Scotia, and perhaps Ontario. He took the third route, helped now by Ed Broadbent, who threatened to withdraw the federal NDP's support for the package if Trudeau refused to take the Supreme Court's ruling to heart and engage the provinces in another round of negotiations.

In the meantime, B.C.'s Bill Bennett had indeed become a bendable, not least because he wanted to escape the fate of Sterling Lyon, his predecessor as chair of the Annual Premiers' Conference, whom the eastern media had branded a cantankerous, inflexible ideologue. Unlike Lyon, Bennett analyzed the situation as if it were a business problem in need of a workable solution. Unlike Lougheed or Blakeney, he hadn't gone to Harvard or Oxford. He simply wanted to put an end to the constitutional bickering so that everyone could get back to dealing with the real problems of the economy. To that end, he held two one-on-one meetings with Trudeau in a search for common ground and beefed up his constitutional team—led by Mel Smith, a hard-nosed conservative—with a couple of younger, less confrontational advisers. James Matkin, a former deputy minister of labour who brought with him a wealth of education and experience in negotiation theories, and Norman Spector, a junior bureaucrat on leave from the Ontario government, did not share Smith's view of Ottawa as the devil incarnate. Neither man was philosophically opposed to a charter of rights. Neither thought the April Accord was going to lead to success if the real goal was to reach a solution rather than simply to stonewall. With their premier's tacit approval, Matkin and Spector set out to establish friendly communications with the other camps and to come up with a "no author single text" that might satisfy everyone by being identified with no particular interests.

Though Matkin once slipped a confidential document to Allan Blakeney while they were riding in a hotel elevator in Montreal— like two spies trying to evade the eyes and ears of the government of Quebec—it was hardly a state secret that B.C. was wavering. The press was full of stories about backroom meetings and trial balloons, and at a ministerial meeting in Toronto on October 27, 1981, Claude Morin denounced Matkin and Spector for conspiring with Roy Romanow. "These gentlemen were no doubt trying to be helpful," he said, "but they are weakening our position."[38]

Quebec was not alone in its concern. Many of the constitutional veterans dismissed Matkin and Spector as boy scouts or rogue warriors, sowing confusion and tension as they improvised their way through a complicated dossier they didn't fully comprehend. When Bennett reported to his colleagues in the Gang of Eight that Trudeau seemed willing to compromise on the amending formula, Michael Kirby methodically set to work to undermine the premier's credibility. If the other premiers believed the B.C. premier, Kirby figured, they'd have no incentive to compromise on the Charter.

"There's always a creative need for crisis and uncertainty to get any deal," Matkin explained. "We wanted to break the Gang and we weren't going to give Trudeau everything he wanted, so of course we were criticized. We were dismissed as dumbheads, but in fact, Trudeau did eventually compromise on the amending formula, which was all that really mattered to British Columbia."[39]

"It seems evident that the anticipated liaison among Saskatchewan, Ontario, and B.C. failed to develop," a confidential review of the provincial positions reported to the prime minister at the end of October. "This was largely because of the B.C. delegation's difficulty in dealing with matters of substance. Further, B.C. does not trust Saskatchewan and even passed a secret draft to Ontario. There is a converging view of the ingredients necessary for compromise by both Saskatchewan and Ontario, but nothing more. There remains the added difficulty that Ontario prefers to deal with B.C., which it perceives to be a leader. Most provinces were, however, dissatisfied with British Columbia's failure to lead the discussion and to encourage the development of a common approach. Indeed, B.C. gave some indications that it is considering reversion to its former position of opposition to a Charter in any form."[40]

The mood heading into the conference, as Saskatchewan saw it, was one of "grudging necessity, persistent mistrust, and modest hope."[41] Very modest hope, in fact. Ottawa had completely rejected the April Accord, yet the Gang of Eight had nothing else to offer. Both Trudeau and Lougheed were convinced that the other would be compelled to give way if confronted by an unyielding opponent. Lévesque preferred failure to any settlement that threatened to diminish Quebec's powers. Lyon kept reiterating that he was opposed to an entrenched Charter, would continue to oppose it, and would never be part of any deal to support it. Bennett remained reluctant to break with the others and preferred "keeping the situation fluid." And there was no indication that Nova Scotia, Prince Edward Island, or Newfoundland was getting ready to make a break. John Buchanan only "wants to be part of the club," federal officials reported, "so he watches to see what constitutes the club at any point and where it is going." Angus MacLean and Brian Peckford might go along with the Charter, but only if everyone else did. Which only left Saskatchewan, with its "exhaustive table of possibilities" but little influence.[42]

"The only factor that continues to hold the group together is the ultimate 'defensive position' of battling the federal government in London, if necessary," the prime minister was informed in his secret briefing notes. "It is now apparent that any move to compromise will have to be taken by individual provinces. They will not move as a group. It is not even possible for the eight to discuss possible compromise proposals. The hardliners are very bitter and vindictive about any possible compromise."[43]

Allan Blakeney was deeply upset by Trudeau's contemptuous dismissal of the Gang's three emissaries on Tuesday afternoon and by his threat of a national referendum or a drawn-out campaign in London. And so, on Wednesday morning, he announced at the Gang of Eight's daily breakfast meeting that he was going to put a compromise proposal on the table when the conference reconvened. None of the other premiers gave any indication of support, and Blakeney himself didn't have an iota of confidence in its success. But since the work was done and the end was approaching, he put it forward anyway, if only to indicate that Saskatchewan was ready to bargain. "Its contents hardly mattered," Blakeney later recalled. "I had no expectation that it would be adopted. I did think it would keep the discussion going for a bit longer. Some of

Allan Blakeney and René Lévesque, with Trudeau, Romanow, and Chrétien behind.

my colleagues disagreed with the tactic. They felt that we should not depart from the position agreed upon by all eight of us in April."[44]

With Sterling Lyon already gone and René Lévesque set to leave at noon, there wasn't the time or will to have a serious discussion about the complexities of the Saskatchewan proposal. Trudeau didn't like the clause that would let the provinces opt in to legal and equality rights, nor was he prepared to demote minority-language education rights to a mere statement of principles. ("I believe you when you say you've drafted it quickly," he teased Blakeney, "because you've even kept the Senate veto in."[45]) Lévesque dismissed the draft as a "non-starter" because it removed financial compensation from the Gang's amending formula without restoring a veto for Quebec. And when Lougheed said that the absence of a *non obstante* clause made the whole thing unacceptable to Alberta as well, that was the end of that.

Allan Blakeney always denied that he had abandoned the Gang of Eight in general and Quebec in particular. The April Accord had been a defensive alliance, he repeated. Once Ottawa rejected it, each signatory was free to explore other avenues towards a settlement, subject only to the understanding, reiterated on Sunday evening, that no one would put forward anything without notifying the others first. Blakeney had done precisely that at breakfast. Now, with his compromise dead at birth, he was back in line with the group. Nevertheless, as we have seen, the Saskatchewan initiative became Lévesque's justification for accepting Trudeau's referendum challenge.

The moment the session adjourned for lunch, Roy Romanow rushed up to Claude Morin and, obviously upset, demanded to know why Quebec had agreed to such a catastrophic plan. "Simple," Morin replied. "Since the common front has vanished, in large part because of your province, why shouldn't Quebec, in its turn, choose to pursue another option? Especially something that it considers reasonable? Hasn't your side been desperate for some time now to come up with a 'compromise'?"[46]

Lévesque wasn't wrong in anticipating the dissolution of the Gang of Eight. Even if he hadn't agreed to the referendum challenge, Saskatchewan and British Columbia were desperate to make a deal. If they went over to Ottawa's side, with Ontario and New Brunswick already there, that might have been enough to satisfy the Supreme Court and the British Parliament, since they represented two of the three largest provinces, all four regions, four different political parties, the national government, and more than 50 percent of the population. And if a deal was going to get done anyway, that might have made it difficult for Nova Scotia, Prince Edward Island, or Newfoundland to resist joining under their own terms. "If Mr. Trudeau picked himself up six provinces," one Quebec official explained, "the job would be harder for the four of us who were left to make an alliance of some kind with the federal Conservatives and go to London to fight the plan."[47]

No, Lévesque's error—and it was unquestionably an error—was to break from the group on the referendum without so much as a by-your-leave. It cost him the cloak of victimhood he later tried to wear anyway. It gave Blakeney and Bennett the freedom to pursue their own course without guilt or obligation. It cast the *indépendantistes* in the eyes of the Anglo premiers as untrustworthy, self-motivated, and destructive. It ostracized Quebec for the rest of the day and set the course for the events that would unfold during the night. "It reinforced in the minds of everyone that the fight between those two guys, Trudeau and Lévesque, was more important to them than a deal," Howard Leeson observed. "If the fate of Canada was left to them, there would be no Canada. To get a deal, we had to force one or the other to choose a third position."[48]

Pierre Trudeau couldn't have known all that. He had assumed from the beginning that he would get all of the Gang or none of the Gang, and when Quebec pulled back from the referendum proposal during the afternoon, he didn't expect Lougheed and the others to give up on Lévesque.[49] All Trudeau knew was that by four-thirty on Wednesday afternoon, the talks had reached another dead end. He was fully prepared to call it quits until Bill Davis berated him for giving up too quickly.

His patience almost exhausted, the prime minister agreed to a half-hour break.

FOURTEEN

The Kitchen Accord

Up and down the corridors of the Government Conference Centre, there was chaos and consternation as the politicians and their officials scrambled to come up with a last-ditch compromise, or at least some reason to keep the negotiations going into the following day. Failure was no longer just one of various scenarios imagined in a briefing book; it was real, imminent, and—to all but René Lévesque—terrifying. The first ministers were risking not just their careers but their country.

"You know, you guys," Chrétien said as he moved from delegation to delegation, "there's going to be a referendum. I don't want one and you don't want one. But I'm telling you, I'm going to go into your provinces, and I'm going to say you're opposed to freedom of religion and equality of women and all that, and I'm going to clobber you."[1] In an aside, however, he said to Roy Romanow, "There's no way I'm going to fight another goddamn referendum."[2]

There had to be a solution among all the permutations and combinations the two buddies had examined during the past eighteen months. For days now, if not weeks, the most obvious compromise had been staring everybody in the face, though no one could move towards it too quickly in the negotiating process. Trudeau clearly cared more about his Charter of Rights and Freedoms than about the federal government's amending formula. Most of the Gang of Eight clearly cared more about their amending formula than about Trudeau's Charter. The best hope for a deal, therefore, was a swap that would give both sides what they most desired. A straight exchange wasn't possible, because the bits that were unacceptable were non-negotiable. But what about the essential parts?

Romanow gleaned from a score of private chats, based on years of camaraderie and discussion, that British Columbia and Nova Scotia might now be open to such a deal. He also knew, through his contacts in the Newfoundland delegation, that Brian Peckford had used the lunch hour to draft a simple one-page proposal that he wanted to present to the conference. Though perceived as a hardliner because of the sound and fury of his rhetoric, Peckford had actually never had much problem with the Charter, and he hated the thought of fighting Canada's constitutional battles in the lobbies at Westminster. He may also have been motivated by the fact that he was "beginning to get some negative feedback at home," according to one federal report, "from his overly combative stance."[3]

"I had the disquieting feeling that the meetings and documents up to that time were falling short of the various degrees of compromise required on the different issues to effect a general concensus [sic]," Peckford later explained in a personal letter to Trudeau. "However, I had also developed by that time a feeling that individually, the vast majority of the First Ministers were expressing such willingness to compromise that there had to be a concensus [sic] in there somewhere."[4]

At that point, Chrétien and Romanow went looking for a quiet space to talk. They withdrew to a narrow kitchenette down the hall from the fifth-floor meeting room, where they were soon joined by Roy McMurtry.[5] (As one pundit wryly noted, that little kitchen would eventually gain "a place in Canadian memorabilia akin to Laura Secord's cow, the

Last Spike and the rope by which Riel was hanged."[6]) On the counter beside the stainless-steel sink, under harsh fluorescent lighting, Romanow, who was under instructions from his premier to get something from Ottawa in writing, jotted down seven points on two sheets ripped from a lined notepad. To satisfy Trudeau, there would be patriation, an entrenched Charter, and no financial compensation in the amending formula. To satisfy the Gang of Eight, there would be a notwithstanding clause for legal and equality rights, which intruded more than did democratic and fundamental rights into provincial jurisdiction. The West would get to protect and exploit its natural resources according to the concession the federal NDP had negotiated; the East would get equalization programs. Finally, to secure Newfoundland's support, there would be a "wiggle" on mobility rights to allow a province with above-average unemployment to protect its own citizens from out-of-province workers, as well

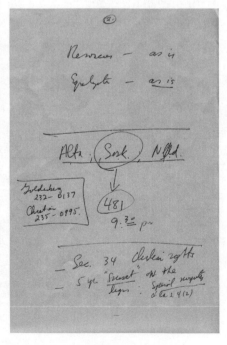

The Kitchen Accord.

Roy McMurtry, Jean Chrétien, and Roy Romanow re-enacting their kitchen deal.

Library and Archives Canada/e010768028

as a referendum in any province that hadn't signed on to the minority-language education rights within two years.

Decades after the fact, there still existed a vigorous debate about whether the so-called Kitchen Accord deserved the importance it subsequently received in press reports and history books as *the* breakthrough moment of the conference. "There are two views," said Hugh Segal. "Those who were in the kitchen think that, next to the signing of the VE treaty, nothing more important ever happened in the history of mankind. And those not in the kitchen think that nothing of substance transpired."[7]

Indeed, many of the premiers were infuriated by the credit given to Chrétien, Romanow, and McMurtry, who were to re-enact their meeting for a television documentary the next afternoon. "One of the great mysteries," Peter Lougheed sputtered decades later, "is how the hell they managed to convince the Ottawa media that they engineered this thing. It astounds me. There were lots of pieces of paper flying around that afternoon, but I didn't even know the Kitchen Accord existed until I read about it in the papers the next day."[8]

"Who signed this accord?" Bill Davis asked, trying to sound amused while he was in fact deeply frustrated. "I didn't sign it, and neither did any other premier. All you had were three people who took a scrap of paper to their first ministers, and none of them knew what Trudeau's reaction was going to be. One of the two Roys—I can't remember which—told me that Blakeney was onside and asked if I would help get Trudeau onside. I'm not minimizing what they did, but it has developed a mythology of its own."[9]

What the three ministers did accomplish, according to Allan Blakeney, was to set down in writing for the first time the terms that the federal government might be ready to accept. That was crucial. Until then, the premiers, ministers, and officials could cook up any option they fancied, but it was useless if Ottawa wouldn't agree. Whether Lougheed and Davis were aware of it or not, the Kitchen Accord was the foundation upon which Blakeney would build a deal later that evening. "Once the feds were prepared to buy a modified Vancouver in exchange for what had to be a substantial measure of their charter," he said, "then the whole thing began to be possible."[10]

The Kitchen Accord may not have been the final settlement, but it came very close. At the time, however, its three godfathers were not under any illusion that their scribbles added up to a done deal. "Never," Chrétien had immediately scrawled beside the idea of a provincial referendum on minority-language education rights. "You guys go sell it to the provinces," he said to the two Roys. "I have a bigger job. I have to sell it to Trudeau."[11] When Romanow reported back to Blakeney, the premier put the likelihood of success at three or four out of ten. But anything was worth a try if it kept the meeting from collapsing and checked a headstrong, macho rush towards a referendum.

Meanwhile, over coffee and pastries in a lounge across the hall from the Centennial Room, Peter Lougheed was making use of the break to try to rally the Gang of Eight back together. Trudeau's referendum was a trap, he argued. If Ottawa got away with being able to legitimize its Resolution by winning the consent of the people, the provincial governments would lose the power of the constitutional convention they had just won in the Supreme Court—and, with it, any hope of blocking Ottawa in London. All the premiers agreed, with Manitoba's attorney general, Gerry Mercier, speaking on behalf of Sterling Lyon.

When they returned to the conference room, Trudeau circulated a new document, 800-15/019, which outlined the procedure by which Ottawa would implement the referendum on the Charter.[12] As they had with the earlier document, and for the same technical reason, the federal bureaucrats again proposed that the Resolution be passed by the Parliament of Canada and sent on to London exactly as it was. But then the process became truly Byzantine: "At the earliest feasible time after the Resolution is sent to Westminster and prior to proclamation, a new resolution to provide authority to implement the Charter Referendum Proposal by way of constitutional amendment would be introduced in Parliament. Provinces would have a period of six months to adopt equivalent resolutions to the new resolution. If new resolutions were adopted in Parliament and all legislatures in that period the Resolution would be proclaimed and the Proposal would be given effect under Section 37 of the Resolution (the unanimity amending formula). If new resolutions were not adopted in Parliament and all legislatures in that period, the Resolution would be proclaimed without modification."

"And they said we made complicated referendum questions," Lévesque observed with bemusement. "Compared to them, we're amateurs." It was, he added, "not far from being Chinese."[13] But when Trudeau went around the table and asked for each province's views, Lévesque said (or was later quoted as saying), "I can go along for obvious reasons. It's not repugnant to the parliamentary system; it would take a great weight off our minds."[14] Another source merely had him agreeing if a majority of the other provinces did, too.[15]

Peter Lougheed was flabbergasted. "To my complete surprise and amazement," he recalled in a letter he wrote to Lévesque, "you reversed your decision and accepted the regional referendum proposal of Mr. Trudeau. The other seven provinces involved in the Group of Eight rejected the Trudeau referendum approach. I considered Quebec's move a very significant departure from the principles inherent in the Accord of April 16, 1981."[16]

Lévesque never challenged Lougheed's version of events, but Claude Morin downplayed its importance. "I wasn't witness to that conversation and Lévesque never spoke to me about it," Morin recalled, "but he had already rejected, in front of all the delegations at the start of the afternoon, the type of referendum Trudeau had in mind. There are two explanations, in my opinion, for what Lougheed and the others thought. Either the referendum to which Lévesque was referring after the coffee break wasn't Trudeau's, and he was talking about the principle of consulting the people, as we had proposed many times between July 1980 and November 1981. Or he expressed himself badly, because he was getting impatient, etc., or he had misunderstood, which is quite possible. Lévesque couldn't logically say, in private, to Lougheed or anyone else, the opposite of what he said in public two hours later."[17]

No matter, the result wouldn't have been any different. Trudeau's "manoeuvre," as Lévesque called the referendum challenge that had been made before lunch, "served to drive a last nail in the coffin of the late common front. I couldn't even be bothered wondering who'd look after the burial."[18]

He couldn't be bothered, no doubt, because he figured he had won the day. His on-again, off-again alliance with Ottawa was now, as he put it, "terribly uncertain." The process was "bizarre and worrisome." The conference was "one of the most fascinating madhouses I've ever seen."[19] Either he was going to get a second chance to take on Pierre

Trudeau in a Quebec referendum (which he thought he could win) or the battle was going to move on to London (where he also thought he could win). Even if some of the others kept talking into the night, he had no fallback position. He never imagined that Trudeau or the Gang of Eight would dare isolate him altogether. His mood was light, and understandably so, given that his goal had always been to block the Resolution. "I'm not a gambling man," he said a short while later, to the laughter of the press corps, "but I'd say the odds are loaded towards failure."[20] Indeed, he had already called for the conference to be adjourned.

The others weren't ready to throw in the towel quite yet, however. Davis and Blakeney declared themselves willing to stay for as long as it took to reach a deal. Chrétien jumped the gun by informing the prime minister that Saskatchewan had a compromise in the works. Peckford wanted to present his proposal. Why the rush, Lougheed asked the prime minister, if it's only to announce failure? Why not take a break, get away from this hothouse, and consult with each other? "I knew about Peckford's ideas in a general way," Lougheed recalled, "and provided that Mr. Trudeau was prepared to make major modifications in the federal position, I thought his ideas had some prospect of acceptance by a significant number of provinces."[21]

"Okay," Trudeau relented, adjourning the conference until nine o'clock the next morning, "but let's go to the television cameras at ten o'clock."[22] If there was no agreement by then, he added, he would push his Resolution through Parliament and be off to London as quickly as possible.

"This guy's serious," Roy McMurtry said to Peter Lougheed as they were packing up their documents at the end of what had been a long ride of twists and turns, and he thought he detected a look of alarm on the Alberta premier's face.[23] "Peter is going to come round at some point," Bill Davis thought to himself, aware that Lougheed had access to the same polling numbers as everyone else, "if we sort things out right."[24]

Allan Blakeney had a quick word with John Buchanan and subsequently cornered Davis, who promised to try to persuade Trudeau to accept a compromise on minority-language education rights. Blakeney and Davis then crossed the room to speak with Trudeau for a few minutes, but they came away no further ahead after the prime minister reiterated his unwillingness to accept the financial compensation provision in the April Accord. Finally, Blakeney stepped into the gap of the horseshoe-shaped desks, with Newfoundland at one end and Alberta at the other. If Saskatchewan was going to find a compromise, it probably needed one or both of them.

"Look," Blakeney said, "we're all tired, edgy, a bit testy. Why don't we get something to eat, maybe have a nap or a run, and send our officials over to my shop at the Château Laurier at nine-thirty?"[25]

At the other end of the room, René Lévesque and Claude Morin were handing out their private phone numbers to various officials, including Dick Johnston, Alberta's minister of intergovernmental relations. "If anything comes up, don't forget to phone us."

"No problem," Lévesque remembered them replying, but he thought they had some difficulty looking him in the eye.[26]

PART 3
Wednesday Night and Thursday Morning November 4 and 5, 1981

FIFTEEN

The Night of the Long Knives

Shortly before seven o'clock, the evening already as black and cold as midnight, the warring parties dispersed to their camps to plot their next moves. Saskatchewan, Nova Scotia, Prince Edward Island, and Manitoba were staying at the Château Laurier, directly across Rideau Street from the Conference Centre but accessible by a tunnel that precluded the need for overcoats and fur hats. Ontario and New Brunswick were together, appropriately, at the swank Four Seasons Hotel, a short limo ride away on Queen Street, as was Newfoundland. British Columbia had rooms at both the Four Seasons and the Château Laurier, not because its premier was attempting to keep his feet in both camps—though that wasn't far from the truth—but because he had one room for his personal use and the other for his role as chair of the Annual Premiers' Conference and de facto chair of the Gang of Eight. Alberta was by itself in a penthouse at the more distant Skyline Hotel, as though brooding in a tent on the edge of the battlefield.

René Lévesque was chauffeured to the Auberge de la Chaudière, across the Ottawa River in Hull, Quebec—a psychological withdrawal as well as a political gesture—where he and Claude Morin debriefed the rest of the Quebec delegation for an hour. The prevailing assumption was that the prime minister wasn't going to move. Some, like Claude Charron, were pleased. "It's going well for us," he said. "Trudeau's threatening to adjourn the meeting at 10 o'clock tomorrow morning, the impasse holds, and that's what we want."[1] Others were busy arranging for yet another delay of the National Assembly's opening.

Lévesque was tired and cranky. At dinner in the hotel's restaurant, he found himself ensnared in an elaborate feast prepared by the chef in his honour. As he waited, a hunk of moose meat was delivered on a garnished platter, preceded by a procession of sparklers and candles. "Could you go a little faster?" Lévesque snapped in the midst of the ceremonious carving. "I'd like to see the ten o'clock news."[2] He and Morin watched the news together over a drink in the Suite du Grand Patron and discussed the day's media coverage, then parted till the morning—without, as the rumour was to have it, playing poker into the wee hours.

Meanwhile, Pierre Trudeau had retired to his residence at 24 Sussex Drive for a quick swim and a brief respite with his three young sons before eight of his most important ministers and five key advisers showed up for a final powwow at nine o'clock. Gathered in the living room of the old stone mansion overlooking the Ottawa River, with a fire crackling in the hearth, a magnificent Riopelle on the wall, and a white-jacketed servant circulating with coffee and drinks, they reviewed the day's events and surveyed tomorrow's possibilities.

Jean Chrétien was the first up. "I think I can perhaps have a deal if we accept the premiers' amending formula rather than our Victoria one, and if we water down the Charter a little bit."

"No, no," Trudeau responded. "The Alberta amending formula is terrible, and as far as the Charter is concerned, there isn't going to be any watering down."[3]

The prime minister's opinion carried a great deal of weight, of course, in a room full of politicians and bureaucrats indebted to him for their power and prestige, but each of them had his own reasons for wanting a veto for Quebec or for disliking the notwithstanding clause. Chrétien, virtually alone, fought back vigorously. The problem with a referendum, he argued, was that the people might well turn it into a vote on the economy or a vote against Trudeau, even though they were all for patriation and the Charter. The West was never going to vote for an amending formula that gave Quebec a veto, Quebec was never going to vote for an amending formula that didn't give it a veto, and most of the premiers would hammer Ottawa for intruding into provincial affairs. Compromise was a safer route and the traditional Canadian way of getting things done.

Perhaps, Trudeau shot back, but the traditional Canadian way hadn't achieved simple patriation in more than fifty years. "Besides," he added, "Romanow can't deliver. The premiers will never buy it. They'll never desert Lévesque."[4]

But at that very moment, in fact, a mile south along stately Sussex Drive, a group of provincial officials were in the midst of doing just that. In response to Allan Blakeney's invitation, Lougheed and Peckford had sent Peter Meekison and Cy Abery, respectively, to meet with Howard Leeson and several legal advisers in Saskatchewan's suite, Room 481, at the Château Laurier. (When British Columbia's minister of intergovernmental relations, Garde Gardom, happened to catch word of the meeting, he was invited to send Mel Smith.) The purpose was to test the Kitchen Accord on two of the most obdurate members of the Gang of Eight. If Alberta and Newfoundland could be persuaded to accept it or some variation, then Nova Scotia, Prince Edward Island, and B.C. would likely accept as well.

The officials worked from two similar drafts: the one that Leeson and his lawyers had drawn up from the Kitchen Accord during the previous two hours, and a second that the Newfoundlanders had brought with them based on the ideas Peckford had been developing since noon. A two-page consensus emerged with remarkable speed. Everybody in the room knew the files thoroughly, and there were only a handful of outstanding issues to consider. Yes to patriation. Yes to the Gang of Eight's opting-out formula, but without financial compensation. Yes to the Charter, but with a notwithstanding clause for legal rights, equality rights, and—at Alberta's insistence—fundamental freedoms. Yes to minority-language education rights, but only for the provinces that opted in to them voluntarily. Yes to the Newfoundland "wiggle" that restricted the application of mobility rights in provinces with high unemployment. Yes to the principle of equalization and the confirmation of provincial jurisdiction over natural resources. No to aboriginal rights, because British Columbia considered them a deal-breaker and the others caved in.

Around ten o'clock, while the redraft of the Newfoundland document was being typed up, Blakeney joined the meeting to answer a few questions and go over the proposed details. He pounced on Alberta's insistence that the *non obstante* clause be applied to fundamental freedoms. The Kitchen Accord, like Hatfield's proposal, had mentioned only legal and equality rights. "Trudeau will never agree," he said.

"That was in the marching orders I received from my premier," Meekison replied. "I'm under instructions, no B.S."

"Well, why don't you phone him and see if he'll drop it?" Blakeney suggested.

Lougheed sounded as though he had been asleep when the call came. Even if still awake, he wasn't pleased. Hadn't he made it clear at dinner that he didn't want to be involved until the morning, because he didn't want to feel bound one way or the other? "My answer stays," he growled at Meekison. "And don't call me again."[5]

At ten-fifteen, having been kept informed by Blakeney of the progress being made at the Château Laurier, Bill Davis said in a casual tone to no one in particular, "We have to get the prime minister onside. I think I'll have a little talk with him." And he went into the bedroom of his suite on the seventeenth floor of the Four Seasons to get away from the noise of his officials, who were dining on Chinese takeout in the sitting room.[6]

When Trudeau went into his study to take Davis's call, Chrétien seized the opportunity to make a final, impassioned argument to his Cabinet colleagues. "If at the end of this meeting you decide on a referendum, I won't be putting on my running shoes again for you," he said, playing on his reputation as a vital participant in the success of the No campaign in Quebec. "I've had enough of families divided, villages divided, French divided against English. A national referendum will be worse. You'll get East divided against West, Protestants divided against Catholics—everything." Pointing to Industry Minister Herb Gray, a notoriously dull speaker with a particularly leaden personality, he added, "You go and sell Ottawa's package. I won't."[7]

Chrétien's plea turned out to be much less consequential than the phone conversation that was taking place across the hall. As wasn't always the case, Davis got straight to the point. "I think our people have worked out something pretty good," he said. "What do you think, Pierre?"

"I think we'd be giving away too much," Trudeau replied.

"Well," said Davis, "I've been talking this thing over with Hatfield, and he seems to feel that—"

Trudeau, sensing what was coming, interrupted to suggest they meet right away, face to face.

"No," Davis replied. His tone was calm and unthreatening, but firm. The Resolution's referendum provisions were unfair to the provinces. The *non obstante* clause was a reasonable safety valve. And maybe the Charter shouldn't force minority-language education rights on anyone until everyone was on board. "Look, Pierre, we have to tell you that this is a good compromise from our point of view. It may not be perfect, but it's better than nothing and it's better than a referendum. Rather than fight this thing to the bitter end, we have to tell you that we won't go to

London, supporting you as we have until now, if you don't accept some sort of compromise of this nature. We can argue the details tomorrow, but we like the outline."[8]

Twenty-five minutes later, Davis returned to his sitting room and said, "Well, everybody, check your watches. It's 10:40. If there's going to be an agreement, this is it." Then he picked up a plate of food, took a bite, and added, "You know, I think the pineapple chicken is better in Brampton."[9]

And thus the native hue of Pierre Trudeau's resolution was sicklied o'er with the pale cast of thought. The call left him feeling cornered. If he lost Ontario and New Brunswick at this stage, he would likely have a major fight on his hands with the parliamentarians in London. Although Margaret Thatcher continued to express support for Ottawa's right to obtain whatever changes it wanted to the BNA Act, the provinces' lobbying efforts had succeeded in alerting a significant number of British MPs, constitutional experts, newspaper editorialists, and old imperial busybodies to the Supreme Court decision, the absence of support in western Canada, the objections of the aboriginal leadership, and the "offence" Trudeau's unilateral Resolution was to federalism. There were no guarantees of what would happen in the event of a disruption to Thatcher's own legislative schedule, a backbenchers' revolt, or a pitched battle in the House of Lords.[10] Even if Trudeau was prepared to mount a full-scale political, constitutional, and public-relations war against Great Britain's interference in the domestic affairs of a sovereign country, he understood the risks of spending the next year or two fighting a referendum or an election in the face of a serious economic downturn, ten opposing premiers, and a discontented, half-attentive population.

"All this led me to believe there was a danger that if we went completely alone, the British might drag their feet and we would have a messy and potentially unpredictable situation," he recalled. "We might have won—but we also might have ended up with nothing. I was a sufficiently long-in-the-tooth politician by then to realize that sometimes you have to take second best."[11]

Trudeau's tone was markedly different when he returned to the living room at 24 Sussex Drive. "Before, he had been impossible," Chrétien remembered, "but now he began asking intelligent questions."

"We may have to go for the compromise solution, even though I don't like it," Trudeau told his ministers and advisers. "Otherwise, we'd be going to London alone. So I'm authorizing Chrétien to work out a deal on this basis—but it better be good." When the meeting broke up around eleven o'clock, he gestured Chrétien into the sunroom off the central hall and said, "Jean, if you can get seven provinces representing 50 percent of the population to accept your solution, I might accept it even if I don't like it. But let me sleep on it."[12]

As Chrétien drove himself home, past the Château Laurier, past the darkened Conference Centre, and along the Rideau Canal to Bower Street, his natural buoyancy returned. Getting home around eleven-thirty, he found three urgent messages waiting for him from Garde Gardom. B.C.'s minister of intergovernmental relations was as folksy and plain-speaking a politician as Chrétien, and the two were fast friends.

"What's this damn piece of paper Romanow's showing around?" Gardom roared with his usual exuberant bluster. "Can you really sell it to Trudeau or is this just another bluff, you damn Frenchman?"

"It's serious, Garde. I think I can sell it."

"Then you'll have a new constitution," Gardom said. "B.C. can buy it, and so can Saskatchewan, Ontario, New Brunswick, P.E.I., Nova Scotia, and Newfoundland."[13]

Chrétien hung up and told his wife, Aline, the historic news. He considered phoning Trudeau but thought better of it, knowing how much the prime minister valued his routines and needed his sleep. He tried calling Romanow's room at the Château Laurier, but without success, for Romanow was on the move between Davis and Blakeney and didn't want to be accused once again of having colluded in secret with Ottawa. So there was nothing more Chrétien could do but toss and turn for the rest of the night and wait to see what the dawn would bring.

By this time, Allan Blakeney felt he had a strong-enough consensus to show some of the other premiers. Angus MacLean was roused from his sleep by his attorney general, Horace Carver. After being reassured that Peter Meekison was involved on Alberta's behalf, MacLean went to Blakeney's suite, where he was asked if Prince Edward Island could sign. Brian Peckford showed up, delighted to have been instrumental in putting together the deal. John Buchanan, waiting at the airport to return to Halifax for his father-in-law's funeral, took a taxi back to the hotel and joined the ever-expanding circle in the sitting room. When Blakeney slipped away for fifteen minutes to phone Ed Broadbent, Peckford and Buchanan tried to unstitch the delicate design their officials had so carefully woven around fundamental freedoms and minority-language education, but they didn't get far before Blakeney returned and put a stop to their mischief.[14]

"A mood takes over after a while," he said. "If the thing is close enough, then you see some people say, 'Well, boys, it's deal time. And you've got to give up that and we've got to give up this because we're going to do a deal.' And that mood began to take hold some time late in the evening."[15]

By now it was after midnight, and the talk turned to tactics. Mel Smith, who had gone off to brief Bill Bennett, phoned from the B.C. premier's room at the Four Seasons to get a few details. Horace Carver said he would call Gerry Mercier, his Manitoba counterpart. Peckford, who everyone agreed should present the proposal the next morning, had got himself into such a pitch of excitement that he seemed to be bouncing around the room, talking quickly and loudly, rarely pausing to hear what anyone else had to say, to the point that some officials worried he might actually think the proposal was his, and his alone, and keep tampering with it.[16]

When MacLean, Peckford, and Buchanan left for the night, Blakeney phoned Bill Davis, despite the risk of waking him up, and brought him up to date. "Premier Davis explained that he had been able to convince the Prime Minister that on minority-language education rights, nothing would be applied in any part of Canada until all of the provinces had agreed," Howard Leeson recorded in the follow-up notes he wrote within a fortnight of the events.[17]

On the other side of the Ottawa River, René Lévesque turned out his light at one o'clock. "Reliving the adventure that had absorbed us since spring and that was now drawing ineluctably to its close," he remembered, "I had some trouble getting to sleep."[18] No one had been in contact with him or his delegation all evening, except for a B.C. official, who had called Claude Morin at around eight o'clock to remind Lévesque of the next morning's breakfast meeting.

"There was then some discussion as to what to do with Quebec," Leeson wrote. "The general conclusion was that Quebec could never agree to this package, because of the lack of compensation in the amending formula. Nevertheless, it was agreed that the proposal must be put to Quebec at the already scheduled 8 a.m. meeting of the Gang of Eight."[19]

Most of the people at work at the Château Laurier hadn't worried unduly about not contacting the Quebecers, caught up as they were in the excitement of the drafting process. The ones who did give it a second thought suspected that Lévesque and Morin would only try to sabotage their efforts. Some had terrible memories of the late-night session in the same hotel the previous April, when Lévesque had almost destroyed the common front before putting his signature on the April Accord. Others took Claude Morin at his word that Quebec would never make any more concessions on the amending formula or the Charter. Others were still furious with Lévesque for betraying the Gang that morning without a trace of remorse.

Allan Blakeney later argued that the draft was nothing more than a work-in-progress for the Gang of Eight to discuss, modify, or reject the next day, with the chances of success a bit better but still no higher than five or six out of ten. "I did not for a minute believe that any official could commit, say, Premier Lougheed to a constitutional text without his having seen it," he said. "Our world did not work that way. I certainly did not believe that the proposal we were hammering out was even close to its final form."[20] He assumed, in fact, that the first ministers would spend all day Thursday haggling over the details, which might or might not lead to a deal.

But it was also true that by one o'clock in the morning, there was a small toast with champagne, a sense of achievement in the air, a bit of celebration and euphoria—if not a closed deal, at least the will to complete a deal, especially after Bill Davis gave his agreement over the phone. It was a fragile piece of work, however, and nobody wanted to see it shattered by the *indépendantistes*. At heart, the drafters felt a bit intimidated, a bit embarrassed, even a bit guilty. "They were afraid to call us," Claude Charron remarked bitterly, and he wasn't wrong.[21] In addition, the only premier whose rapport with Lévesque remained good enough to have made such a call—Peter Lougheed—was also absent.

"I obviously suspected that the other provinces would be talking during the night (and that Chrétien would be involved)," Morin remembered. "At one point I had a thought of taking a tour of the hotels to see if something was going on without us, but Lévesque and I finally decided to do nothing. Everyone had been informed of where they could find us, and everyone knew we were available for any sort of discussion. It was up to them to reach us, or at least to talk to us if need be. Consider this: if someone had invited us to the discussions, if someone had phoned us to propose this or that, we would have been opposed (because the federal project didn't suit us at all), but at least the other governments would have been able to say later on that we had been consulted. That wasn't the case, and it was the mistake."[22]

It was undoubtedly bad politics as well as bad manners not to have phoned Lévesque and Morin and invited them to come over. The results probably would have been the same, but the courtesy would have taken some of the sting from the wounds and played better with the people of Quebec. "The saddest part is that Lévesque was never told," Davis reflected. "I'll never understand that. He had been working with the others. He was hurt."[23]

As it happened, nobody phoned Richard Hatfield either, albeit for a different reason. They didn't trust him not to blab the news to the press. While the negotiations were under way on the fourth floor of the Château Laurier, Hatfield was downstairs in the Cock and Lion pub listening to Sneezy Waters sing the greatest hits of Hank Williams. When the show was over, as was the premier's wont, he invited a few reporters and hangers-on back to his suite at the Four Seasons to continue talking and drinking. Sometime around one-thirty in the morning, Aidon Charlton, one of Roy Romanow's assistants, knocked on Hatfield's door with a confidential envelope in his hands. He was supposed to deliver it to Roy McMurtry, who in turn was supposed to pass it to Bill Davis and the federal officials, but Charlton couldn't find any of the Ontario delegation and had been drawn to the noise coming from New Brunswick's room. Hatfield, his curiosity piqued, phoned Romanow, who read him the draft but insisted it was far from final. Hatfield then phoned Roy McMurtry's room to find out what Ontario was thinking. McMurtry, pretending to be his own executive assistant, said that the minister had probably gone to bed and he didn't know where.

"Young man," scolded Hatfield, inebriated enough to have fallen for the deception, "an executive assistant should always know where his minister is."

Later, when asked why he had done it, McMurtry replied, "I had to. Richard would have told all the reporters."[24]

Early the next morning, the premier of New Brunswick refused at first to get out of bed. "I know what today is going to bring," he moaned. "Failure."[25]

SIXTEEN

A Mean Process

The sun had not risen before Jean Chrétien was up and on the phone to Roy Romanow. Seven of the provinces were indeed on board, Romanow reported, "and in half an hour Lougheed will be woken up by Dick Johnston and told of the deal. We're expecting Alberta to agree."

"What about Quebec?" Chrétien asked.

"Quebec will never sign anything. We'll tell them what we've done at breakfast and see how they react."

"In that case, make sure Manitoba doesn't sign. It will be difficult for us if Quebec is the only holdout."

"Don't worry," Romanow assured him. "Lyon will never agree to the Charter."[1]

Romanow hung up, still uncertain whether Trudeau was ready to agree to an override clause on fundamental rights or to leaving the entrenchment of minority-language education rights to the discretion of each province. "Listening to Chrétien," he remembered, "it seemed as though the accord had not in fact bridged the gulf between the federal government and the dissenting provinces, and that more negotiations might stall the momentum for agreement."[2]

Michael Kirby delivered much the same warning when he turned up at the Four Seasons at 6:00 a.m. to meet with Bill Davis, who was still in his robe and pyjamas. The proposal is probably okay if everybody but Quebec and Manitoba are onside, Kirby told the premier, but there could still be trouble with the notwithstanding clause, the minority-language education opt-in, and—adding what Chrétien had not—the elimination of the referendum mechanisms in Ottawa's amending formula. All three were potential deal-breakers.

In fact, Jean Chrétien wasn't too worried. He knew what none of the others did: Trudeau had asked for at least seven provinces; Chrétien had delivered at least eight. "Mr. Prime Minister," he said over the phone at seven o'clock, "if you agree now with what you agreed last night, then you have a new constitution."

"Jean," Trudeau replied, "if you were here, I'd give you a hug." Then he invited his justice minister to breakfast at 24 Sussex to go over the provinces' proposal with him and a few senior officials.[3]

"He didn't like it, but he had to compromise," Chrétien recalled of their meeting that morning. "The acceptance of compromise by Trudeau between five o'clock in the evening and seven o'clock in the morning is unbelievable. I didn't have to convince him. He was very happy."[4]

Peter Lougheed, who was even less likely than Pierre Trudeau to hug one of his ministers, was nonetheless pleased by the news he heard when Dick Johnston and Peter Meekison showed up at his suite around that same time. A consensus had been reached overnight by a number of provinces, they told him. It satisfied Alberta's two primary objectives: an amending formula based on the equality of the provinces and an override provision in the Charter. Even if Trudeau rejected it, nobody would be able to blame Alberta for not trying its best. Canadians wanted a deal and wouldn't stand for another failure. The draft was to be passed around and discussed at the Gang of Eight's regular breakfast meeting, set for eight o'clock sharp in British Columbia's suite at the Château Laurier.

Lougheed, Bennett, Peckford, MacLean, and Blakeney were there on the hour and ready to get down to business. John Buchanan had initialled the document before heading back to Halifax. Sterling Lyon, presumably still asleep in Winnipeg, would be brought up to date by a phone call from Lougheed before the start of the conference at nine o'clock. René Lévesque, typically, was late. Since time was pressing and there was nothing that hadn't been discussed ad nauseam, the five leaders conducted a quick review and decided that the proposal was acceptable to each of them.

Lévesque finally arrived. "What's this?" he said with a scowl, picking up the two sheets of paper that had been placed beside his plate.

"We were just building blocks through the night," replied Brian Peckford, who still put the chances of success at sixty-forty. "One block at a time. Now it's your turn."[5]

Lévesque took a quick look and exploded with fury. He began shouting and storming around the table.[6] It was a take-it-or-leave-it proposition, he raged, put together by his colleagues without any consultation with him, probably in cahoots with Ottawa. Moreover, he saw it as a compromise achieved at the expense of Quebec: no financial compensation for opting out and a Charter that was a direct infringement on the powers of the National Assembly. "I went to breakfast and discovered that seven had got together to tear up an agreement signed by everybody," he said later that day. "It never crossed my mind that I would be asked to wipe out all the essential guarantees that we had decided to maintain together."[7]

While the others slipped away to prepare for the final session, Lougheed stayed behind to go over the previous night's events with Lévesque. There had been, he said, "no attempt to develop something behind the back of any province."[8] He explained that he himself hadn't been present during the negotiations; he hadn't agreed to the draft proposal until this morning at breakfast. Furthermore, Lyon hadn't come on board yet, and there was still an opportunity for everyone to propose changes when the first ministers reconvened. He specifically invited the Quebec premier to try to get financial compensation reinserted into the amending formula and to raise whatever objections he had about the Charter. But Lévesque was outraged. "It was the procedure much more than the content that was intolerable," he remembered. The "shady dealing," the "trickery."[9]

"But if anyone had a right to be angry, it was more me than him," Lougheed reflected afterwards, "because he had already planned not to sign. I was surprised by the final position he took. Not greatly surprised—I had my suspicions—but I didn't know until he said no that morning."[10]

When the two premiers parted from their tense and fruitless exchange after about twenty minutes, Lougheed wasn't sure what René Lévesque was going to do next. Nor did he know for certain what Pierre Trudeau was going to say. The Gang of Eight was in a strong position because of the Supreme Court ruling, he felt, but he never underestimated Trudeau's intelligence, his strength of character, or his will to win. The Alberta premier had been face to face with the prime minister across a negotiating table often enough to know that Trudeau wasn't going to fold until he absolutely had to. All would be revealed soon enough. "Our final acceptance," he recalled, "was subject to Mr. Trudeau indicating quickly at the conference that the proposal was—perhaps with some modifications—acceptable to the federal government."[11]

Lougheed then went off to phone Sterling Lyon. "We can only get what we want if we swallow the Charter" was the core of his message to the Manitoba premier, and the notwithstanding clause would let him argue that Parliament was still supreme.[12] But Lyon had already received a blunter and perhaps more convincing message from his campaign adviser, Nate Nurgitz, who had been awakened in the night by a call from Roy McMurtry. "It's crunch time," Nurgitz had told his premier.

"They're going to hang you out to dry as the guy who sided with the separatists."[13]

By the time Richard Hatfield arrived at the Government Conference Centre around nine o'clock, Trudeau and Davis were already there, waiting to walk him through the deal. Hatfield, clutching a cup of black coffee, was aghast at the concessions the federal side was being asked to make, particularly when it came to the notwithstanding clause. "All right, Pierre," he finally said, "but don't ask any more of me. I've given all my clothes away."[14]

It was a disheartened and embittered René Lévesque who entered the fifth-floor conference room just before the final in camera session was called to order at 9:25 a.m. He immediately indicated his wish to speak. Would the prime minister, he asked, return to yesterday's offer to put everything on the back burner for another two years of negotiations? "Let's not run it through with such haste," he pleaded.[15] Trudeau wasn't unsympathetic, but he didn't want to go down that road again if the premiers were going to keep fighting him tooth and nail. All the first ministers had to put some water in their wine, he said, if they wanted to get a constitutional deal right away, which was better than dragging out the process towards an uncertain result later on. Then he invited Brian Peckford to speak.

It was later claimed that the prime minister, out of concern that Lévesque might change a few minds or sway a few hearts with a dramatic last-minute appeal, had cleverly selected Peckford. If the provinces were invited to speak in the reverse order by which they had joined Confederation, Newfoundland would go first and Quebec last. It would also be a nice symbolic touch to have the makings of the new Confederation presented by the premier of the youngest province. But in truth, Peckford had been chosen by the negotiators in the Château Laurier the night before. His interventions had proven helpful, and the proposal was thought to have a better chance if presented by a hardline member of the Gang of Eight. With Lévesque and Lyon obviously out and

Lougheed at risk of provoking Trudeau, the premier of Newfoundland was handed the job—and he was tickled to do it.

No one was willing to break the awkward silence when Peckford finished reading. Then British Columbia spoke up and said it would stand by the package, including the entrenchment of minority-language education rights, no matter how politically unpopular. Alberta agreed, though it too had to take "a great swallow" on language rights. Then Saskatchewan came on board, with changes to suggest but only if changes were permitted. Then a qualified acceptance from Manitoba, subject to the approval of its legislature. Then Prince Edward Island, Nova Scotia, Ontario, and New Brunswick—yes, yes, yes, yes. All eyes turned to Quebec; ears had to strain to hear Lévesque's subdued voice. "I'll be brief," he said. "We've had a veto for 114 years. Yank out compensation and there's nothing left. Quebec says no."[16]

All eyes shifted two seats to the left, to the prime minister of Canada, who was studying the text, head down and eyes lowered through his horn-rimmed reading glasses. Lévesque's last remaining hope lay, ironically, with Pierre Trudeau. Hadn't Trudeau vehemently opposed the Gang's formula, even without financial compensation? Wouldn't he, the champion of rights and freedoms, refuse the notwithstanding clause? Mightn't he startle everyone one more time by demanding the restoration of Quebec's veto for the sake of a deal? Hadn't he just been seen shaking his head at the opt-in provision for minority education? "Trudeau the actor frowned and looked unhappy," Chrétien observed at his side. "Lévesque and Morin smiled and looked pleased."[17] Roy McMurtry's heart sank at the grumpy expression on Trudeau's face, and he thought to himself, "Oh God, please don't bugger it up now."[18] Beneath the table, however, unseen by anyone, Trudeau gave Chrétien's leg a playful kick.

"Not bad, nice work," he said at last. "It makes a lot of sense."[19]

Claude Morin couldn't believe it. "Perhaps it's paradoxical to mention it in view of the circumstances and the treatment inflicted on Quebec," he later wrote, "but Trudeau disappointed me at that moment. Though I never had any particular reason to admire him, I never expected such a *volte-face* on his part."[20]

"But what about this?" the prime minister quickly added.

On the amending formula, he felt that it was "a mistake not to be able to go to the people," but he too was prepared to swallow hard.[21] He then resurrected the idea of requiring provinces to get a two-thirds vote in their legislatures before opting out of a national program that infringed on their jurisdiction. It was "a bit late in the day," he admitted when the suggestion was greeted frostily, and he acknowledged that his strong reservations about the opting-out provision didn't add up to a refusal.

As to the Charter, he asked if the provinces would accept a "sunset" provision that would compel their legislatures to renew any invocation of the *non obstante* clause every five years. If there was a political price to be paid for using it, he wanted to make governments pay over and over again. Though Trudeau pretended that the thought had just occurred to him, it had been included as an option in his briefing book and had even been scribbled in the margins of the Kitchen Accord.

"Sure, I can live with that," said Lougheed, who had been told it was coming, and nobody else was willing to upset the deal over it.

Remarkably, Trudeau let pass Alberta's insistence that the notwith-standing clause could be applied to fundamental freedoms. Perhaps, having heard reports of Lougheed's stubbornness the night before and at breakfast, or having just witnessed the negative reaction to Davis's plea to exempt it, he simply abandoned this item as a lost cause.[22] In retro-spect, however, Peter Meekison felt certain that Lougheed would have sacrificed it for the sake of a final agreement—an accident of history with tremendous potential consequences.[23] "So I agreed to accept the clause with a heavy heart," Trudeau recalled, "exhorting anyone willing to listen to put pressure on the provinces so that we might dispense with it in future negotiations."[24]

Next, he noted that aboriginal rights had been dropped. Initially he himself had been reluctant to entrench these in the constitution, uncertain what they implied and fearful they would be interpreted as a form of special status or territorially based "ethnic nationalism." But Trudeau allowed himself to be persuaded by Jean Chrétien, Ed Broadbent, and the government lawyers that they were just, reasonable, and absolutely necessary to smooth the Resolution's passage through Parliament and Westminster.[25] Sensing the trouble that was indeed to come, he suggested the first ministers at least agree to hold another conference in the near future to discuss the issue. Done.

Finally, there was the question of the right to minority-language education. Knowing how important it was to Trudeau, and repeatedly warned that he'd never accept an opt-in clause, the Anglo premiers pre-empted a clash of principle by simply saying on record, then and there, that the right would be entrenched in their provinces once everyone was in. "I appreciate that nine of you would accept," Trudeau said.[26] He then turned to Lévesque. Since the English-speaking provinces have agreed to guarantee the right of French-speaking citizens to primary and secondary schooling in their language wherever the numbers warrant, would Quebec agree to guarantee the same right to its English-speaking minority?

"No," Lévesque snapped, "there would be riots in the streets of Montreal."

"I can't accept a constitutional amendment that will treat Anglos different," Trudeau responded. "It's the responsibility of Ottawa to protect minority education everywhere in the country, but I am willing to continue discussing it."

"I will never give up one iota of our responsibility for education," Lévesque countered, "a power fundamental to the protection of the only French-speaking island in the English-speaking ocean of North America."[27]

As had happened so often in the past, the other first ministers found themselves looking on like spectators at a final grudge match between two old boxers, each determined and desperate to win one last bout before hanging up his gloves. At one point, Brian Peckford had to interrupt their quarrel to remind them that there were other players in the room. The English-speaking premiers were trapped once again between the two competing and contradictory visions of Quebec, between Pierre Trudeau and René Lévesque, both with strong mandates from the voters of Quebec, and they would have to choose one or the other if they wanted to get a deal. On the one hand, as a matter of both principle and politics, most of them remained firmly opposed to Ottawa's intruding unilaterally into an area of provincial jurisdiction. They'd fought the Charter and the NEP for that very reason. On the other hand, could they really side with the avowed *indépendantiste* who had deserted them to try to save his own skin, rather than with the ardent federalist who had won an undeniable victory the only time the choice was put directly to the people of the province?

Peter Lougheed was especially conflicted. He believed in a federalism in which the provinces had clear constitutional responsibilities, not the least of which was education. He believed that the federal government's true agenda, to be fiercely challenged whenever and wherever it reared its ugly head, was to turn Canada into a unitary state. He believed that Trudeau had not lived up to the spirit of the promise he'd made to Quebecers during the referendum campaign. He believed that isolating Quebec at this moment in history would damage national unity in the long term. "It causes me great concern," he said of minority-language education. "It is not up to me to impose my will on another province."[28]

In the end, however, Lougheed simply wasn't prepared to unite in solidarity with Lévesque. Would going to the wall with Quebec have increased the odds of getting the PQ premier's signature on a final deal? At what cost to Alberta's own interests? The amending formula? The notwithstanding clause? The deal itself? "It might have been better politically," said Peter Meekison, "but it wasn't worth losing what we wanted.

Trudeau was determined to do this thing."[29] And so, after huddling with Chrétien in a corner of the room during a brief coffee break, Peter Lougheed decided "with great reluctance" to leave the issue of education rights in Quebec for the federal and provincial French Canadians to sort out among themselves, within the family, so to speak.[30]

"That was a tough one for us," Lougheed confessed, "but we were winning in so many other places. It was part of the compromise. If that's what we had to do for the deal, okay, because we thought the deal was very important."[31]

The rest of the English-speaking provinces agreed to accept immediate entrenchment—except for Manitoba, where approval would require a legislative vote—and Ottawa could do what it thought best as far as Quebec was concerned. "All right," Blakeney told the prime minister, "but be it on your head."

To which Davis replied drily, "Yes, that's right. But, Allan, I wouldn't put it just that way to the public."[32]

"Come on, surprise me," Trudeau poked Lévesque in a quiet aside in French. "Make some kind of gesture now that you've lost this inning. Come along and we'll all do this together." And he started down the list. "You're a progressive, René, so what's wrong with a charter of rights for all citizens? Are you opposed to freedom of speech?"

"Of course I'm for freedom of speech," Lévesque barked.

"Good, good," Trudeau purred. "And are you for freedom of religion?"

Lévesque saw the trap. If he accepted some human rights, how could he not accept them all? So he returned to his objections to labour mobility and minority education.

"Okay, then," Trudeau said, "how about a referendum on them in Quebec? If you win, we'll reopen the accord."[33]

Instead, Lévesque went back to demanding either financial compensation or a veto. Compensation could be negotiated on an administrative basis, Trudeau replied, but he didn't see how he could commit future governments by entrenching it in the constitution. As for a Quebec veto, Trudeau had always been supportive of it, but the moment was gone, he said. Bourassa had rejected it along with the Victoria Charter; Lévesque had accepted the principle of equality in the April Accord. And besides, wasn't opting out from future amendments a kind of veto?

A month later, in a telex to the prime minister dated December 2, 1981, René Lévesque gave his formal response. "If Quebec was able to block your previous formulas," he wrote, "why could it not block your present formula, especially since, in addition to contradicting what Quebecers understood to be your referendum promises, it threatens the rights and powers of Quebec as no other formula has ever done? Since you are unwilling to respect a right that has always been respected since the beginning of Confederation, we have no choice but to have that right recognized by the Courts."[34]

"On April 16," Trudeau fired back two days later, with a display of the legal precision and irrefutable logic that invariably drove Lévesque to distraction, "your government subscribed to the notion of the equality of the provinces, and there was no question then of Canadian duality or even of a special status for Quebec! If Quebec, then, were to have a veto, one would have to say that each of the other provinces also had a veto too, and the amending formula would have to be unanimity to respect the equality of the provinces. But the Supreme Court in its decision on the *Patriation Reference* stated that unanimity is *not* required for constitutional amendments. Therefore, if the provinces are equal and unanimity is not required, there is no veto either for Quebec or for any other province."

The Supreme Court reached the same conclusion a year later. Quebec, it was to rule on December 6, 1982, had never had a veto by law or convention.

It was now eleven-thirty on Thursday morning, November 5, 1981. "If you don't want to sign," Trudeau said to René Lévesque and Claude Morin, "we will finish the work among ourselves."[35] At this point, arguably, Quebec's bargaining strength had never been greater. Who knows what price the other first ministers would have paid to get Lévesque's signature if he had pushed? Wasn't this just the first step to prepare the ground for the Powers' Package that was still to come? But Lévesque and Morin were in no frame of mind to negotiate. Not only was this constitutional renewal such a long way from the new powers and special status they had always envisaged, but they were too distraught to think rationally or strategically. "They weren't left out," Bill Davis observed. "Lévesque made a decision not to come in."[36]

In the weeks that followed, it was left to the federal government to improve the deal on Quebec's behalf, if only to secure the support of Claude Ryan's Liberals in the National Assembly and the soft nationalists in the province. First, Ottawa arbitrarily amended the deal to alleviate the demographic concerns of many francophone Quebecers. Minority education rights in Quebec would not apply to every citizen whose mother tongue is English—the Charter's so-called universal clause—without the consent of the National Assembly. Until that time, the right would be restricted to the children of those who had received their schooling in English in Canada or to children who themselves had already been schooled in English.[37] Not only had Lévesque agreed in principle to just such a "Canada clause" at meetings with the other premiers in St. Andrew's, New Brunswick, in 1977 and Montreal in 1978, but there was even a provision for it in the PQ's draconian language laws. And second, Trudeau agreed—very much against his will, admittedly—to entrench financial compensation for any province that opted out of an amendment affecting education or culture.

Vanquished, agitated, emotional, Lévesque made ready to leave. "You won't get away with this" were his departing words to Trudeau. "The people will stop it."

"The people have already decided, René, and you lost."[38]

Now there remained little more for the others to do but tie up a few loose ends. "We'll sign it here," Trudeau said, ending the session

Library and Archives Canada/e010768035

Lévesque alone.

with the same emphatic sense of occasion by which Donald Smith had hammered the last spike into the rail lines at Craigellachie. "I'm not taking any chances."[39]

Bone tired and eager to be done, none of the participants caught the small detail that would blow up into a major controversy as soon as reports of the deal reached the street.[40] By agreeing to apply the notwithstanding clause (section 33) to equality rights (section 28), the first ministers provoked the full fury of women's organizations, who feared it would be used not to protect affirmative-action programs but to override gender equality. Allan Blakeney, the last holdout against reopening the deal, finally buckled after almost two weeks of demonstrations, petitions, and personal attacks, though his price was to get British Columbia and Alberta to agree to insert the "existing" rights of the aboriginals into the Charter at the same time. Thus, on

November 23, 1981, Canada could claim to have the first and only constitution ever negotiated anywhere in the world by telephone.

That was still ahead, as the unsuspecting players and supporting cast made their way down to the Main Hall on the ground floor to announce their agreement to the public. They were experiencing the full gamut of thoughts and emotions. Triumph mitigated by disappointment. Exhilaration offset by exhaustion. Defeat unaccompanied by consolation. "Let's face it," Pierre Trudeau admitted to a member of his staff, "it was a mean process."[41] Like John A. Macdonald, he had been forced to compromise the purity of his national vision in the face of powerful regional interests and formidable provincial barons. "I have one regret," he said at the closing ceremony. "I put it on the record. I will not return to it. I have the regret that we have not kept in the amending formula a reference to the ultimate sovereignty of the people as could be tested in a referendum." When all was said and done, however, he had achieved the near impossible: the legal independence of Canada, a consensus by which to change the constitution, and in his own words, "the best Charter in the world."[42]

Allan Blakeney felt that the result, coming so fast and with so many "grubby compromises," was anti-climatic.[43] Though he won some points on natural resources and the amending formula, he lost on the principle of the Charter and would have gained more for Saskatchewan if he had struck a bilateral deal with the federal government instead of joining the Gang of Eight. (Indeed, all the premiers would have gained more for their provinces if they had settled with Ottawa in September 1980, and even more in February 1979.) True to his agonizing self, Blakeney remained haunted by one of the most interesting what-ifs of Canadian history. "If Mr. Trudeau had proceeded unilaterally and if the Imperial Parliament had given their assent," he wrote in his memoirs, "the eight dissenting provinces would have been incensed. I know the Saskatchewan government would have been. The government of Quebec would have been particularly angry. But they would not have been alone or isolated.

Would Canada have been better served by eight angry provinces or just one—an angry and isolated Quebec?"[44]

In retrospect, as well, Canada might have been better served if the first ministers hadn't decided, in their rush for a consensus, that nine signatures were better than eight. Quebec wasn't alone that day. In fact, Manitoba didn't sign the agreement until after Sterling Lyon lost the election to the New Democrats on November 17, 1981. Lyon, out on the campaign trail, even tried to claim victory by arguing that the Charter wasn't really enshrined in the constitution because of the notwithstanding clause. "If it makes somebody down there have jollies to talk about an entrenched charter," he told the press, "they can have all the jollies they want. I know that the clause going into it is such that it permits the Government of Manitoba to override it."[45] (Lyon may have got the final word on the Charter in the end: he became a judge.)

Bill Bennett flew back to British Columbia relieved that he could finally turn his attention to the economy, but exhausted by almost a week of tension. "I'm home," he sighed as the plane landed in Kelowna. "Relax."[46] Richard Hatfield secured equalization payments for his province, language rights for the long-suffering Acadian people, and a landslide victory for his party in 1982. (Following his criminal charges for marijuana possession and his crushing defeat in 1987, he also secured his dream of a seat in the Senate.) Brian Peckford, Angus MacLean, and John Buchanan, despite having done little but stand in the way of patriation and the Charter for more than a year, now strutted and preened as the new Fathers of Confederation. "Am I a hero?" Peckford crowed to the press, while officials from Ontario and Saskatchewan scrambled behind the scenes to put his last-minute contribution back into perspective. "No, many were involved beside myself."[47]

Peter Lougheed, with Alberta's energy now protected and its amending formula the fundamental law of the land, beamed like a quarterback who had just scored the winning touchdown. "It all shook out as a pretty good solution, except for the Quebec factor," he reflected.

"We came through with a constitution that was good for the country, one that I was prepared to sign on to. In hindsight, under the circumstances of dealing with a separatist government, we got blindsided. There was no way they were going to sign. But I only came to that conclusion looking back at it."[48]

When Bill Davis walked into the Ontario delegation's offices on the first floor, he was hailed by Tom Wells, his natty minister of intergovernmental affairs, as the man whose skill and decency had made the new constitution happen. The premier was too moved to speak, then started to cry and couldn't stop. As the tears poured down his cheeks, everyone gave him three rounds of "Hip, hip, hurray!"[49]

"There was a sense of accomplishment," Davis remembered. "When the history books are written, it will be one of the determining points in our history. I'm quite a modest soul, but I think I played a small part in making it happen. Canada was finally sovereign. We have a charter better than most. And though there was disappointment that Quebec didn't sign, getting close to perfection is better than nothing. Certainly the alternative didn't appeal to me very much."[50]

There were tears, too, among the Quebec delegates, but theirs were tears of rage and frustration rather than of relief or fatigue. When Lévesque phoned his wife, she had never heard him sound so broken. Not angry but totally defeated, like a child in need of consolation. "That day," said Claude Charron, who was himself in a state of shock from the unexpected turn of events, "he hated *les Anglais* enough to kill them."[51] It took all of Charron's persuasive skills to convince the premier to stay long enough to address the people of Quebec.

It was an electrifying moment—part tension, part relief—when Lévesque scurried, late and distraught, into the Main Hall. The spectacular room, formerly the train station's gargantuan waiting room—its stone walls, Corinthian columns, and vaulted ceiling modelled after both the Baths of Caracalla in Rome and Pennsylvania Station in New York City—had been transformed by the klieg lights and TV cameras

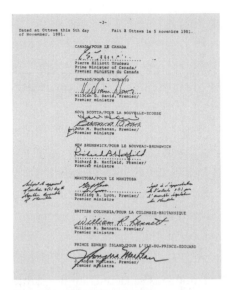

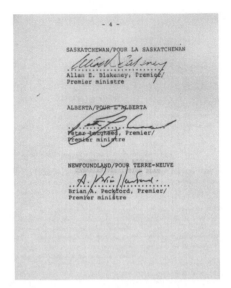

The November 5 signatories.

Main Hall, Government Conference Centre, November 5, 1981.

into an enormous stage set. There, some 150 officials, more than 600 accredited journalists, and over two million viewers had been waiting all morning for news from the fifth floor.

Lévesque smoked feverishly while the other premiers heaped praise upon themselves, as giddy as boys let out of school, slapping each other on the back and grinning like football players after a winning series, with only a pro forma word of regret that Quebec was not with them. In his eyes, the majority English-speaking government in Ottawa had just joined with nine English-speaking governments in the provinces—led, he thought, by a bunch of "rug merchants who wouldn't hesitate to walk over their mother for an ice cream cone"—to ask the English-speaking parliamentarians in London to reduce the powers of the only French-speaking government in North America without its consent.[52]

"I am deeply sorry to see Quebec back in the place the federal regime has traditionally reserved for us: once again Quebec is all alone," Lévesque said when it came his turn to speak. "It will be up to the people of Quebec, and to them alone, to draw what conclusions they can ... When they have done that, I think you may feel a little less joyful than you seem to be now."[53]

EPILOGUE

SEVENTEEN

A Beautiful Risk

They tried to make a big hoopla out of the signing of the Royal Proclamation of the Constitution Act, 1982. The Queen and Prince Philip came over from London with an entourage that included a doctor, a hairdresser, three footmen, equerries, secretaries, and one duchess. There was a gala event at the National Arts Centre and a "young achievers" dinner at the Holiday Inn (to which the prime minister invited the actress Margot Kidder and his mentor, Frank Scott). Jean Chrétien hosted a glittering banquet at the Château Laurier to thank 350 politicians and officials for their efforts. Some thirty thousand Canadians gathered on Parliament Hill to watch the noontime ceremony on April 17, 1982. The spring sun shone, flags fluttered in a humid breeze, cannons boomed, choirs sang, bands marched, four hundred pigeons soared in imitation of doves, and the monarch in a turquoise dress and her prime minister in a morning suit strode onto an enormous makeshift stage erected on the lawns in front of the Peace Tower. None of the provincial premiers had been invited to share the glory, an insult that annoyed Bill Davis but spared Allan Blakeney the awkwardness of being photographed at

Pierre Trudeau's side in the middle of the Saskatchewan election. This was the last scene of the last act.

Never did Trudeau, spot-lit under the striped canopy and amplified through the gigantic speakers, seem more like an actor coming to the end of a great performance. "It is my deepest hope," he said, "that Canada will match its new legal maturity with that degree of political maturity which will allow us all to make a total commitment to the Canadian ideal. I speak of a Canada where men and women of aboriginal ancestry, of French and British heritage, of the diverse cultures of the world demonstrate the will to share this land in peace, in justice, and with mutual respect. I speak of a Canada which is proud of and strengthened by its essential bilingual destiny, a Canada whose people believe in sharing and in mutual support, and not in building regional barriers. I speak of a country where every person is free to fulfill himself or herself to the utmost, unhindered by the arbitrary actions of governments."[1]

Thunder rumbled in the distance and dramatic black clouds rolled in from the east, over the Gatineau Hills on the other side of the Ottawa River. The sky darkened during the signing ceremony, turning the theatrical set into a surreal box of brilliant light. A splash of rain smudged the ink, and when the pen was handed to Jean Chrétien with a broken nib, he muttered *"Merde!"* under his breath, to the Queen's evident amusement. No sooner had she begun her remarks than a torrential downpour, accompanied by hail and hurricane-force winds, battered the spectators, who screeched or laughed in response. Her words were blown away by the gale, drowned by the deluge, lost in the magnified flapping of the canvas walls. Scores of dignitaries, not wishing to meet Her Majesty at lunch looking like soaked rodents, tossed aside the rules of protocol and fled for shelter; some covered their heads with plastic garbage bags or used their chairs as umbrellas. Many women plunked their husbands' top hats over their expensive and now ruined coiffures.

Given that the angry storm had swept in from Quebec to rain on Trudeau's parade, it was taken as a symbol, a metaphor, a curse from

René Lévesque, a sign from God that Quebecers were enraged. On November 5, the moment he could get the hell out of Ottawa, Lévesque had flown back to his own capital aboard the government's F-27. During the flight he spilled a cup of coffee over his justice minister, Marc-André Bédard, who was playing poker with Claude Morin. A simple accident? Bad nerves? Probably, but it was also interpreted as a manifestation of his deep unhappiness with his two principal advisers. There was no one to greet or console him when he landed in Quebec City, except for a mob of striking taxi drivers who had blockaded the airport. Instead of returning as a conquering hero, he was the first and only premier of Quebec to lose constitutional powers for the province. As much as he would try to blame others, he knew he would be blamed, and he blamed himself, too. "I didn't have many illusions," he said, "but I don't have any illusions left."[2]

The bitter recriminations were swift in coming and lasted decades, thanks in no small part to the mischief of Jacques Parizeau, who took his revenge for not being invited to Ottawa by pointing his finger at his old nemesis, Claude Morin. Based on a single, spontaneous, and extremely brief visit paid to the delegation's hotel suite in Hull, Parizeau later described a party atmosphere, with Lévesque in the centre of a harem of female staff members, Charron and Bédard playing cards with two assistants, and a general air of disorder, distraction, and disrespect.[3] Martine Tremblay, who was in the room but not mentioned in Parizeau's list of the women fawning over the premier, took issue with the details, and especially with the implications.

"Quebec wasn't done in, in November, by grave tactical errors," she concluded, "or because its delegation had let down its guard and gone to bed just as the knives of English Canada were being unsheathed. It wasn't because Claude Morin was conspiring with the RCMP to betray the *souverainistes*, or because Claude Charron didn't know anything about constitutional matters, or because the minister of justice, Marc-André Bédard, couldn't speak English! … The mistake, if there was a mistake, occurred after the victory of 1981, when René Lévesque and his team, reinvigorated by the renewed support of the voters, thought that their strategy, put in place months before and never seriously contested by anyone since then, had a real chance of stopping the Ottawa steamroller. And their confidence, reinforced by the length of the process, created, in my opinion, a false hope that held right up to the final stage of the November conference."[4]

In the weeks that followed, in the National Assembly and in the press, Lévesque raged against the betrayal, the treachery, the contempt, the banditry, and the humiliation of what the media came to call the "Night of the Long Knives."[5] Nothing better illustrated the existence of two distinct nations in Canada, Lévesque told his legislature, or how small a price the rest of the country put on the rights of Quebec. "I couldn't find words strong enough to express my burning resentment," he recalled. "For the first time, I even went so far as to suggest that we might think of administering to Anglo-Québécois some of the 'school medicine' our minorities were forced to swallow in the rest of Canada. It was a release I badly needed, but it became excessive."[6]

Not just excessive but reckless, for it unleashed the black dogs of ethnic nationalism to run wild through the Parti Québécois convention in early December. Vengeance, even violence, was in the air. The delegates voted to dump the word "association" and every other connection to the rest of Canada from the party platform. They tossed out the promise of consulting the people in a referendum before declaring independence. They applauded the presence of one of the Marxist terrorists who had murdered a Quebec Liberal Cabinet minister in 1970. Horrified by what he had done, Lévesque moved to save the PQ from self-destruction. First he threatened to resign, then he arranged an internal referendum that asked the broad membership to repudiate what the delegates had decided. Of the half who responded, 95 percent supported Lévesque.

The National Assembly passed a motion, 70–38, calling for changes to the agreement, to no effect. Flags were ordered flown at half-mast throughout Quebec the day the Resolution was approved in the House of Commons, by a vote of 246–24. The PQ introduced a spiteful law that automatically applied the notwithstanding clause to every piece of provincial legislation. The *indépendantistes*, wonder of wonders, begged the British government to keep Canada a constitutional colony. "Never before in our history has the British Parliament been asked to diminish the rights and powers of Quebec's legislature and government without their consent," Lévesque wrote to Prime Minister Thatcher. "The proposed legislation is an unprecedented attack on the powers that allow North America's only French-speaking society to defend and promote its language and culture."[7]

The truth was, outside the political class and away from the media, most Quebecers remained profoundly indifferent to what had happened at the First Ministers' Conference in November. On April 17, 1982, at the same hour as the proclamation ceremonies in Ottawa, the PQ government organized a protest march to denounce what Lévesque termed "an unprecedented centralization of all economic levers and fiscal powers."[8] But it attracted a disappointing fifteen thousand people. While the demonstrators donned black armbands, waved the fleur-de-lys, wore "*Québec j'aime*" buttons, and carried placards condemning the federal "traitors" and the "charter of genocide," the polls showed that 48 percent of Quebecers disagreed with Lévesque's position, 32 percent were in favour, and the rest either didn't know or didn't care.[9]

"A gamble lost; a gamble won—big deal!" Pierre Trudeau observed. "Quebec public opinion, with its usual maturity, applauded the players, and then, yawning, turned to other matters."[10] And he pirouetted once again behind the back of the Queen after bidding her farewell at Ottawa airport.[11]

Though René Lévesque and the Parti Québécois were undoubtedly the losers, Quebec was not. For the first time since Confederation, it and the other provinces had a legal veto over significant sections of the constitution. Quebec's powers and responsibilities were protected by the new amending formula, which now included financial compensation if the province ever chose to opt out of any amendments affecting education and culture. It had a notwithstanding clause that it could invoke if the Charter impinged in an unacceptable way on the will of the National Assembly. Without being forced to fully reciprocate unless and until their provincial legislature consented, Quebecers were assured of French-language schooling in the rest of Canada, wherever the numbers warranted, for any citizens who had French as their mother tongue. They also had the right to work anywhere in the country, while mobility rights would not apply to Quebec if and when the province's employment rate dropped below the Canadian average. The principle of equalization was engraved in stone. And last but not least, no matter what demographic changes the future might bring, the equality of English and French in all institutions and services of the federal government and the government of New Brunswick was protected, even from the *non obstante* clause.

With interest rates, inflation, and unemployment on the rise, Quebecers focused their attention on keeping their jobs, their homes, and their businesses, rather than on the argument that they had forfeited some hypothetical special status in the constitution. Three months after the November conference, in fact, Lévesque had to set aside his feelings and return to Ottawa to discuss the Canadian economy with the very men he accused of stabbing him in the back.[12] He sat down with them again in March 1983 to talk about aboriginal rights, joking that the Native leaders in attendance should post watchmen during the night. In 1984, with Pierre Trudeau retired, the federal Liberals defeated, and the Progressive Conservatives under Brian Mulroney making unprecedented overtures towards Quebec nationalists, Lévesque even convinced himself and his party that Canada might be "a beautiful risk" after all.

"If federalism should function less badly, and even actually improve," he mused at a PQ meeting on September 22, 1984, "doesn't that risk smothering our fundamental option and sending sovereignty to never-never land? Obviously, there is an element of risk. But it is a *beau risque*, and we don't have the luxury of not taking it."[13] Two months later, on November 19, he declared, "We must certainly resign ourselves, at least for the next elections, to the fact that sovereignty shall not, in whole, or in parts more or less disguised, be an issue."[14]

In 1985, after Lévesque retired from politics and was replaced by Pierre-Marc Johnson, the Parti Québécois moved even further away from sovereignty towards "national affirmation." Even so, the PQ was defeated at the end of the year by the Liberals under Robert Bourassa, who had returned from his political Elba still bearing an accountant's attachment to Canada and a nationalist's yearning for a special status for Quebec.

In other words, in the three years that followed the First Ministers' Conference in November 1981, all the evidence pointed to just one conclusion: the independence movement, severely wounded by the loss of the 1980 referendum and bleeding from the cuts it had received in the constitutional battle (some from Pierre Trudeau, some from the Gang of Eight, some from its own hand), was moribund. But that didn't prevent the *souverainistes* and their sympathizers in the universities, the media, and the arts from sowing falsehoods like dragon's teeth, ready to rise up like an army of fierce warriors when nurtured in the hothouse of Quebec politics. "Lévesque Trahi Par Ses Alliés," wailed the *Journal de Québec* in a large front-page headline accompanied by a photograph of Trudeau and Chrétien sharing a laugh at the end of the November conference. The headline could just as accurately have read "His Allies Betrayed by Lévesque," and the picture left the insidious and totally misleading impression that the two federalists had been caught grinning in their triumph over Quebec rather than enjoying, as was actually the case, a joke by Bill Davis.

In May 2005, on the occasion of the twenty-fifth anniversary of the 1980 referendum, *Le Devoir* summed up the prevailing narrative among Quebec historians and journalists: "The defeat of the sovereigntist camp during the referendum of 1980 led to the unilateral repatriation of the

Canadian Constitution in 1982 by Prime Minister Pierre Elliott Trudeau, who profited from the weakness of René Lévesque's government."[15]

In fact, as we have seen, Trudeau hadn't acted unilaterally in the end. He was compelled to accept a compromise deal, forced on him by nine premiers, to get what the Supreme Court termed a "substantial level of provincial support." And rather than taking advantage of the No side's victory to do something harmful to the interests of French-speaking Canadians, he had leveraged the *strength* of the nationalists in Quebec to get English Canada to entrench the protection of the French language and minority-language education across the country. Nevertheless, in this and a thousand other ways, the legend of the Night of the Long Knives was recounted again and again, like a spooky bedtime story told behind the invisible curtain of language.

EIGHTEEN

Power to the People

The situation following the proclamation of the Constitution Act, 1982, might have remained much as it had after the British North America Act became law in 1867: a perpetual tug-of-war for money and power between Ottawa and the provinces, with a yank of centralization followed by a pull of decentralization, and vice versa; the sabre-rattling ultimatums of the politicians; the backroom brokering of the bureaucrats; the weary indifference of the voters; and the periodic outbursts of Quebec nationalism, Atlantic grievance, Ontario chest-pounding, and western alienation. What upset the routine was the overthrow of Joe Clark as leader of the Progressive Conservative Party of Canada by Brian Mulroney, an electrician's son from the hinterland of Quebec who had grown rich as a corporate lawyer and branch-plant CEO in Montreal with his street smarts, his back-slapping charm, his raw ambition, and his gift for Irish blarney in both official languages.

Mulroney captured the leadership in June 1983 by convincing his fellow Conservatives in Ontario, the Maritimes, and western Canada that they would never be able to form an enduring majority government without a major breakthrough in Quebec, which had been a Liberal stronghold since the day the Tories hanged Louis Riel in 1885. They first needed to elect a fluently bilingual son of the province as their leader—with Mulroney himself the only candidate who happened to have those specific qualifications. They then needed to show themselves open to the dreams and aspirations of the province's anti-Liberals, made up of hardline *indépendantistes*, soft-core nationalists, and the sworn enemies of Pierre Elliott Trudeau. However much it stuck in the craw of the party's Loyalist remnants and its anti-French rednecks, Mulroney's strategy prevailed and carried them to triumph in 1984, winning them fifty-eight of Quebec's seventy-five seats.

There was one small bump on the road to power. Unlike Joe Clark, Brian Mulroney had been an enthusiastic supporter of Trudeau's unilateral package in 1980—"not because he had thought about it for five minutes," said one of his closest advisers, "but because he was thrilled by the sheer bravado of it all."[1] Mulroney dealt with that inconvenient truth by ignoring it. In August 1984, in Sept-Îles, Quebec, he delivered a major campaign speech—written by his law school buddy, a federalist turned separatist turned federalist named Lucien Bouchard—in which he declared that the people of Quebec had suffered "a collective trauma" because of Trudeau's actions. "Not one person in Quebec authorized the federal Liberals to take advantage of the confusion that prevailed in Quebec following the referendum in order to ostracize the province constitutionally," he railed. "My party takes no pleasure in the politically weak position in which these deplorable events have placed Quebec."[2]

As prime minister, Mulroney saw an opportunity to right this perceived wrong—and solidify his party's gains in Quebec—when Robert Bourassa was returned to office in December 1985. Though Bourassa was a Liberal and a flag-of-convenience Canadian, he shared Mulroney's intense dislike of Pierre Trudeau, not least because the former prime minister had insulted him repeatedly and in public for reneging on the

Victoria Charter in 1971 and for passing the "politically stupid" bill that had made French the official language of Quebec in 1974. Bourassa was indeed a cautious, indecisive, and conflicted leader who valued economic development and social stability ahead of political adventurism and cultural wars, but he was neither unintelligent nor a quitter. The son of a minor federal bureaucrat who was required to speak English on the job in Montreal, Bourassa had been educated at the same elite school as Pierre Trudeau, earned degrees in law and economics from Oxford and Harvard, married into a wealthy Quebec dynasty, and got himself elected the youngest premier in Quebec history at the age of thirty-seven. Before being frightened off by the economic unknowns of independence, he had flirted with René Lévesque's sovereignty-association movement as a backbencher and, as premier, had retained Claude Morin to advise him on constitutional matters. Though a federalist, he seemed to have no emotional feelings towards Canada. "I have no prejudices one way or the other," Bourassa once replied in answer to a question about sovereignty. "In politics I always worked at the Quebec level. But in terms of economics, there are advantages for Quebec if it stays within a Canadian community."[3]

Perhaps realizing that he had let slip a historic opportunity to secure language rights across Canada and a permanent veto for Quebec in 1971, he was open to Mulroney's offer to renegotiate the constitution so that Quebec could sign it "with honour and enthusiasm." And so it came to pass, on April 30, 1987, thanks to the prime minister's extraordinary skills as a negotiator, that a fresh batch of first ministers (with Brian Peckford, John Buchanan, and Richard Hatfield the only holdovers) signed the Meech Lake Accord to secure the one thing that had eluded Trudeau—the government of Quebec's signature. The price was a number of major concessions. Going forward, the federal government would have to make appointments to the Senate and the Supreme Court from lists provided by the provinces (including, presumably, a Parti Québécois government in Quebec). Ottawa surrendered its control over the reception and integration of immigrants. It limited federal spending in areas of provincial jurisdiction. It guaranteed the provinces, as Trudeau had refused to do, financial compensation for opting out of an amendment involving a transfer of provincial power to the federal government. Most controversially, it recognized Quebec as "a distinct society" within the constitution and affirmed the role of the government of Quebec "to preserve and promote the distinct identity" of the province.[4]

No one knew for certain what that meant or what its legal implications would be for either the divisions of power or the Charter of Rights and Freedoms. While Mulroney downplayed distinct society to English Canada as a mere political and sociological fact, with no additional powers or privileges attached, Bourassa trumpeted it in Quebec as the entrenchment of the special status or associated statehood the soft nationalists had long desired.[5] "It must be stressed," he told the National Assembly, "that the entire Constitution, including the Charter, will be interpreted and applied in the light of the distinct-society section. Since it is directed towards the exercise of legislative powers, we will be able to consolidate what has already been achieved, and gain new ground."[6] When Bourassa set up a party committee to explore "the political autonomy necessary for the development of Quebec's identity," its recommendations left Ottawa with little more than defence, tariffs, currency, and equalization payments—or else another referendum, another knife to the throat, another threat to separate.

"If the recognition of Quebec as a distinct society turns out not to mean anything," Claude Morin observed from the sidelines, "Quebecers will begin fighting again."[7]

To sell the Meech Lake Accord as the perfect remedy, Mulroney had to come up with some terrible ills. Trudeau had excluded Quebec from "full and active participation" in Canada's constitutional evolution, he alleged; Trudeau had betrayed his solemn promise to Quebecers and had "isolated and humiliated" the province.[8] The Constitution Act, 1982, was the worst injustice ever inflicted on Quebec. It was a Major Error in the nation's history. It wasn't worth the paper it was written on. "Do you think the Queen would have come over here and there would have been a big party in front of Parliament Hill with everybody in striped pants celebrating a Constitution without the industrial heartland of Ontario?" he roared with his typical Irish hyperbole, recklessly stirring the pot among francophone Quebecers.[9]

Pierre Trudeau struck back. "*If* the Ontario provincial government had obstructed all attempts since 1927 to repatriate the Constitution," he retorted, "if that government in 1964 and 1971 had withdrawn its support for a repatriation formula that it had itself proposed or accepted, if it had been told by the Supreme Court that it had no constitutional veto, if that government was the one that wanted Canada broken apart and had just lost a referendum on this issue, if more than 95 per cent of Ontario's Members of Parliament had supported a constitutional reform that Quebec and the eight other provinces wanted, why, yes! I believe we would have proceeded without the approval of Queen's Park. But clearly, as the Viennese say, if my grandmother had wheels, she'd be a bloody bus!"[10]

As Trudeau saw it, there was nothing wrong with trying to put together a Powers' Package as the next step to constitutional reform. He himself had offered to do it. Mulroney's mistake was to proceed by running down the People's Package. Nor did Trudeau see any pressing need for the federal government to reopen the file. All was quiet on the constitutional front; the fundamental law, including the Charter of Rights and Freedoms, applied as much in Quebec as it did in every other province. And yet Mulroney was prepared to give up important powers over the central institutions, immigration, and shared-cost programs without asking for anything in return.

"The proof that Quebec was not badly treated in 1981," Trudeau said, "is that it was not attempting to correct the things that happened in 1981; the whole operation was one of leverage, of trying to tell Canada that it could have its Constitution providing it gave the Province of Quebec more power. That was the sole grievance after the negotiations of 1981 and the Constitution Act, 1982. Quebec had not succeeded in using its leverage to acquire more power. That is where Mr. Lévesque went wrong."[11]

Above all, Trudeau objected to distinct society for the same reasons he had always argued against special status, especially one entrenched as an interpretative clause in the constitution. "The possibility of building one Canada will be lost forever," he declared. "Canada henceforth will be governed by two Constitutions, one to be interpreted for the benefit of Canada and one to be interpreted for the preservation and promotion of Quebec's distinct society—two Constitutions, two Charters, promoting two distinct sets of values, and eventually two Canadas—well, one Canada and something else."[12]

His interventions proved instrumental in turning public opinion in English Canada against the Meech Lake Accord, as did Bourassa's ill-timed invocation of the notwithstanding clause to salvage a law banning the use of English on outdoor signs in Quebec.[13] Yet in truth, the Parti Québécois didn't care for the accord either, and a change of governments in New Brunswick, Manitoba, and Newfoundland threw support for Meech Lake into doubt during the three-year ratification period required by Canada's brand-new amending formula. By the deadline of June 23, 1990, it had failed to get through the Manitoba legislature owing to a filibuster by a lone aboriginal MLA, Elijah Harper, and thus wasn't put to a vote in the Newfoundland House of Assembly.

Brian Mulroney had gambled with a toss of the dice that he could get his deal by stoking passions in Quebec, then blackmailing the rest of the country to submit or face dreadful consequences. Three months *before* the Meech Lake Accord collapsed, the sense of humiliation among francophone Quebecers—inculcated by a prime minister of Canada, no less—had reached such a pitch that support for sovereignty surpassed 50 percent for the very first time. The independence movement, which had been thought dead and buried, was back in force. Lucien Bouchard, who had become one of Mulroney's most powerful ministers, quit the Cabinet at the threat of a compromise (also prior to the deal's demise) and became a separatist once more. In other words, it wasn't English Canada's resistance to the Meech Lake Accord that reignited the independence option so much as the hysterical marketing pitch that preceded it.

The accord failed not just because of its content, but also because of its process. More than 70 percent of Canadians wanted to have their say in a national referendum. The first ministers got the message. Before trying to contain the nationalist frenzy he had created in Quebec, Mulroney launched the Citizens' Forum on Canada's Future to solicit the advice and opinions of ordinary people. Similarly, Bourassa established the Commission on the Political and Constitutional Future of Quebec to conduct public hearings across the province. A federal parliamentary committee, set up to review the amending process, recommended the introduction of a non-binding referendum that would need majorities in the four regions as well as nationally, not unlike Trudeau's old Victoria formula. Three provinces—British Columbia, Alberta, and Quebec—passed laws requiring that any proposed constitutional amendments be put to a direct vote. In 1982 the Northwest Territories held a plebiscite regarding its division, and in 1992 the northern territory of Nunavut was created after obtaining the approval of its citizens.[14]

In August 1992, after a truly remarkable feat of horse-trading and arm-twisting, Mulroney and the ten premiers managed to reach a second unanimous agreement during a meeting in Charlottetown, Prince Edward Island. The Charlottetown Accord was Meech refined, with a lot of extras thrown in for the anglophone premiers and aboriginal leaders to broaden the base of support. And this time, to help solidify its acceptance, the leaders submitted their new package to the people of Canada in two concurrent referendums, the one promised to Quebecers by Bourassa and the other arranged by Ottawa in the rest of the country.

Would they be binding or non-binding? Did a Yes vote require a national majority alone—or a majority of the provinces, the regions, or Quebec as well? These questions, never adequately answered, proved moot when, on October 26, 1992, 54 percent of the population and the majorities of six provinces, including Quebec, voted No.

The negative result suggested that Jean Chrétien, Bill Davis, and the Anglo premiers in the Gang of Eight had been right in warning Trudeau about the divisive and unpredictable risks of referendums. The rejection reflected the deep unhappiness Canadians felt towards Mulroney and his government on a host of issues as much as—or more than—any particular dissatisfaction with the complicated clauses of the constitutional package. But just as the passionate protests of women's groups and aboriginal leaders in November 1981 had given the premiers a taste of what might have happened in their provinces had Trudeau taken his Charter to the people, so the Charlottetown vote revealed how deeply Canadians felt about their ownership of the constitution, and how unwilling they were to entrust it to the machinations of the political elite. It was now *theirs*.

"The Canadian people did exactly what I had hoped they would do," Trudeau noted with pleasure, not least because he had opposed the distinct-society provision in the Charlottetown Accord just as vehemently as he had opposed it in the Meech Lake Accord. "They established that the locus of the sovereignty of Canada is the people, and they were telling every practicing politician in the land: 'You guys think one thing, we think another—and what we think is what will prevail.' What they did really amounted to a revolt of the people against the political class."[15]

NINETEEN

To the Precipice

The next few years were difficult ones for Canadian federalists. The nationalists continued to feed the fires in Quebec for their political advantage. In the aftermath of the Meech Lake fiasco, Lucien Bouchard formed a new party, the Bloc Québécois, to promote independence from within the Canadian House of Commons. In 1993, it captured the majority of seats in Quebec from both the federal Conservatives and the federal Liberals. A year later, the Parti Québécois returned to power in the province under the leadership of the hardline *indépendantiste* Jacques Parizeau, who vowed to hold another referendum on a clear question as quickly as possible, while secretly conniving to use a Yes victory as a mandate for immediate and full independence.

On the surface, it looked as though Pierre Trudeau's great exercise in nation-building had only succeeded in bringing Canada to the brink of breakup. Beneath the surface, however, things weren't so dire. The popular vote for the Bloc Québécois never exceeded 50 percent, and the party won its seats not because it promoted a platform of independence but because it was seen as the more trusted defender of the province's interests in Ottawa, or because of the split among the federalist parties. Similarly, the PQ regained office with less than 45 percent of the vote, and Jacques Parizeau's determination to ask the kind of simple, direct question he had accused René Lévesque and Claude Morin of being too cowardly to ask in 1980 faltered in the face of polls that showed it would lose by 60–40 once again. Anxious to avoid another debilitating setback for his cause, Parizeau hoisted the frayed banner of sovereignty-association once again and, in the middle of a lacklustre campaign, passed the leadership of the Yes side to the Bloc's Lucien Bouchard. On October 30, 1995, the results see-sawed minute by minute until the final ballot was counted at 11:15 p.m. and the No side eked out a victory at a mere 50.5 percent.

The unexpected rush to the edge of the precipice wasn't the result of a lemming-like enthusiasm for sovereignty among the people of Quebec. In part, it was due to the charismatic appeal of Bouchard the man—or rather, the saint—whose recent brush with death from a viral infection seemed to sanctify him as a resurrected messiah ordained by God to lead his people into the promised land. In part, too, it was due to soft nationalists who, in the wake of Mulroney's two failures, simply wanted to send a strong message to English Canada for an equal partnership within the federation. Indeed, according to the polls, the closeness of the result frightened a large number of them away from the dangerous game of chicken they had been playing with Canada, while Parizeau's ugly insinuation on the night of the referendum that "money and the ethnic vote" had denied old-stock Quebecers their rightful destiny forced him to resign as premier in favour of the more moderate Bouchard.

Among the ironies of history was the fact that the PQ government's chief opponent in the campaign was none other than Jean Chrétien, who had vowed in the living room of 24 Sussex Drive on the evening of November 4, 1981, that he would never again put on his running shoes to fight another referendum battle in Quebec. He had no choice. On June 23, 1990, by chance the very day the Meech Lake Accord was pronounced dead, Chrétien had been elected leader of the Liberal

Party of Canada. On October 25, 1993, he was elected prime minister of Canada, though his Liberals were reduced to only nineteen seats in his home province and he himself had had to seek a safe riding in New Brunswick. For Chrétien was forced to pay a very heavy personal and political price for the role he had played in patriating the constitution in 1982. His boastful re-enactment of the Kitchen Accord for the TV cameras fed the rumours that he was integral to the behind-the-scenes, middle-of-the-night intrigues that had kept Quebec from the final deal-making. His on-again, off-again opposition to Meech Lake and its distinct-society clause led to his being ostracized by a majority of his own people, egged on by the historical fabrications and partisan exaggerations of Brian Mulroney and Lucien Bouchard.

In a televised address during the referendum campaign, for example, Bouchard portrayed patriation as the original sin that sovereignty alone could expunge, and he cast Pierre Trudeau and Jean Chrétien as the devils who had torn up "the constitution of our ancestors," imposed a new one that reduced Quebec's powers in the areas of language and education, and conspired with the English-speaking provinces in a hotel room in the dark of night to consummate the pact that excluded Quebec from the Canadian constitutional family. As proof, Bouchard dramatically interrupted his speech to hold up an enlarged copy of the fourteen-year-old front page of the *Journal de Québec* with its provocative headline and the photograph of Trudeau and Chrétien apparently laughing in the face of a weak and wounded René Lévesque. "Everyone will recall that sad episode in the history of Quebec and Canada," Bouchard intoned mournfully.

As if anxious to pass the buck, Peter Lougheed seemed to agree. "Quebec takes a walk," he said in a televised exchange with Trudeau in 1994, "and we've got a country where the *legitimacy* of the constitution is questioned by that."

"Quebec wouldn't have walked if you hadn't broken up the Gang of Eight," Trudeau was quick to remind him. "My feeling, going into that conference, is, we'd get you all or we wouldn't get any of you. I never dreamt that you people would break your Gang of Eight, and perhaps in my heart I was hoping that you wouldn't."[1] As for legitimacy, Quebec hadn't been left out of the new constitution by law or by convention, signature or no signature, as Premier Bourassa's use of the notwithstanding clause had demonstrated.[2]

Canada's narrow escape from chaos, if not disintegration, forced Prime Minister Chrétien's hand. To appease the soft nationalists in Quebec and rebuild his party in the province, he introduced a motion recognizing Quebec as a distinct society.[3] He went on to pass a law giving all five regions a veto on future constitutional amendments, and he made a commitment not to use federal spending power to create new shared-cost programs in areas of exclusive provincial jurisdiction without the consent of a majority of the provinces. Unlike Meech Lake and Charlottetown, however, these concessions were subject to repeal at any time, and though it might be politically difficult for a future government to discard them, they bore no constitutional consequence. And unlike Mulroney, Chrétien didn't give without getting something more important in return. Fed up and furious with the deceit of the PQ's two referendum questions, he risked arousing the sleeping dogs of separatism by implementing the Clarity Act, which basically declared that no Canadian Parliament would ever negotiate the secession of any province without the approval of a clear majority of its citizens to a clear question in a fair referendum.

When Quebecers accepted it as a reasonable condition rather than a high-handed attack on their right to self-determination, Lucien Bouchard realized—just as René Lévesque had in 1982—that his dreams of sovereignty were going nowhere, and he quit politics shortly afterwards. In 2000, more Quebecers voted for Chrétien's Liberals than for the Bloc Québécois. In 2003, the Parti Québécois was defeated by the provincial Liberals under Jean Charest, a former Mulroney Cabinet minister and the most federalist leader of the province since Jean Lesage.

TWENTY

Charter Canadians

As Pierre Trudeau warned, as Jean Chrétien witnessed, as Robert Bourassa experienced, and as Brian Mulroney learned, the constitution is a battlefield from which few politicians return unscathed. But battles make a history and often make a nation. Certainly Canada emerged transformed after 1982. It had cut its last significant colonial link, with only the monarchy still to go. It had decided on how to amend its own constitution, based on the equality of provinces. It had entrenched the official status of English and French at the national level and in New Brunswick, minority-language education wherever the numbers warranted it, provincial ownership of natural resources, the principle of equalization, and the existence of aboriginal rights and multicultural communities. The unilateral power of the federal government had been checked. The self-interested ambitions of the premiers had been tamed. The *indépendantistes* had been bested. Canadians had been pushed irrevocably towards breaking with their old customs of deference to authority, rule by elites, and an inward-looking provincialism.

Trudeau's vision of a bilingual, multicultural country rooted in individual freedom and social justice—a civic patriotism, in other words, rather than an ethnic nationalism—was embraced with remarkable alacrity by English Canada and new Canadians. But it proved a harder sell in French Quebec, slower to take root and maybe even impossible. Francophone Québécois see themselves as a majority shackled by history to an equal and opposite majority, and crises follow as night the day whenever events remind them of their actual minority status. Despite ongoing attempts to cast their nationalism as liberal and pluralistic, its very essence is to conserve a distinct society in which change and *les autres* aren't really wanted.

Thus, thirty years after the introduction of the Charter of Rights and Freedoms, it was still possible to hear a Parti Québécois MLA declare, "Multiculturalism may be a Canadian value, but it's not a Quebec one. We haven't signed the constitution of Canada because it contains this notion of multiculturalism."[1]

The ethnic dualism upon which most Quebecers want to construct a political and constitutional dualism remains a utopian fantasy. Understandable, to be sure, but refuted by history and unachievable in practice. Quebec has never been ethnically pure, even in the days of New France, and neither has the so-called Rest of Canada. And while Confederation was, in part, a dualistic arrangement between two socio-logical nations divided by language and religion, it also recognized the rights of the English-speaking, Protestant minority within the territory of Quebec and the French-speaking, Roman Catholic minority without—imperfectly protected in the past, but now entrenched in the supreme law of the land.

Caught between the rock of individual freedom and the hard place of collective survival, between national unity and two nations, Canada may be doomed. The question isn't whether Trudeau's strategy of official bilingualism and entrenched language rights has or has not succeeded according to his plan. The question is whether a strategy of two unilingual territories and a two-headed partnership with one province would have succeeded any better. The independence of Quebec may indeed prove the only workable option.

But there are rays of hope for those who believe in the Canadian experiment as a model of diversity and tolerance for the world. This hope doesn't depend on any more quixotic attempts to satiate the nationalists' demands for power, money and a special status. It lies, however flickering and easily extinguished, with the next generation of francophone Quebecers. Though their hearts undoubtedly belong first and foremost to Quebec, young Québécois have become more confident about their language, their culture, and themselves than their parents or grandparents ever were. The Conquest of 1763 no longer looms like a bogeyman in their lives. There aren't any priests or despots trying to keep them poor and frightened (except, of course, for the nationalist elites and language police who want to deny them the bilingualism necessary to earn better salaries or to pursue opportunities in a bigger world). They rarely experience the sting of being denied a management job because they are French-speaking or the shame of racist taunts from a privileged minority on top of the hill. They take pride, not shame, at welcoming thousands of out-of-province students to their campuses, tens of thousands of American tourists to their festivals, and the jobs brought by multinational companies. While they may remain for the most part unfamiliar and uncomfortable with anglophone Canadians, more and more of them travel for business or pleasure, pick up a second language for work or fun, cheer when the Maple Leaf is raised at an Olympic medal ceremony or international hockey tournament, and get to know people of different races and cultures in their schoolyards, their neighbourhoods, or their offices. They are adapting to realities that have almost nothing to do with Canadian politics or even Quebec independence: the unprecedented migration of peoples, the need of an aging and declining population for skilled and unskilled labour, and the displacement of French as a global asset by English, Spanish and Mandarin.

Quebec nationalism isn't about social justice or linguistic equality anymore. It's about the survival of the French language and a unique culture in contemporary North America. As in the past, so in the future, there will be those who will argue, eloquently and passionately, even with some logic, that the way to survive is to retrench behind laws in the only jurisdiction where French Canadians constitute a majority. On behalf of the people, they will say, the state must constrict the rights and freedoms of individual citizens, francophones and non-francophones alike. They will wave flags, sing anthems, lead crusades against kirpans and niqabs to deflect attention from the true nature of their power-mongering.

Yet there will always be brave souls who will resist the "state of siege" mentality and go over the barricades as the best chance for survival. They will point to Bombardier or Cirque du Soleil, to Paul Desmarais or Robert Lepage, to Wajdi Mouawad or Alexandre Bilodeau, as evidence that the best in Quebec can be among the best in Canada and in the world. Unless they are already among the elites who can afford to send their children to English private schools, they will realize that their own children are more disadvantaged by Bill 101 than are the multilingual children of immigrants. If nationalist-driven economics compels them to leave the province in search of jobs, as happened so tragically around the turn of the twentieth century, they will find their right to work elsewhere in Canada protected by the constitution; they will find French-language services guaranteed by the federal government and the government of New Brunswick; and they will find French-language schooling wherever the numbers warrant.

Moreover, when the percentage of francophone Quebecers diminishes decade after decade, as it most certainly will, the French language will remain an official language of Canada. Bilingualism will continue to be an advantage, if not a prerequisite, for anyone aspiring to the highest positions in politics or the public service. Its strength in Ottawa in turn will strengthen it across Canada and North America, at the United Nations and the G20, within the NATO alliance and the Asia-Pacific

Economic Cooperation meetings, in a way that no independent government of Quebec could ever come close to matching.

Great nations aren't built in a generation or even a century. Good constitutions aren't written for short-term politics. And Pierre Trudeau was rare among politicians in having an almost Chinese perspective of the long march of history. He spoke of crafting a constitution that would last a thousand years. Canada was still a very young country in his eyes. It had yet to master the patience to bear a week of crisis or even a decade of darkness with equanimity and faith. Its unity and identity were still to be forged. He knew, too, that the most enduring legacy of the Constitution Act wasn't the mechanics of the amending formula or the absence of Quebec's signature but the entrenchment of the Charter of Rights and Freedoms. Faster and more thoroughly than Trudeau had ever imagined, however, the Charter had crystallized into a symbol of national pride, national identity, and national citizenship that began to bind Canadians of every region, language, and ethnicity to a set of values and principles as tightly as the steel rods of the Canadian Pacific Railway had bound the scattered and diverse communities from sea to sea almost exactly one hundred years earlier. In one poll conducted on the tenth anniversary of the November 1981 First Ministers' Conference, Canadians placed the Charter ahead of the national anthem, the flag, the monarchy, bilingualism, and the CBC as an important symbol of Canadian identity.[2] More than a symbol, it changed the political and legal system of the country as surely as the CPR had changed its economics and demographics.

While scholars and lawyers continue to debate the Charter's impact for good or evil—whether judges have twisted it to intervene unduly in the political process or failed to go far enough; whether it is breeding a litigious, rights-conscious culture of entitlement or nurturing a fairer, more egalitarian society; whether it ought to be able to overturn laws or merely send them back to the elected politicians for improvement— nobody questions that it has had a radical, almost daily influence on public policy, from criminal procedure to racial discrimination, from language to abortion, from Sunday shopping to refugee processing, from health care to same-sex marriage.

The Charter has also remained extraordinarily popular. In 2002, on the occasion of its twentieth anniversary, a poll found that 88 percent of Canadians—*and 91 percent of Quebecers*—considered it a good thing.[3] So good, in fact, that very few politicians dared to touch the notwithstanding clause in the first twenty-five years of the Charter's history. In 1982, René Lévesque used it holus-bolus on every piece of provincial legislation past or present to protest the Constitution Act, but that rather petulant override lapsed as soon as he left office. In 1986, a Conservative government in Saskatchewan used it to force its striking civil servants back to work, though the Supreme Court subsequently decided that the legislation didn't violate freedom of association anyway. When Robert Bourassa bragged about suspending fundamental liberties to protect his outdoor-sign legislation in 1988, the backlash cost him three anglophone Cabinet ministers and contributed to the death of the Meech Lake Accord. In other words, while there are always a few politicians and interest groups who demand the notwithstanding clause be invoked whenever a court reaches a decision they don't like, governments and citizens alike are rarely willing to pay the price. Far from saving the nation from the ravages of Charter law, as Sterling Lyon and others had hoped, it has proven to be a "paper tiger."[4] Peter Lougheed himself came to argue that omnibus applications such as Quebec's or pre-emptive uses such as Saskatchewan's should be outlawed, and he returned to the idea that the override provision should require 60 percent of the legislators rather than a simple majority.[5]

Of course, it might be argued that Canada's demographic revolution has been much more significant. Waves of recent arrivals from Europe, Asia, Africa, and South America have shaken up the old cultures and cityscapes of English and French Canada to an astonishing degree. However, it is the Charter that has provided the intellectual, legal, and moral structure to accommodate that rapid and overwhelming impact with relative peace and continuity. Gone, or at least numbered, are the days of the discriminatory laws based on race or religion that stained Canada's history and reputation. The Charter stands at the centre of Canadian society as a beacon, a lodestone, a guarantee of freedom and tolerance. As such, it has saved and advanced the dream of the original Fathers of Confederation to create a new nation, open to all the nationalities of the world, respectful of difference, protected by community but grounded in individual liberty and two official languages. One people, one country, one Canada.

In 1968, shortly after he became prime minister, Pierre Trudeau had a private meeting with Louis St. Laurent in Quebec City. To Trudeau's consternation, his elderly and distinguished predecessor, whom he greatly admired, was depressed by the rise of Quebec nationalism and kept admonishing himself for not having done more for the rights of French Canadians. The Confederation bargain remained broken; Laurier's dream had yet to be fulfilled. Trudeau came away with a personal resolve: when it came his turn to retire, he was never going to roll in regrets and second-guessing.[6]

True to his resolve, he normally dismissed the might-have-beens of his time in office with a shrug. He had done his best under the circumstances; he had been cast in the role of pragmatic politician rather than intellectual perfectionist. The rest he left to history. One day in 1992, however, while riding home in a taxi from a television interview, Trudeau let down his actor's guise. Though he was sometimes heard to admit that the notwithstanding clause hadn't turned out to be as bad in practice as he'd once feared, he continued to oppose it in principle. Even its temporary application violated his sense of justice.

"You know," he reflected, "I didn't give a completely candid answer to that question about the First Ministers' Conference in November 1981. It's true I felt I had no choice but to accept the provinces' deal after Davis's call. But I now think it was a mistake. I should have gone for an election or a referendum. Quebec wouldn't have been able to say it was 'left out,' because everybody would have been 'left out,' and Canada would have got a better amending formula and a better charter."[7]

Perhaps, but he seemed to have forgotten, for the moment at least, what the Viennese say about grandmothers, wheels, and a bloody bus.

TIMELINE

May 20, 1980	The Quebec government holds its referendum on sovereignty-association. The No side wins 60–40.
June 9, 1980	Trudeau meets with the ten provincial premiers at 24 Sussex Drive. He presents them with a list of twelve items to be negotiated by federal–provincial ministers and officials over the summer.
September 8–13, 1980	The disastrous First Ministers' Conference on the Constitution takes place in Ottawa. It begins with the premiers' fury over the so-called Kirby report and ends with Trudeau's rejection of the provinces' Château Consensus.
October 1980	Trudeau unveils the federal government's Resolution, nicknamed the People's Package, which is to be approved by the Canadian House of Commons and the Senate before being sent to the British Parliament in London.

The Resolution proposes unilateral patriation of the BNA Act, an amending formula based on the one that had been accepted by all eleven ministers in Victoria in 1971, and a charter of rights.

According to the Victoria formula, changes to the division of powers would require the consent of Ottawa and the four regions (Ontario, Quebec, the Atlantic provinces, and the West). Trudeau adds two referendum mechanisms to break future deadlocks.

Ontario and New Brunswick support the Resolution. Saskatchewan and Nova Scotia with-hold judgment. The others form the Group of Six and dedicate themselves to fighting Ottawa's *coup de force* in the courts, in London, and in their provinces.

Winter 1980–81   The Resolution's legality is challenged in the courts of Manitoba, Newfoundland, and Quebec, with inconclusive results.

A British parliamentary committee questions the Resolution's constitutional legitimacy, throwing doubt on Westminster's quick and automatic approval.

Saskatchewan and Nova Scotia join the Group of Six, now called the Gang of Eight, after failing to find common ground with the federal government.

The Parti Québécois government is re-elected in Quebec on April 13, 1981.

April 16, 1981   The Gang of Eight meets in Ottawa and agrees to an alternative patriation plan, dubbed the April Accord. This accord rejects a charter of rights and puts forward another amending procedure, first proposed by Alberta but known as the Vancouver formula.

The Vancouver formula would require changes in the division of powers to be approved by at least seven provinces representing more than 50 percent of the population. Provinces that choose to opt out of any such amendment would receive financial compensation.

September 28, 1981   The Supreme Court decides that Ottawa's Resolution is legal but "unconstitutional," because it does not meet the convention of requiring substantial (though not unanimous) provincial agreement.

Trudeau is forced back to the negotiating table for one last attempt at a deal.

NOVEMBER 2 TO 5, 1981—FIRST MINISTERS' CONFERENCE IN OTTAWA

Monday Morning	Trudeau, Davis, and Hatfield offer concessions on the Charter of Rights and Freedoms and the amending formula at the televised opening session in the Main Hall.
Monday Afternoon	The first ministers reconvene in private in a fifth-floor meeting room. They discuss the amending formula, without reaching an agreement.
Tuesday Afternoon/ Evening	Three emissaries from the Gang of Eight, with Bill Davis as go-between, present a compromise proposal to Trudeau, who angrily rejects it. The Ontario and Saskatchewan delegations meet by chance during dinner at an Ottawa restaurant.
Wednesday Morning	Saskatchewan puts forward its own compromise, with no success. Lévesque breaks from the Gang of Eight by agreeing to Trudeau's challenge to take the Charter and the amending formula to the people in separate referendums.
Wednesday Afternoon	Ottawa presents two plans to initiate referendums on the amending formula and the Charter. The Kitchen Accord proposes exchanging the Gang of Eight's Vancouver formula (without financial compensation) for Ottawa's Charter (with a notwithstanding clause added).
Wednesday Night	A group of premiers, ministers, and officials meet in Blakeney's suite at the Château Laurier to draw up a final compromise—without inviting Quebec.
Thursday Morning	Ottawa and nine provinces reach an agreement, which will be further modified by phone in the weeks to come. Quebec refuses to sign.

NOTES

PROLOGUE

TWO: A CAN OF WORMS

1. The constitution of Canada is more than the British North America Act, 1867, and its amendments. It includes various British laws and orders in council; certain federal and provincial acts; a number of judicial rulings in London and Ottawa; and a myriad of constitutional conventions, one of which is to play a very important role in this narrative. See James Ross Hurley, *Amending Canada's Constitution: History, Processes, Problems and Prospects* (Ottawa: Ministry of Supply and Services, 1996), p. 11. If truth be told, the United States Constitution (often confused with the Declaration of Independence) is itself a rather turgid read, except for its short, rousing preamble.

2. "I see in the not remote distance one great nationality bound, like the shield of Achilles, by the blue rim of ocean." Thomas D'Arcy McGee, quoted in Christopher Moore, *1867: How the Fathers Made a Deal* (Toronto: McClelland and Stewart, 1997), p. 232.

3. Gerald M. Craig, ed. *Lord Durham's Report* (Toronto: McClelland and Stewart, 1963), pp. 23, 146.

4. "A form of double-majority principle was observed in many instances (but violated in others), according to which issues of concern to a region could be decided only with concurrence of a majority of the region's members." Kenneth McRoberts, "The Sources of Neo-nationalism in Quebec," in Michael D. Behiels, ed., *Quebec Since 1945: Selected Readings* (Toronto: Copp Clark Pitman, 1987), p. 81.

5. Legislative Assembly, February 6, 1865. Quoted in Janet Ajzenstat, Paul Romney, Ian Gentles, and William D. Gairdner, eds., *Canada's Founding Debates* (Toronto: University of Toronto Press, 2003), p. 279.

6. Quoted in ibid., pp. 279–80. This important caveat challenges the assertion, often put forward by Quebec politicians, that English Canada is a monolith thwarted in its dream of a unitary state by the demands of French Quebec. It also confirms that Confederation was more than a dualistic bargain between anglophones and francophones, except with regard to language.

7. As the historian Peter Waite observes in his close study of the speeches and newspapers of the time, the Fathers of Confederation paid much less attention to the division of responsibilities than they did to regional representation at the centre, especially in the Senate. P.B. Waite, *The Life and Times of Confederation 1864–1867: Politics, Newspapers, and the Union of British North America* (Toronto: University of Toronto Press, 1962), pp. 108–9, 111, 288, 327.

8. "Since the Great Depression, the hot issues have been those in provincial jurisdiction: health, education and social services. The feds have the cash, they set the rules of encounter. And playing one province off the next is the sport. This is all dressed up in the need for national standards and for a common level of services in social-issue areas." Bob Plecas, *Bill Bennett: A Mandarin's View* (Vancouver/Toronto: Douglas and McIntyre, 2006), p. 93.

9. The Supreme Court of Canada put it to death in September 1981, a few weeks before the November conference.

10. The five were Australia, New Zealand, Newfoundland, the Union of South Africa, and the Irish Free State.

11. There wasn't even an agreement on the words "patriation" and "repatriation." The advocates of the former argued that since the BNA Act had always resided in London, it wasn't being brought *back* to Canada. The proponents of the latter insisted that the BNA Act had been drafted in the Canadian colonies, and that "patriation" wasn't a genuine word. See Hurley, *Amending Canada's Constitution*, p. 25.

12. A federal document in 1965 admitted the principle of "prior consultation and agreement with the provinces," though not "the nature and degree of provincial participation." See Roy Romanow, John Whyte, Howard Leeson, *Canada … Notwithstanding: The Making of the Constitution 1976–1982* (Toronto: Carswell/Methuen, 1984), pp. 137–38; Hurley, *Amending Canada's Constitution*, pp. 18–21.

13. Trudeau, in Thomas S. Axworthy and Pierre Elliott Trudeau, eds., *Towards a Just Society: The Trudeau Years* (Toronto: Penguin Books, 1992), p. 418.

THREE: TIME FOR A CHANGE

1. Keith Banting and Richard Simeon, eds., *And No One Cheered: Federalism, Democracy and the Constitution Act* (Toronto: Methuen, 1983), p. 51.

2. Trudeau, in Axworthy and Trudeau, *Just Society*, pp. 419–20.

3. Denis Monière, *Ideologies in Quebec: The Historical Development* (Toronto: University of Toronto Press, 1981), pp. 230–31; *Royal Commission on Bilingualism and Biculturalism*, book 3A, *The Work World* (Ottawa: Queen's Printer, 1969), pp. 22–24; Behiels, *Quebec Since 1945*, p. 59.

4. Pierre Elliott Trudeau, *Federalism and the French Canadians* (Toronto: Macmillan of Canada, 1968), pp. 47–48.

5. See Trudeau, in Axworthy and Trudeau, *Just Society*, p. 439, for a list of the six demands Jean Lesage presented to the federal-provincial conference in July 1960.

6. "Jean Lesage himself had no precise idea of the content of special status; it was for him in large part a convenient slogan to appease the nationalists in his own

government and party and to be used in competition with his opponents." Dale C. Thomson, *Jean Lesage and the Quiet Revolution* (Toronto: Macmillan of Canada, 1984), p. 134.

7. *A Preliminary Report of the Royal Commission on Bilingualism and Biculturalism* (Ottawa: Queen's Printer, 1965), p. 13.

8. Canada, House of Commons, *Debates*, December 17, 1962, p. 2723. Pearson perpetuated a false duality, it could be argued, by failing to include the aboriginals among Canada's "founding races." And Trudeau took issue with the idea that Canada was a "bicultural" society, since it is made up of people from many cultures. Also: "My viewpoint was one of sympathy to the provinces, especially to Quebec, in their desire for more control and for more resources ... By enforcing centralism perhaps acceptable to some provinces but not to Quebec, and by insisting that Quebec must be like the others, we could destroy Canada. This became my doctrine of federalism." *Mike: The Memoirs of the Right Honourable Lester B. Pearson*, vol. 3 (Toronto: University of Toronto Press, 1975), p. 239.

9. *Maclean's*, February 8, 1964. In Pierre Elliott Trudeau, *Against the Current: Selected Writings 1939–1996* (Toronto: McClelland and Stewart, 1996), p. 214.

FOUR: THE SCHOOL OF BLACKMAIL

1. Michel Vastel, *Bourassa* (Toronto: Macmillan of Canada, 1991), p. 56. Bourassa also said, "I asked for ten days to reflect on it and the fact that I asked for a delay shows that I hadn't yet reached a decision ... It had only been six months since the October Crisis. There was a nationalist surge in Quebec; I couldn't take the risk of reigniting another seven or eight years of political violence. The climate did not allow me to take incalculable risks." Michel Vastel, *Trudeau le Québécois* (Montreal: Les Éditions de l'Homme, 1989), pp. 220–21. As a matter of fact, Saskatchewan didn't ratify it either, because Premier Ross Thatcher was defeated by Allan Blakeney in the election on June 30, 1971.

2. Pierre Elliott Trudeau, *Memoirs* (Toronto: McClelland and Stewart, 1993), p. 234. Peter Lougheed and Allan Blakeney, attending their first First Ministers' Conference a month after the collapse of the Victoria Charter, were shocked by the virulence with which Trudeau attacked Bourassa over dinner: "If you had any guts, this problem would be over." Allan Blakeney, *An Honourable Calling: Political Memoirs* (Toronto: University of Toronto Press, 2008), p. 85.

3. Quoted in Monière, *Ideologies in Quebec*, p. 299. Quebec separatists don't like being called separatists. They consider it pejorative, akin to referring to Blacks as Negroes or *Québécois* as *Canadiens français*. Their real problem is that outright separation has never been able to win support among more than a third of the province in the polls. To try to circumvent that awkward fact, the separatists coined a new meaning for the word "sovereignty" and marketed themselves as *souverainistes*. Academics and journalists bought into this Orwellian newspeak, despite—or because of—the fact that it implied something less than independence. Although René Lévesque and other moderates sincerely desired an amicable association with the rest of Canada, their first purpose was to take control of the levers of power—that is, to separate. "My intentions are to get out," Lévesque stated

flatly, to the shock and concern of his fellow premiers at their first meeting after his victory. Graham Fraser, *PQ: René Lévesque and the Parti Québécois in Power* (Montreal and Kingston: McGill-Queen's University Press, 2001), p. 87.

4. Trudeau, *Memoirs*, pp. 247–48.

5. Transcripts, First Ministers' Conference on the Constitution, September 8, 1980.

6. Donald Johnston, ed., *Pierre Trudeau Speaks Out on Meech Lake* (Toronto: General Paperbacks, 1990), p. 17.

7. Government of Alberta, "Harmony in Diversity: A New Federalism for Canada," Government of Alberta Position Paper on Constitutional Change (October 1978), Appendix A, p. 26.

8. "The general tactical position of the other provinces was to promote their devolutionary demands by linking up with Lévesque's. However, the premiers never precisely defined how far in that direction they were prepared to go, even though that question would inevitably present a fundamental point of departure. Moreover, the pervasive sense of suspicion and mistrust about Ottawa's intentions occupied more of the premiers' attention than the motivations of Lévesque, especially when the list of provincial demands was endorsed by the new premier. In retrospect, the provincial 'shopping list' was too unwieldy, general, and unrealistic, especially in light of Trudeau's growing apprehension about the centrifugal forces within Canada." Romanow, Whyte, Leeson, *Canada … Notwithstanding*, p. 5.

9. See Fraser, *PQ*, chapter 12; Pierre Duchesne, *Jacques Parizeau*, tome 2, *Le Baron, 1970–1985* (Montreal: Éditions Québec Amérique, 2002), chapter 15.

10. Robert Sheppard and Michael Valpy, *The National Deal: The Fight for a Canadian Constitution* (Toronto: Macmillan of Canada, 1982), p. 33; John English, *Just Watch Me: The Life of Pierre Elliott Trudeau*, vol. 2, *1968–2000* (Toronto: Alfred A. Knopf Canada, 2009), pp. 452–54. Jean Chrétien remembered the decision being taken at a lunch a couple of days before the speech. "And it was at that moment that, after a lot of planning for this part of the agenda, we decided he would say that if we were to win the referendum, there would be a big push to change this country, and to give all Canadians, especially the Francophones in Quebec, a sense of real equality within our society." Jean Chrétien, "The Negotiation of the Charter: The Federal Government Perspective," in *Litigating the Values of a Nation: The Canadian Charter of Rights and Freedoms*, Joseph M. Weiler and Robin M. Elliot, eds. (Toronto: Carswell, 1986), pp. 5–6.

11. Sheppard and Valpy, *The National Deal*, p. 32.

12. Trudeau, in Axworthy and Trudeau, *Just Society*, p. 419.

PART 1

FIVE: THE PLAYERS

1. The delegations were supposed to be restricted to one first minister, one Cabinet minister, and one official. But most couldn't resist bringing along at least one more elected politician (including Brenda Robertson, New Brunswick's minister of health, the only woman in the room) and a few more advisers. Although there were

sound technicians hidden in booths behind dark glass, there weren't any recording secretaries or simultaneous translators.

2. "Pierre Elliott Trudeau: Memoirs," vol. 2, ep. 2 (Montreal: Productions La Fête, 1994).

3. English, *Just Watch Me*, pp. 349–50. In a private conversation with the author, Trudeau insisted that his pirouette was completely spontaneous.

4. George Radwanski, *Trudeau* (Toronto: Macmillan of Canada, 1978), p. 210.

5. Trudeau, *Memoirs*, p. 270.

6. Trudeau wasn't alone in that view. In 1979, the Economic Council of Canada warned that the federal government was becoming "increasingly powerless" to manage the national economy. The C.D. Howe Research Institute reported in April 1980 that it was concerned about the "process of disintegration." Richard Gwyn, *The Northern Magus* (Toronto: McClelland and Stewart, 1980), pp. 256, 285.

7. "The federal government is the balance wheel of the federal system, and the federal system means using counterweights. If one province is very rich and another very poor, my view is that there should be some redistribution of resources, with the federal government in charge of making sure that the distribution is done fairly." Trudeau, *Memoirs*, p. 290.

8. Canada, House of Commons, *Debates*, March 23, 1981, p. 8519.

9. Fisheries, in fact, was added at the meeting by Premier Brian Peckford.

10. "If we permit the erection of barriers at provincial boundaries, then we are on the path to setting up quasi-sovereign states. Surely, if being a Canadian means anything, it means the liberty to move anywhere in the country." "Briefing for the Delegation of the Government of Canada," September 8–12, 1980, LAC MG32-G15, vol. 12, file 6, p. C.7. Mobility rights were considered doubly important because they contributed to national unity and equality of opportunity. The right of a Canadian citizen to own property in any province was in, then out, then in, then out again over the course of the negotiations.

11. Trudeau, *Memoirs*, p. 300.

12. André Burelle, *Pierre Elliott Trudeau: L'intellectuel et le politique* (Montreal: Éditions Fides, 2005), p. 65, footnote 107.

13. Quoted in Stephen Clarkson and Christina McCall, *Trudeau and Our Times*, vol. 1, *The Magnificent Obsession* (Toronto: McClelland and Stewart, 1990), p. 277. Trudeau also replaced Gordon Robertson, a sage and experienced mandarin, for being "too much of a gentleman." Trudeau quoted in ibid., p. 281. André Burelle, one of the rare "soft" nationalists in the PMO, claims he was frozen out of the inner circle of advisers, because his vigorous denunciation of the federal government's post-referendum strategy troubled the prime minister "to the point that he risked being paralyzed." Burelle, *Trudeau: L'intellectuel*, p. 81.

14. Trudeau's invitation wasn't simply good manners. "This will convey the image of determination to work continuously and, if the invitation is accepted, will minimize the opportunity for the group of eight to use the lunch hour to paper over any cracks which may develop in their common front during the opening session." Government of Canada, "A Scenario for the FMC," October 31, 1981, LAC MG32-G15, vol. 15, file 7, tab A, p. 3.

15. Howard Leeson, "The Patriation Minutes" [hereafter Leeson notes], p. 24.

16. Sheppard and Valpy, *The National Deal*, p. 39.

17. Angus MacLean, *Making It Home: Memoirs of J. Angus MacLean* (Charlottetown: Ragweed Press, 1998), p. 246.

18. Canada, "A Scenario for the FMC," p. 7. Many participants, both at the time and decades later, dismissed Premier Buchanan as a nobody at the conference, a hanger-on, a cipher who seemed incapable of stating a clear position one way or another. He never responded to several requests for an interview for this book.

19. John English, *Citizen of the World: The Life of Pierre Elliott Trudeau*, vol. 1, *1919–1968* (Toronto: Alfred A. Knopf Canada, 2006), p. 61. According to English, Trudeau was moved to tears after first reading it as a teenager.

SIX: THE PIERRE AND RENÉ SHOW

1. Sheppard and Valpy, *The National Deal*, p. 274.

2. Canada, "A Scenario for the FMC," p. 6.

3. Blakeney, *An Honourable Calling*, p. 85.

4. Gérard Pelletier, *Years of Impatience, 1950–1960*, Alan Brown, trans. (Toronto: Methuen, 1984), p. 27; English, *Citizen of the World*, p. 261.

5. René Lévesque, *Memoirs* (Toronto: McClelland and Stewart, 1986), p. 323.

6. Pelletier, *Years of Impatience*, p. 26. Also in Lévesque, *Memoirs*, p. 150; English, *Citizen of the World*, p. 310. The exact year is uncertain.

7. Pelletier, *Years of Impatience*, p. 27.

8. Trudeau, *Memoirs*, p. 241.

9. André Laurendeau, quoted in Fraser, *PQ*, p. 7.

10. "In times of stress—and the stress grew steadily during his premiership—his natural conservatism led him to resist aspects of that very Quiet Revolution that he had initiated. French-Canadian nationalist sentiments, stimulated by him during his first years in office, became a nightmare. At times he gave the impression he was riding a tiger and was unable to dismount." Thomson, *Jean Lesage*, p. viii.

11. See Max Nemni and Monique Nemni, *Young Trudeau 1919–1944: Son of Quebec, Father of Canada*, William Johnson, trans. (Toronto: McClelland and Stewart, 2006), and English, *Citizen of the World*, chapter 2, for a full account of Trudeau's brief flirtation with Quebec nationalism.

12. René Lévesque, *An Option for Quebec* (Toronto: McClelland and Stewart, 1968), p. 14.

13. His aides never saw him angrier than when his wife, Corinne, inadvertently gave what looked like a Nazi salute at the end of a few remarks she made during a referendum rally. Martine Tremblay, *Derrière les portes closes: René Lévesque et l'exercice du pouvoir, 1976–1985* (Montreal: Québec Amérique, 2006), p. 58.

14. René Lévesque, "For an Independent Quebec," *Foreign Affairs* 54, 4 (July 1976), in Behiels, *Quebec Since 1945*, p. 268.

15. Fraser, *PQ*, p. 54.

16. Lévesque, *Option*, p. 26.

17. See Trudeau, *Federalism*, p. 180.

18. Quoted in Radwanski, *Trudeau*, p. 81. As a provocative essayist in the 1950s, Trudeau personally experienced intimidation and punishment for not conforming to the collectivist mentality. But he was spared the more extreme xenophobia encountered by Native Canadians, francophone immigrants from Haiti or Senegal, and Jews.

19. Trudeau, *Memoirs*, pp. 72–73. See also Pierre Elliott Trudeau, "Lettre ouverte aux Québécois," *La Presse*, July 15, 1980.

20. Trudeau, *Federalism*, p. 4.

21. Ibid., p. 158.

22. Radwanski, *Trudeau*, p. 179.

23. Lévesque, *Memoirs*, p. 228.

24. Moore, *1867*, pp. 149, 142.

25. Behiels, *Quebec Since 1945*, p. 16.

26. Lévesque, *Memoirs*, p. 201, my italics. "Ever since I began working with him, René Lévesque seems to me to have understood and empathized with the contradictions facing every Québécois which compel him to strive for liberation and at the same time prevent him from achieving it," said Camille Laurin, a psychiatrist as well as a Cabinet minister (quoted in Fraser, *PQ*, p. 14). Lesage was torn between his loyalty to Quebec and his loyalty to Canada (see Thomson, *Jean Lesage*, p. 130). Bourassa's own ambiguity was reflected in his proposed version of the 1980 referendum question: "Do you wish to replace the existing constitutional order by two sovereign states associated in an economic union, a union which would be responsible to a parliament elected by universal suffrage?" Vastel, *Bourassa*, p. 73.

27. Lévesque, *Option*, p. 27. This clear statement should put to rest the idea that Lévesque wasn't really a separatist, or that sovereignty didn't really mean independence.

28. Tremblay, *Derrière les portes closes*, p. 224. Most francophone voters who chose Yes in the referendum still believed they would be sending MPs to Ottawa, and polls consistently showed that more than two-thirds of Quebecers said they were deeply attached to both Canada and Quebec at the same time. See also Godin, *René Lévesque*, p. 148.

29. Lévesque, *Memoirs*, p. 201, my italics. In other words, the group was to be equal, not the individual. "Because they are a conquered people and a minority, French Canadians have always been chiefly concerned with group rights. Their public philosophy might be called Rousseauian: the expression of a 'general will' to survive. The English Canadian, as is equally befitting his majority position, is far more concerned with individual rights and with that characteristic North American middle-class ideal, equality of opportunity. The English Canadian's public philosophy might be somewhat grandly described as Lockean." Ramsay Cook, *Canada and the French-Canadian Question* (Toronto: Macmillan of Canada, 1966), p. 146.

30. Lévesque to Robert Bourassa, quoted in Fraser, *PQ*, pp. 41–42.

31. Trudeau, in Axworthy and Trudeau, *Just Society*, p. 441.

32. "Considering the past and so many claims so often reiterated, any right-minded person couldn't help thinking that nothing less than greater autonomy and better guarantees for Quebec were in question. If not, it was just an airy promise, or else something no democratic politician could permit himself at this moment—sheer deceit." Lévesque, *Memoirs,* p. 308.

33. Pierre Elliott Trudeau, *Essential Trudeau*, Ron Graham, ed. (Toronto: McClelland and Stewart, 1998), p. 147. There's an expanded version in Trudeau, *Memoirs*, p. 283. Critics who argued that Trudeau had not gone far enough in offering Quebec new powers forgot that his efforts to negotiate a Powers' Package hit an impasse in September 1980 because there was no give to the premiers' take.

SEVEN: *COUP DE FORCE*

1. Roy McMurtry, interview with author; Sheppard and Valpy, *The National Deal*, pp. 4–5.

2. *Ottawa Citizen*, August 22, 1980.

3. Claude Morin, *Lendemains piégés: Du référendum à la nuit des longs couteaux* (Montreal: Boréal, 1998), p. 113. My translations.

4. Government of Canada, "Report to Cabinet on Constitutional Discussions, Summer 1980, and the Outlook for the First Ministers' Conference and Beyond" [hereafter Kirby report], August 30, 1980, LAC R12685, vol. 5, file 14, p. 60 (his italics).

5. Transcripts, First Ministers' Conference, September 1980.

6. Kirby report, p. 38.

7. Government of Canada, "Briefing for the Delegation of the Government of Canada," LAC MG32-G15, vol. 15, file 1, p. 3. On the front of another confidential document regarding the Charter from Roger Tassé, dated August 5, 1980, Trudeau scrawled by hand, "I believe in some concessions now, and more later, to increase the scope of the consensus."

8. Michael Kirby, interview with author. Kirby also noted that the leak of his memo, though not deliberate, might have helped the process in the long run by convincing the premiers of Ottawa's determination to move ahead, and therefore pressuring them to negotiate.

9. Sheppard and Valpy, *The National Deal*, p. 64. Trudeau responded by saying, "The people of Quebec showed last May that they didn't agree with the view of Canada held by Mr. Lévesque."

10. MacLean, *Making It Home*, pp. 242–43. MacLean surprised many people by the vigour with which he attacked the federal government in his opening statement at the September conference: "Canada is much more than our federal government. We as provinces have views and perspectives which are integral to our national well being. Being cast as opponents to some supposed national will is as uncomfortable as it is unreasonable ... In other words, a common economy has come to mean that it is common for some sections of the country to prosper, and common for others to cope with built-in economic disadvantages." "Notes for an Address to the First Ministers' Conference," September 8, 1980, doc. 800-14/015.

11. Trudeau, *Memoirs*, p. 306. André Burelle argues that the Château Consensus was the straw that broke Trudeau's back. It upset the delicate balance that Burelle claims had existed between the prime minister's communitarian, personalist reason and his anti-communitarian, individualist passion. "For the real question one must ask is not why M. Trudeau decided to crush Lévesque and the other premiers, but why, having decided to move without their consent, he didn't profit from the opportunity to put in place the minimum renewal [of the constitution] promised during the referendum and offered to Quebec in September 1980." Burelle, *Trudeau: L'intellectuel*, pp. 65–66, 68, 88.

12. Johnston, *Pierre Trudeau Speaks Out*, p. 54.

13. Trudeau, *Memoirs*, pp. 307–09.

14. "Statement by the Prime Minister on the Canadian Constitution," Ottawa, October 2, 1980, p. 4.

15. Kirby, interview with author.

16. Clarkson and McCall, *Magnificent Obsession*, p. 361.

17. "The concept of acting unilaterally can give rise to accusations of arrogance, contempt and bad-faith bargaining. It will be easier for the provinces to campaign against arrogance than to campaign against detailed constitutional changes." Kirby report, p. 35.

18. Angus MacLean of Prince Edward Island actually hesitated a day before joining the other five premiers. "Caught between sizable transfer payments from Ottawa and Conservative party ties, the political economy of the island dictated no clear position. Reluctantly, the government chose to emphasize its fraternal connections with the federal Conservative party and the opposing provinces." Romanow, Whyte, Leeson, *Canada ... Notwithstanding*, p. 108.

19. "If the Canadian Parliament asks me for something and it has a majority supporting a resolution, there is nothing much I can do to prevent it." Margaret Thatcher to Pierre Trudeau, Johnston, *Pierre Trudeau Speaks Out*, p. 59.

20. Government of Canada, "Patriation of the Constitution: Validity of Unilateral Action," August 26, 1980, LAC MG32-G15, vol. 15, file 4, p. 1. Also: "It may therefore be fairly safely assumed that if the question somehow came before a Canadian court, it would uphold the legal validity of the U.K. legislation effecting patriation. The court might very well, however, make a pronouncement, not necessary for the decision, that the patriation process was in violation of established conventions and therefore in one sense was 'unconstitutional' even though legally valid." Kirby report, p. 51. The federal government was particularly skittish because its attempt to reform the Senate in 1978 had been ruled unconstitutional by the Supreme Court. But Trudeau ruled out the referendum option during the winter of 1980–81 as "a 'revolutionary' step, involving too sharp a break with the original British basis of Canada's constitutional system." Edward McWhinney, *Canada and the Constitution 1979–1982: Patriation and the Charter of Rights* (Toronto: University of Toronto Press, 1982), p. 46. As late as the summer of 1981, the prime minister was still arguing that a referendum would be too divisive and too difficult to win. Vastel, *Trudeau le Québécois*, p. 269.

21. A secret memorandum from Michael Kirby to the prime minister highlighted how reluctant the British government was to force a Commons vote, despite Mrs. Thatcher's earlier promise to do so "as expeditiously as possible." She was having trouble with a sizeable number of her Conservative backbenchers. Emotions were running high among some MPs, her House Leader was "extremely apprehensive" about Ottawa's timetable, and there was pressure to wait for the results of the provinces' three court challenges. "Report on Mr. Chrétien's London Trip," March 27, 1981, LAC MG32-G15, vol. 15, file 9. For a wry account of provincial operating methods, see Plecas, *Bill Bennett*, p. 150.

22. Gil Rémillard, "Legality, Legitimacy and the Supreme Court," in Banting and Simeon, *And No One Cheered*, p. 203.

23. See www.canlii.org/en/ca/scc/doc/1981/1981canlii25/1981canlii25.html, p. 909.

24. Ibid. p. 905.

25. McMurtry, interview with author.

26. Laskin lecture, in Trudeau, *Against the Current*, p. 256. Others saw it as a brilliant compromise between the letter of the law and the spirit of Confederation.

27. Ibid.

28. Trudeau, *Memoirs*, p. 316. In fact, Trudeau's advisers were divided on the need to respond to the Supreme Court's decision, and those who thought there was a need were divided between the question of constitutional legitimacy and the question of practical politics. It was an important debate because it affected whether Ottawa had to make a compromise offer or not.

29. Ibid., p. 317. One federal official suggested leasing a giant electronic billboard in Piccadilly Circus with the message "Let Our People Go!"

EIGHT: DEADLOCK

1. Government of Canada, "Prime Minister's Briefing Book—Meeting of First Ministers—November 1981," October 30, 1981, LAC R12685, vol. 5, file 2, tab 2(e), no pagination.

2. Earlier versions also required the support of at least 50 percent of the population in the western and Atlantic regions, but that requirement had been dropped by the final draft in an attempt to satisfy Alberta and Prince Edward Island.

3. Canada, House of Commons, *Debates*, March 23, 1981, p. 8513.

4. "The idea and details of a referendum as a way to amend the Constitution had never been debated by the CCMC or the first ministers before its appearance in the resolution." Romanow, Whyte, Leeson, *Canada ... Notwithstanding*, p. 106. A secret federal poll, conducted during the summer of 1980, revealed that 71 percent of Canadians wanted a referendum—which had to carry in every province to win—if there was no agreement between Ottawa and the provinces. Government of Canada, "Results of a Survey on Attitudes to Constitutional Change," July 18, 1980, LAC MG32-G15, vol. 15, file 6, p. 3. The idea was well lodged in Trudeau's mind going into the September 1980 conference. "If it appears that there is near unanimity, you might focus the discussion on the federal proposal for a referendum at the initiative of the electorate in the event of *dissent* of

Parliament or a legislature." Canada, "Briefing for the Delegation," p. 32.
See also Burelle, *Trudeau: L'intellectuel*, p. 79, footnote 124.

5. Kirby, interview with author.

6. The Vancouver formula, later incorporated into the final agreement, also set a
    time limit of three years for approval of a constitutional amendment by Parliament
    and the provincial legislatures, starting from the day it was initially approved
    anywhere. That technicality was to lead to the dramatic collapse of the Meech
    Lake Accord in 1990. "The net effect of this new amending formula, little appreci-
    ated at the time, was to stack the odds heavily against any major modifications in
    the constitution." Patrick J. Monahan, *Meech Lake: The Inside Story* (Toronto:
    University of Toronto Press, 1991), pp. 16, 28–36. Jean Chrétien, among others,
    countered that constitutions should be difficult to amend, lest they be changed too
    often and according to the political fashions of the day. Interview with author.

7. "I said quite clearly that if it were the only thing that were needed to create a
    consensus on a package, I would go along, so it was not dismissed out of hand,
    but it is a concept of Canada which once again incorporates the notion of a free
    association of provinces. We hold that Canada is a free association of peoples."
    September 13, 1980, quoted in *Globe and Mail*, November 4, 1981. Trudeau's
    officials only recommended acceptance on two conditions: one, the issue of
    financial compensation be dropped, and two, if seven provinces approved an
    amendment and Ottawa did not, 3 percent of the electorate could initiate a
    national referendum on the issue. Government of Canada, "Patriation, including
    Amending Formula: Notes for an Introductory Statement by the Prime Minister,"
    September 5, 1980, LAC MG32-G15, vol. 12, file 7, p. B.4.

8. *Globe and Mail*, November 3, 1981.

9. Leeson notes, p. 3.

10. See Ajzenstat et al., *Canada's Founding Debates*, chapters 11 and 12.

11. Axworthy and Trudeau, *Just Society*, pp. 247–48, my italics.

12. It was more a symbolic than substantive shift, since Ontario's population virtually
    guaranteed it a veto under the Vancouver formula. It was also a signal to the Gang
    of Eight that Trudeau's commitment to the Victoria formula wasn't carved in stone,
    though Ottawa didn't want to be seen as giving up on a veto for Quebec.

13. Leeson notes, p. 18. There was a technical glitch that would cause Ottawa some
    difficulty later in the day. Under the terms of the proposed Resolution, the Gang of
    Eight's Vancouver formula couldn't be put up against Ottawa's Victoria formula in
    a national referendum because, with Ontario opposed, it didn't meet the 80 percent
    population threshold. Trudeau offered to change the rule and, failing any other
    options, to present the two alternatives to the public. According to parliamentary
    procedure, however, the Resolution that was now before the House of Commons
    could not be changed without unanimous approval.

14. Ibid., p. 19. At this point Trudeau was not prepared to surrender his referendum
    idea or to give the provinces the right to initiate a referendum of their own.
    But he was probably prepared to allow six or more of them, representing more
    than 50 percent of the population, the power to block a federal referendum—a
    concession he had already made to Saskatchewan the previous January.

NINE: RIGHTS AND FREEDOMS

1. Montreal *Gazette*, November 4, 1980.
2. Canada, "Prime Minister's Briefing Book," Annex II, p. 2.
3. Trudeau, *Federalism*, p. 57.
4. Leeson notes, p. 21.
5. "Notes for a Statement on the Entrenchment of a Charter of Rights," September 9, 1980, doc. 800-14/072. The same debate took place in 1867. See Ajzenstat et al., "Part Five: How to Make a Constitution." Not everyone was convinced: "The language of parliamentary supremacy was a rhetorical device to protect province-building against the nationalizing philosophy of the Charter." Alan Cairns in Banting and Simeon, *And No One Cheered*, p. 42. Besides, Parliament and the legislatures are never supreme in a federation in which the courts can rule legislation unconstitutional.
6. Lyon to Premier Bill Bennett, James G. Matkin, "The Negotiation of the Charter of Rights: The Provincial Perspective," in Weiler and Elliott, eds., *Litigating the Values of a Nation*, p. 29.
7. Trudeau always made a clear distinction between the individual and the person. In essence, personalism put the individual in the context of a community, socially aware rather than self-centred. For a fuller discussion, see Burelle, *Trudeau: L'intellectuel*.
8. Trudeau, in Axworthy and Trudeau, *Just Society*, p. 401. Trudeau's thesis at the London School of Economics was on "Liberties in the Province of Quebec." His favourite slogan in the 1950s was "Democracy first!"
9. Burelle, *Trudeau: L'intellectuel*, p. 70.
10. Sandra Djwa, *The Politics of the Imagination: A Life of F.R. Scott* (Toronto: McClelland and Stewart, 1987), pp. 232–33.
11. Ibid., p. 326.
12. To which Scott later added, "He didn't learn enough!" Scott was opposed to the notwithstanding clause and other details in the final deal. Graham Fraser, *Sorry, I Don't Speak French: Confronting the Canadian Crisis That Won't Go Away* (Toronto: McClelland and Stewart, 2006), p. 83.
13. Canada, "Briefing for the Delegation," pp. C.1–2.
14. Sheppard and Valpy, *The National Deal*, p. 67.
15. Hugh Segal, interview with author.
16. Trudeau, in Axworthy and Trudeau, *Just Society*, p. 407.
17. Both languages were already protected in the legislatures and courts of Quebec and Manitoba by the BNA Act, 1867, and the Manitoba Act, 1870.
18. The mother tongue qualification was added with the specific purpose of helping francophones outside Quebec, since many of them had not had access to French-language schooling in the past. The qualification also meant there wasn't absolute freedom of choice for every citizen.
19. Norman Spector; Plecas, *Bill Bennett*, p. 167; Clarkson and McCall, *Magnificent Obsession*, p. 355; Sheppard and Valpy, *The National Deal*, p. 6.

20. Blakeney, *An Honourable Calling*, p. 176; also interview with author. See also Kenneth McRoberts, *Misconceiving Canada: The Struggle for National Unity* (Toronto: Oxford University Press, 1997), p. 170. It is extremely significant that while Trudeau reluctantly accepted an override clause on fundamental freedoms in the Charter, he never would have agreed to apply it to language and education rights.

21. See Waite, *Life and Times of Confederation*, p. 288. At the time of Confederation, many French Canadians wanted their rights protected by the federal government, which was why Cartier was a centralist.

22. Lévesque, *Option*, p. 14. In practice, despite recent efforts to build a more tolerant society in Quebec, many francophones from Europe, Africa, Asia, the Middle East, and the Caribbean have found that language alone isn't enough to make them fully accepted Québécois.

23. Unfortunately, that is hardly an exaggeration. See Fraser, *Sorry*, pp. 54–55. "The separatists of both Quebec and the West well understood what was happening. Conscious that their ultimate goal presupposed an exclusively English-speaking Canada and an exclusively French-speaking Quebec, they abandoned their minorities in other provinces—French-speaking and English-speaking—and fought tooth and nail against the policy of bilingualism, which in their terms was the work of traitors and double-dealers." Trudeau, in Axworthy and Trudeau, *Just Society*, p. 411.

24. "In terms of *realpolitik*, French and English are equal in Canada because each of these linguistic groups has the power to break the country. And this power cannot yet be claimed by the Iroquois, the Eskimos, or the Ukrainians." Trudeau, *Federalism*, p. 31.

25. Quoted in *Globe and Mail*, September 15, 1980.

26. *Maclean's*, February 8, 1964; Trudeau, *Against the Current*, p. 216. "Our approach was indisputably more effective and more respectful of the dignity of Canadians. However, it made things awkward for Quebec nationalist politicians because it made them largely redundant; the moment the survival of 'the race' no longer depended on them, their racist preachings became superfluous." Trudeau, in Axworthy and Trudeau, *Just Society*, p. 412. See also pp. 409–412, 435ff.

TEN: CAT AMONG THE PIGEONS

1. Lévesque, *Memoirs*, pp. 328–29; Tremblay, *Derrière les portes closes*, p. 269.

2. *Globe and Mail*, November 2, 1981.

3. Godin, *René Lévesque*, p. 158.

4. Ibid., pp. 154, 155. Also Pierre Duchesne, *Jacques Parizeau, Le Baron*, pp. 403–16; Tremblay, *Derrière les portes closes*, p. 292, footnote 44.

5. Banting and Simeon, *And No One Cheered*, p. 50. The PQ lost four by-elections in November 1980 and trailed badly in the polls. Ottawa knew there would be disadvantages as well as advantages in dealing with Claude Ryan as premier, so it didn't focus unduly on the outcome of the Quebec election. Since it couldn't control the results, its strategy was simply to move forward and deal with whatever presented itself. Kirby, interview with author.

6. See Godin, *René Lévesque*, p. 154.

7. Morin's motives have been a subject of great debate. Since he gave the money to the Parti Québécois and various religious charities, he could hardly be described as a mercenary. (The PQ returned his donations when the scandal broke in 1992.) He himself claimed he was a kind of double agent, getting more for Quebec than he gave to Ottawa. Others have suggested that he was Ottawa's mole, planted inside the separatist movement to sabotage independence. Or perhaps he was simply in love with the game. It's a Byzantine tale, full of intrigue and contradiction, fuelled by hardline nationalists who blamed Morin for Lévesque's gradualism and failures. See Claude Morin, *Les choses comme elles étaient: Une autobiographie politique* (Montreal: Boréal, 1994), pp. 197–210, 325–45, 379–82, 402–06, 453–66; Claude Morin, *L'Affaire Morin: Légendes, sottises et calumnies* (Montreal: Boréal, 2006); Duchesne, *Jacques Parizeau, Le Baron*, chapter 20; Godin, *René Lévesque*, chapter 18; Daniel Poliquin, *René Lévesque* (Toronto: Penguin Canada, 2009), p. 182.

8. Morin, *Lendemains piégés*, p. 19.

9. Eddie Goldenberg, *The Way It Works: Inside Ottawa* (Toronto: McClelland and Stewart, 2006), p. 169.

10. Government of Quebec, "Opening Statement by the Quebec Minister of Intergovernmental Affairs, Claude Morin," July 8, 1980, Continuing Committee of Ministers on the Constitution, Department of Intergovernmental Affairs, LAC MG32-G15, vol. 17, file 6.

11. Morin, *Lendemains piégés*, p. 78. "I found him a proud man, who tended to speak down to people, and a skilful schemer, whose only goal was to make our work fail." Jean Chrétien, *Straight from the Heart* (Toronto: Key Porter, 1985), p. 174.

12. Chrétien, *Straight*, p. 174; Trudeau, *Memoirs*, pp. 302–3. "If we end up making a deal with Ottawa, how are we going to explain that to our rank-and-file?" Marc-André Bédard, quoted in Poliquin, *René Lévesque*, p. 181.

13. Godin, *René Lévesque*, p. 39.

14. Tremblay, *Derrière les portes closes*, p. 261.

15. Letter from Claude Morin to Roy Romanow, January 29, 1982; Morin, *Lendemains piégés*, p. 369.

16. The issue seemed more one of process than of content, since a sovereign Quebec would have had to agree to mobility rights under the terms of an economic association, and Lévesque had already agreed to the principle of extending education rights to anglophones who had been educated in English in Canada.

17. "Opening Statement," First Ministers' Conference on the Constitution, September 8, 1980, doc. 800-14/037. See also his open letter to Quebecers, "*Un coup de force qui est aussi une trahison*," *La Presse*, October 25, 1980.

18. "The three issues that contributed most to arouse national feeling and stimulate the pro–French-Quebec movements of these years were the Québécois' economically dependent situation, immigrant identification with the English group, and the attendance of English schools by children from French-speaking families." Monière, *Ideologies in Quebec*, p. 256.

19. Trudeau argued that calling French the "official" language did more harm than calling it the "principal" language (as Lesage had done), the "working" language,

or even the "national" language. Vastel, *Bourassa*, p. 57. English was still protected in the laws and courts of the province by section 133 of the BNA Act.

20. That reciprocal arrangement was provided for in section 86 of Bill 101. It was also approved in principle in two agreements Lévesque signed with the other premiers, one in St. Andrew's, New Brunswick, in 1977, and the other a year later in Montreal. Neither agreement was ever implemented. Trudeau later argued that with the Charter, Ottawa was able to achieve what the government of Quebec couldn't do on its own.

21. Lévesque, *Memoirs*, p. 288.

22. The Supreme Court ruled that both were unconstitutional. As Lévesque often noted, it had taken the court ninety years to come to the aid of the francophone minority in Manitoba, but almost no time to defend the rights of the anglophone minority in Quebec.

23. Quoted in Fraser, *PQ*, p. 106. See also Burelle, *Trudeau: L'intellectuel*, p. 76. Chief Justice Jules Deschênes went further, saying: "Quebec's argument is based on a totalitarian conception of society to which the court does not subscribe. Human beings are, to us, of paramount importance and nothing should be allowed to diminish the respect due to them." Quoted in Axworthy and Trudeau, *Just Society*, pp. 29–30.

24. Tom Axworthy, "Colliding Visions: The Debate Over the Charter of Rights and Freedoms 1980–81," in Weiler and Elliott, eds., *Litigating the Values of a Nation*, p. 16.

25. Lévesque, *Memoirs*, p. 327. Quebec even objected to a limited charter, because it had nothing to do with the province's demands for new powers, might be interpreted by the judges as a way to encroach into provincial jurisdiction, and could lull the others into a belief that constitutional renewal was over. "For us there was no question of endorsing this hypocritical verbiage essentially aimed at wresting from Quebec its sovereign authority in education." Ibid., p. 329.

26. Romanow, Whyte, Leeson, *Canada ... Notwithstanding*, p. 123.

27. Peter Meekison, ed., *Constitutional Patriation: The Lougheed–Lévesque Correspondence* (Kingston: Institute of Intergovernmental Relations, Queen's University, 1999), p. 17.

28. Morin, *Lendemains piégés*, p. 225. The decisions of the courts in Manitoba and Quebec in support of Ottawa's unilateral action also put pressure on Lévesque to maintain the common front. A confidential memo to Michael Kirby offered a revealing insight into B.C.'s thinking at that time: "British Columbia officials, in particular Garde Gardom, are quite concerned about developments they see taking place in the province of Quebec. They have found that Quebec has more and more isolated itself from the other provinces, in that they have their own game plan for the post-patriation period. They see the provincial government strengthening Bill 101 and, some time after patriation of the constitution (and some bad news on energy and fiscal arrangements), holding a referendum." Russell Anthony, "Constitution," June 23, 1981, LAC MG32-G15, vol. 13, file 11.

29. Tremblay, *Derrière les portes closes*, pp. 264–65. According to one federal poll, 63 percent of Parti Québécois voters had chosen the PQ because it provided good

government, while only 11 percent had voted for it because of its commitment to sovereignty-association.

30. Fraser, *PQ*, p. 282. It was officially called the Canadian Patriation Plan.

31. "Some people pretend that Quebec gave up its claim to a veto. They forget that in the accord (for as long as it held), the right to a veto had been replaced by a right to opt out *with compensation*. It follows logically that if the accord didn't hold, Quebec would return to its traditional position. Therefore it's false to say that we simply dropped the right to a veto." Claude Morin, correspondence with author, November 12, 2009.

32. Lévesque, *Memoirs*, p. 326. In French: "*D'étape en étape, je le répète, on pourrait ainsi se faire quelque chose comme un pays.*" This was in keeping with Morin's strategy of *étapisme,* a step-by-step approach to full independence: "We'll separate from Canada the same way that Canada separated from England," he said. "We'll sever the links one by one, a little concession here and a little concession here and a little concession there, a move here and a move there, and eventually there will be nothing left." Quoted in Chrétien, *Straight*, p. 151.

33. English, *Just Watch Me*, p. 499. Also: "I knew then, for certain, that Lévesque would never negotiate a deal. His only purpose was to use the Gang of Eight to block us, and he must have felt very sure that he would succeed." Trudeau, *Memoirs*, p. 314.

34. Morin, *Lendemains piégés*, p. 282; Axworthy and Trudeau, *Just Society,* p. 348.

35. Johnston, ed., *Pierre Trudeau Speaks Out*, p. 136. "Following the election in April, Premier Lévesque has reiterated to his party at a meeting of its Conseil National that his ultimate goal remains the independence of Quebec ... The press has seized on this talk and has begun to speculate on the possibility of a referendum with respect to patriation and the constitutional package. There is also speculation that the next election will be fought on the issue of a mandate either to separate or to negotiate separation although Premier Lévesque has recently pronounced himself against a referendum election." Unsigned, "Memorandum to Michael Kirby: Strategy Paper Re: Quebec," September 23, 1981, LAC MG32-G15, vol. 13, file 11.

36. "It was an affiliation of disparate personalities and widely divergent positions. Forced by the relentless pressure of Ottawa's determination to proceed, even in the face of widespread controversy, members of the opposing alliance submerged their differences, which ranged from the pursuit of separatism to the maintenance of the status quo, in order to stop unilateral federal action." Romanow, Whyte, Leeson, *Canada ... Notwithstanding*, p. 132.

37. Lévesque to Lougheed, in Meekison, *Constitutional Patriation*, p. 14.

38. Leeson notes, p. 29.

39. Lévesque, *Memoirs*, p. 330.

40. Morin, *Lendemains piégés*, p. 300.

41. Ibid., p. 371.

42. Trudeau, *Memoirs*, p. 319; Leeson notes, p. 27.

43. Godin, *René Lévesque*, p. 164.

44. Sheppard and Valpy, *The National Deal*, p. 284; Leeson notes, p. 30. There remains no certainty about whether this famous exchange took place in English or in French. Because of the absence of simultaneous translators, Trudeau and Lévesque were comfortable speaking to each other in English for the benefit of the other first ministers, with occasional one-on-ones in French. Leeson's minutes seem to prove that Lévesque's acceptance of the referendum challenge, at least, was understood by everyone. The minutes also contradict the memories of Trudeau and other participants that the meeting was, at that point, immediately adjourned for lunch (see Trudeau, *Memoirs*, p. 319). In fact, there followed quite an animated discussion about any referendum, both as an idea and as a process.

45. Lévesque, *Memoirs*, p. 331.

46. English, *Just Watch Me*, p. 453.

47. Correspondence with author, November 13, 2009. Some hardline nationalists later claimed that Morin, in his role as an RCMP informant, had told federal officials in advance that Lévesque would accept a referendum. There is no credibility to such an accusation. Though Lévesque had been calling for a referendum on patriation, Trudeau didn't expect him to risk one. Trudeau, Chrétien, and Kirby all denied having received information from Morin or even knowing of his relationship with the RCMP. Kirby, interview with author; Morin, *L'Affaire Morin*, pp. 161–72.

48. Godin, *René Lévesque*, p. 163.

49. Tremblay, *Derrière les portes closes*, p. 270. See Duchesne, *Jacques Parizeau, Le Baron*, pp. 409–10, and Godin, *René Lévesque*, p. 166, for the reaction of various Quebec officials and the Quebec media.

50. Montreal *Gazette*, November 5, 1981.

PART 2

ELEVEN: HIGH NOON

1. Peter Lougheed, interview with author.

2. Leeson notes, p. 36. The historian Ramsay Cook recorded Trudeau's off-the-record opinion of Peter Lougheed: "Well … he is hard to hate, he is so earnest, so lacking in humour, so concerned about appearances. Duplessis at least had a sense of humour and didn't take himself so seriously. He could be hated—but not Lougheed, who just wanted to do right by Alberta." Ramsay Cook, *The Teeth of Time: Remembering Pierre Elliott Trudeau* (Montreal and Kingston: McGill-Queen's University Press, 2006), pp. 143–44. See also Sheppard and Valpy, *The National Deal*, p. 9, for an unusual insight into the relationship between the two men.

3. Government of Canada, "Results of a Survey," p. 2. Not only was Peter Lougheed considered more selfish than Réné Lévesque, but he was also viewed as very selfish in both Saskatchewan and British Columbia. The survey noted that 85 percent of Canadians supported Ottawa's proposed bill of rights, including mobility rights, with the same proportion of support in Alberta.

4. Cited in Douglas Owram, "The Perfect Storm: The National Energy Program and

the Failure of Federal–Provincial Relations," in Richard Connors and John M. Law, eds., *Forging Alberta's Constitutional Framework* (Edmonton: University of Alberta Press, 2005), p. 391. See also Michael D. Behiels, "Premier Peter Lougheed, Alberta and the Transformation of Constitutionalism in Canada, 1971–1985," in ibid., p. 426.

5. David G. Wood, *The Lougheed Legacy* (Toronto: Key Porter, 1985), p. 170.

6. Canada, House of Commons, *Debates*, April 15, 1980, p. 33.

7. Clarkson and McCall, *Magnificent Obsession*, p. 301–2.

8. See Jeffrey Simpson, *Faultlines: Struggling for a Canadian Vision* (Toronto: HarperCollins Canada, 1993), pp. 120, 127; Nelson Wiseman, *In Search of Canadian Political Culture* (Vancouver and Toronto: UBC Press, 2007), pp. 244–50. Also: "From the very first settlement, Alberta has been unique in the extent of American influence, especially in the southern part of the province. The early white settlers were ranchers from Montana. Their numbers were later augmented by Mormon farmers and still later by oil-industry workers from across the western states, an influence that continues to this day. These American immigrants were numerous enough to create a political culture with no particular reverence for the standard Canadian brands—Liberal and Conservative—inherited from Britain." Tom Flanagan, "Alberta's One-Shot Wonders," *Globe and Mail*, January 23, 2010.

9. W.L. Morton, quoted in Barry Cooper, "Western Political Consciousness," in Stephen Brooks, ed., *Political Thought in Canada: Contemporary Perspectives* (Toronto: Irwin Publishing, 1984), p. 228. "Considered together," Cooper explained, "the elements that constitute the bias of prairie politics amount to a sort of nationalism." Ibid., p. 229.

10. "Aberhart's government tried to provide much-needed social and economic reform to alleviate human suffering during the Depression, but a number of his policies verged on fascism. Much of his legislation was quashed by the federal government because of its illegality." David R. Elliott and Iris Miller, *Bible Bill: A Biography of William Aberhart* (Edmonton: Reidmore Books, 1987), p. viii. On the other hand, it has been argued, support for both the United Farmers of Alberta and Social Credit was more about regional identity than party programs. "Accordingly, glib chatter from Marxian and eastern intellectuals about funny-money and fascism is but a mildly irksome insult." Cooper in Brooks, ed., *Political Thought in Canada*, p. 231.

11. Ironically, the idea for a Heritage Fund may have come from Trudeau himself. See Sheppard and Valpy, *The National Deal*, p. 62, footnote. Lougheed vigorously denied the story. Interview with author.

12. Romanow, White, Leeson, *Canada … Notwithstanding*, p. 25. See Marc Lalonde, "Riding the Storm: Energy Policy, 1968–1984," in Axworthy and Trudeau, *Just Society*, p. 93ff.

13. Trudeau, *Memoirs*, p. 293.

14. Ibid., pp. 293–94.

15. "The Constitution Act proposals were seen as a means to constitutionally entrench the NEP, while the NEP was seen to foreshadow the dangers ahead should the Constitution Act become the law of the land. Thus the details of Ottawa's

constitutional proposals were examined from a very narrow perspective; what would be their impact on the resource base of the western Canadian economy?" Roger Gibbins, "Constitutional Politics and the West," in Banting and Simeon, *And No One Cheered*, p. 124.

16. G. Bruce Doern and Glen Toner, *The Politics of Energy: The Development and Implementation of the NEP* (Toronto: Methuen, 1985), p. 268.

17. See www.canlii.org/en/ca/scc/doc/1981/1981canlii25/1981canlii25, p. 873.

18. Lougheed, interview with author.

19. Ibid. See Sheppard and Valpy, *The National Deal*, p. 185.

20. Lougheed, interview with author.

21. Trudeau to Ramsay Cook, *Teeth*, p. 144. René Lévesque reciprocated by referring to Richard Hatfield as Trudeau's "ventriloquist's dummy."

22. *Calgary Herald*, November 6, 1981. Lougheed certainly kept the federal advisers guessing right up to the last minute. "Under favourable circumstances," they informed the prime minister on the eve of the conference, "Alberta may support the entrenchment of a Charter either of diminished scope or with a number of overriding provisions. However, it is more likely that Alberta would stay on the side of Quebec and Manitoba if a consensus of seven provinces emerged in support of some form of charter." Canada, "Prime Minister's Briefing Book," October 30, 1981, tab 2(d), p. 2. This suggests that while Ottawa never expected Quebec to sign, it also never expected Quebec to be isolated.

23. Lévesque, *Memoirs*, p. 42.

24. Lougheed, interview with author.

25. Meekison, *Constitutional Patriation*, p. 20.

26. Lougheed, interview with author.

27. It's perhaps significant that only Quebec and Alberta felt certain that the federal government's Resolution would ultimately fail in London if the Gang of Eight held strong.

28. Meekison, *Constitutional Patriation*, p. 23.

29. Canada, "Prime Minister's Briefing Book," October 30, 1981, tab 2(d), p. 1.

30. Meekison, *Constitutional Patriation*, p. 23.

31. Lougheed, interview with author.

32. "We felt strong about our position because of the court ruling, but we weren't sure whether, in the end, Trudeau would fold or not, because he was such a brilliant negotiator. I was involved because I wanted to judge the probability of whether we were going to make something go, how much give there was." Lougheed, interview with author. Both Quebec and Manitoba gave a nod without committing themselves to the proposal itself, just to see what would happen. This is a puzzle, since neither of them was prepared to compromise at this point. The only explanation is that they were sure that Trudeau would reject Bennett's proposal.

33. Lougheed, interview with author.

34. Trudeau, in Axworthy and Trudeau, *Just Society*, p. 422. Trudeau was referring to an exchange of dialogue in the film *Last Year at Marienbad*:

"I know a game I always win."
"If you can't lose, it's no game."
"I can lose, but I always win."

35. "The lesson of the Quebec referendum was that the demands of provincial governments did not necessarily correspond to the wishes of the people and that Ottawa could appeal directly to the electorate to support its position. The traditional intergovernmental process, while still having an impact, lost much of its former authority." Romanow, Whyte, Leeson, *Canada … Notwithstanding*, p. 102.

36. Trudeau, *Memoirs*, p. 365.

37. Montreal *Gazette*, November 5, 1981.

38. Correspondence with author, November 12, 2009.

39. Leeson notes, p. 36.

40. Sheppard and Valpy, *The National Deal*, p. 287.

41. Hugh Segal in Claire Hoy, *Bill Davis: A Biography* (Toronto: Methuen, 1985), p. 367.

TWELVE: BLAND WORKS

1. Bill Davis, interview with author.

2. Sheppard and Valpy, *The National Deal*, p. 287.

3. "Davis told them he would be onside for any series of reasonable compromises necessary to get this thing to go forward. He would not be onside for a weakened federal government, for radical institutional change, or for an amending formula that didn't protect Ontario's interests. But he also wasn't onside for unilateralism if a compromise became possible." Hugh Segal, interview with author.

4. Hoy, *Bill Davis*, p. 360. "Davis did not want to let down his province or his country—to disappoint through some failure or lack of courage or resolve. That fear permeated the operations of the Ontario government on the constitutional issue and the discussions about Ontario's strategy and tactics." Nathan Nurgitz and Hugh Segal, *No Small Measure: The Progressive Conservatives and the Constitution* (Ottawa: Deneau Publishers, 1983), p. 108.

5. Segal, interview with author.

6. Davis, interview with author.

7. Telex from Davis to Trudeau, October 1, 1980. LAC MG32-G15, vol. 11.

8. "I had the temerity to suggest there were a lot of things everybody could be doing to make things easier, but Davis simply said, 'The point is, we should not find ourselves singing from different hymn books.' Which is as tough a statement as you're going to get from Davis." Segal in Hoy, *Bill Davis*, pp. 364–65.

9. Roy McMurtry in ibid., p. 350.

10. *Globe and Mail*, November 2, 1981.

11. Nurgitz and Segal, *No Small Measure*, p. 105.

12. Ibid., p. 110.

13. Roy McMurtry, interview with author.

14. Davis, interview with author. Like Trudeau, Davis didn't see Lévesque's signature

on the April Accord as proof that the PQ government could have signed a deal, since everyone knew that it would be unacceptable to Ottawa. "Nothing puzzled Ontario more than the ease with which some provincial premiers associated themselves with the Lévesque government's position." Nurgitz and Segal, *No Small Measure*, p. 36.

15. Lévesque, *Memoirs*, p. 329.
16. Transcripts, First Ministers' Conference, September 8, 1980.
17. Davis, interview with author.
18. Segal, interview with author.
19. Allan Gregg, in Nurgitz and Segal, *No Small Measure*, p. 31.
20. Speech to Empire Club, reprinted in full in *Toronto Star*, March 6, 1981.
21. Davis, interview with author.
22. Nova Scotia and Prince Edward Island shared the Loyalist heritage of Ontario and New Brunswick, but not the francophone element. Manitoba was very similar to Ontario, but Sterling Lyon (though born in Ontario) was on an ideological crusade that prevented him from joining the federal side.
23. McMurtry, interview with author.
24. Allan Blakeney in Nancy Southam, ed., *Remembering Richard* (Halifax: Formac Publishing, 1993), p. 82. Though Bill Davis probably meant no harm, his tease was interpreted by some as an allusion to rumours about Hatfield's sexual orientation and use of marijuana. When Hatfield was questioned about his extensive travels, he answered that he had been elected to govern New Brunswick, not live there.
25. Barry Toole in Southam, *Remembering Richard*, p. 43.
26. Lowell Murray in ibid., p. 42. Though Claude Morin leaked the Kirby report to the premiers in September 1980, Hatfield was probably the one who leaked it to the press. See Sheppard and Valpy, *The National Deal*, p. 59; Morin, *Lendemains piégés*, p. 121.
27. "There is no question that Clark's efforts to find some balance on the energy issue that respected the interests of both the East and the West were perceived by Ontarians as the inability to decide in the interests of the whole country. The idea of nation, of national governments capable of making national decisions, is part of the psyche of Ontario voters and the list of demands they have traditionally made of national political parties." Nurgitz and Segal, *No Small Measure*, p. 34.
28. Canada, House of Commons, *Debates*, March 23, 1981, pp. 8519–20.
29. "Pierre Elliott Trudeau: Memoirs," vol. 3, ep. 5.
30. Davis, interview with author.
31. Roy McMurtry, "The Search for a Constitutional Accord—A Personal Memoir," *Queen's Law Journal* 30 (1982–1983), p. 30.
32. Hoy, *Bill Davis*, p. 365; McMurtry, interview with author.
33. Davis, interview with author. "That wasn't deceptive—it was tactical. We had to get the premiers back to thinking about their province's interests rather than the interests of the cabal. In terms of games theory, we had to change the dynamic of side A versus side B, full stop. So if side A had differences of opinion, it was kosher for side B to have differences of opinion as well." Segal, interview with author.

34. Allan Blakeney, interview with author.

35. Davis, interview with author.

36. Sheppard and Valpy, *The National Deal*, p. 9. In his befuddling way, Hatfield himself had threatened the monarchy in remarks he made in London on January 14, 1981: "If an appeal to the Queen of England is rejected by the Queen of England, or her answer is, I'm sorry, there will be people who will understand that we have to get rid of the Queen of England." Richard Starr, *Richard Hatfield: The Seventeen-Year Saga* (Halifax: Formac Publishing, 1987), pp. 150–51.

37. "On the basis of preliminary discussions with provincial officials, it would appear that a 'notwithstanding' clause has some appeal to the provinces. We, however, continue to have considerable reservations about its desirability and, indeed, its necessity, particularly if the legal rights are more clearly defined." In response, the prime minister scribbled in the margins, "I agree." Memo from Roger Tassé, deputy minister of justice, to Trudeau, "Charter of Rights," August 5, 1980, LAC MG32-G15, vol. 15, file 1, p. 9. Also: "Federal officials raised doubts respecting the necessity of an override clause but suggested that if there should be one, it should be restricted by requirements that any law enacted under an override provision be adopted by a 60% majority of the legislative body and expire after a specified time (e.g., 5 years)." Kirby report, p. 5.

38. See Paul Weiler, "The Evolution of the Charter: A View from the Outside," in Weiler and Elliot, eds., *Litigating the Values of a Nation*.

39. Canada, "Prime Minister's Briefing Book," tab 6, p. 2. Also: "The danger of accepting a notwithstanding clause is that it might work its way into fundamental rights & language rights." Trudeau, handwritten note, "Constitutional Strategy, August–September 1980," August 20, 1980, LAC MG32-G15, vol. 8, file 6, p. 3.

40. Davis, interview with author.

41. McMurtry, interview with author. The notwithstanding clause wasn't used in Alberta or Saskatchewan before 1981; it was invoked only once in Ottawa, by Trudeau himself during the October Crisis in 1970; and it was applied seven times in Quebec under its own charter.

42. See Trudeau's arguments in *Just Society*, pp. 414–15. McWhinney, *Canada and the Constitution*, p. 56, found "no less than five weasel-word exceptions in the single qualifying clause."

43. Trudeau, *Memoirs*, p. 322. See Weiler, "The Evolution of the Charter," in Weiler and Elliot, eds., *Litigating the Values of a Nation*, for a vigorous defence of the idea.

44. Sheppard and Valpy, *The National Deal*, p. 276.

45. Kirby, interview with author.

46. Leeson notes, pp. 16–17.

47. Davis, interview with author.

48. Chrétien, *Straight*, p. 182.

49. Davis, interview with author.

50. Sheppard and Valpy, *The National Deal*, p. 282.

51. Davis, interview with author.

52. Segal in Hoy, *Bill Davis*, p. 367.
53. Ibid., p. 368.

THIRTEEN: LAST IN, FIRST OUT

1. Blakeney, *An Honourable Calling*, p. 186. "Anything offered by Ottawa was too little for Quebec, and anything requested by Quebec was too much for Ottawa." Romanow, Whyte, Leeson, *Canada ... Notwithstanding*, p. 103.
2. Blakeney, *An Honourable Calling*, p. 175.
3. Ibid., p. 179.
4. Allan Blakeney, interview with author. See ibid., pp. 130–31, for more details.
5. See ibid., p. 26; David E. Smith, *The Regional Decline of a National Party: Liberals on the Prairies* (Toronto: University of Toronto Press, 1981), pp. 40–41.
6. Roy Romanow, interview with author.
7. As premier of Saskatchewan, Douglas fought for an entrenched bill of rights at a federal–provincial conference in 1950 and again, alongside Jean Lesage, in 1960.
8. "What my concession ultimately meant, however, was that the only change in the division of powers between the federal and provincial governments as a result of our entire patriation exercise was a strengthening of provincial powers over natural resources. So much for all the talk about a federal power grab!" Trudeau, *Memoirs*, p. 310.
9. Ibid., pp. 272–73. In his memoirs, Trudeau speculated that Broadbent "feared that his party would lose its power and credibility" by joining the government. According to the historian Ramsay Cook, Trudeau thought that Broadbent had agreed and then was scared off by the Ontario NDP and the Canadian Labour Congress. "Anyway," Trudeau added, "they just had 'no balls.'" Cook, *Teeth*, p. 143.
10. Romanow, interview with author.
11. Ed Broadbent, interview with author.
12. John Whyte, interview with author.
13. Romanow, Whyte, Leeson, *Canada ... Notwithstanding*, p. 110. See also p. 117 for an insiders' account of Premier Blakeney's thinking in October 1980. Whether it was because of his Nova Scotian roots, his Oxford education, or his socialist bent, Blakeney certainly had a bigger vision of Canada than Peter Lougheed did, though it cost him the strength of Lougheed's single focus.
14. Canada, "Re discussions with Saskatchewan officials on Patriation Resolution," October 17, 1980, LAC MG32-G15, vol. 15, file 5, pp. 5–6.
15. Trudeau's reason for rejecting that demand offers insight into his general thinking. "It is only when the whole nation (i.e., Parliament) wants something and the provinces don't that there is a deadlock," the prime minister explained in a note he scribbled in the margin of a memo. "If several provinces want an amendment but not the whole nation (i.e., Parliament) why consult the whole nation by referendum?" Ibid., p. 2.
16. As examples, Blakeney often cited the difficulty a provincial legislature might encounter if affirmative-action programs were judged discriminatory or laws against hate speech and pornography were ruled violations of free expression.

17. Canada, "The NDP Position on the Constitution: Premier Blakeney and the NDP Caucus," January 16, 1981, LAC MG32-G15, vol. 15, file 8, pp. 10–11.

18. Chrétien, *Straight*, p. 182.

19. Canada, "The NDP Position on the Constitution," Appendix D, p. 4.

20. Chrétien, *Straight*, p. 180; Romanow, interview with author. Chrétien was probably remembering a front-page report published in the *Globe and Mail* on January 23, 1981, of a speech Romanow had delivered at McMaster University the previous day. It seemed to signal that Saskatchewan was ready for a deal if Ottawa gave ground on international trade and the referendum provisions in its amending formula. Another article, that same day, highlighted Saskatchewan's objection to property rights in the proposed Charter.

21. Canada, "Notes of Events Surrounding Negotiations with the Province of Saskatchewan in the Period from Thursday, January 22 to Tuesday, January 27, Inclusive," memo from F.A.G. Carter, January 31, 1981, LAC MG32-G15, vol. 12, file 19, p. 23. It's not clear whether Romanow was talking about the difficulty of supporting only the existing Resolution or *any* unilateral resolution.

22. It is interesting to note, in light of what happened in November 1981, that Blakeney had dropped his principled objections to the Charter of Rights and Freedoms by February. He already understood that Trudeau was not going to give way unless the Gang of Eight conceded some form of charter, especially when it came to language rights, and the battles over the Charter were threatening to pull the NDP asunder.

23. Jean Chrétien, interview with author.

24. Romanow, interview with author. Blakeney didn't remember being quite so firm, but there's no doubt he wanted to move forward. Under tremendous pressure from his Cabinet not to join Trudeau, he saw this as his last shot before joining the Gang of Eight. Blakeney, interview with author.

25. Canada, "Notes of Events," p. 16. According to jottings kept at the time by Ramsay Cook, Trudeau was especially "mad at Blakeney and Romanow. Said Blakeney played public role of 'great Canadian,' but in closed sessions was narrow or worse than other western premiers. Said Romanow very narrow and unwilling to give in on language rights." Cook, *Teeth*, p. 143.

26. Romanow, interview with author.

27. Canada, "Notes of Events," p. 16.

28. Whyte, interview with author.

29. Blakeney, *An Honourable Calling*, p. 176. As it turned out, under the terms of the Gang of Eight's amending formula, which Trudeau was forced to accept in November 1981, the Senate could only delay a constitutional change for 180 days, not veto it permanently. After quite a bit of heavy arm-twisting, most of the Liberal senators realized they were in no position to block a hard-earned deal that had the support of nine premiers and the majority of the House of Commons.

30. Blakeney, interview with author.

31. Chrétien, *Straight*, p. 180.

32. Romanow, interview with author.

33. Meekison, *Constitutional Patriation*, p. 18. Lougheed himself didn't seem to be bothered by the contradiction between his insistence on the equality of provinces and the April Accord's embrace of asymmetrical federalism.

34. Morin, *Lendemains piégés*, p. 369.

35. Claude Charron, *Désobéir* (Montreal: VLB éditeur, 1983), p. 46.

36. Meekison, *Constitutional Patriation*, p. 7. Also Howard Leeson, "Memorandum from Howard Leeson: First Ministers' Conference on the Constitution, Ottawa, November 2–5," November 16, 1981, p. 12. Memories differ about the exact date of this incident.

37. Howard Leeson, interview with author.

38. Matkin, "The Negotiation of the Charter of Rights," in Weiler and Elliot, eds., *Litigating the Values of a Nation*, p. 38.

39. James Matkin, interview with author.

40. Canada, "Prime Minister's Briefing Book," tab 2(c), no pagination. A secret memo to Michael Kirby from Eddie Goldenberg, dated October 31, 1981, reported on private talks with Jim Matkin: "Leaving Lévesque aside, the toughest members of the eight are Lougheed, Lyon and Peckford. The position of British Columbia will be to stick with them for as long as possible in order to try at the appropriate time to bring them along. British Columbia wants to act as a mediator and will therefore sit back and say nothing for a long time. In looking at each Premier, they believe that Peckford is close to Bennett and will in the end do what Bennett wants. Buchanan very much wants a deal. His only major concern is the referendum. McLean [*sic*] is tougher than Buchanan, but in the end will follow Buchanan." LAC MG32-G15, vol. 13, file 11.

41. Romanow, Whyte, Leeson, *Canada … Notwithstanding*, p. 193.

42. Canada, "Prime Minister's Briefing Book," tab 2(d), pp. 2–5.

43. Ibid., tab 2(e), no pagination.

44. Blakeney, *An Honourable Calling*, p. 186.

45. *Globe and Mail*, November 5, 1981.

46. Morin, *Lendemains piégés*, p. 302.

47. Fraser, *PQ*, p. 296.

48. Leeson, interview with author.

49. Trudeau, *Memoirs*, p. 320.

FOURTEEN: THE KITCHEN ACCORD

1. Chrétien, *Straight*, p. 183.

2. Romanow, interview with author.

3. Canada, "Prime Minister's Briefing Book," tab 2(e), p. 5.

4. Brian Peckford letter to Pierre Trudeau, January 27, 1982, LAC MG32-G15, vol. 15, file 15.

5. McMurtry arrived too late to have much input, but there was a public-relations benefit to be gained by having the document come from one Liberal from Ottawa, one New Democrat from the West, and one Tory from the East.

6. Donald Smiley in Banting and Simeon, *And No One Cheered*, p. 92.

7. Segal, interview with author.

8. Lougheed, interview with author. One of the answers to the mystery is the excellent rapport the three ministers had established with the Ottawa media during the summer negotiations in 1980. As well, the Kitchen Accord offered a visual, human-interest angle that the television reporters loved.

9. Davis, interview with author.

10. Montreal *Gazette,* November 7, 1981. Also Leeson, "First Ministers' Conference," p. 1. In fact, Trudeau had already signalled his openness to the idea at the Wednesday morning session. "I'd think about exchanging the [April] Accord formula for the Charter if you include the fundamental, legal and equality clauses, or as per Hatfield, legal, equality and aboriginal. Then I will go for the Accord formula minus compensation." But the Gang of Eight hadn't broken apart yet, so Trudeau's offer was dismissed, Leeson notes, p. 26.

11. Chrétien, interview with author.

12. Some journalists tried to make a conspiracy out of the fact that this document was numbered out of sequence, as though Ottawa had been holding it back as a trick. The more plausible explanation is clerical error under extreme pressure. Though federal officials had been hearing talk of a referendum for a week or so, no drafts had been requested or prepared.

13. *Globe and Mail*, November 5, 1981.

14. Sheppard and Valpy, *The National Deal*, p. 290.

15. Romanow, Whyte, Leeson, *Canada … Notwithstanding*, p. 207.

16. Meekison, *Constitutional Patriation*, pp. 24–25.

17. Claude Morin, correspondence with author, November 13, 2009.

18. Lévesque, *Memoirs*, p. 331.

19. Montreal *Gazette*, November 5, 1981.

20. Ibid.

21. Meekison, *Constitutional Patriation*, p. 25; Segal in Hoy, *Bill Davis*, p. 368.

22. Sheppard and Valpy, *The National Deal*, p. 290. "He would have come back. He would have told me if he was going for a referendum." Chrétien, interview with author. Perhaps, but Mary Dawson, a justice department official at the time, was assigned the task of drafting the implementation proposals into legalese. She worked in her office almost to the dawn of Thursday morning, only to be told at eight o'clock that she needn't have bothered—the first ministers had reached a deal after all. Dawson, interview with author.

23. McMurtry, interview with author.

24. Davis, interview with author.

25. Blakeney, interview with author.

26. Lévesque, *Memoirs*, p. 331.

PART 3

FIFTEEN: THE NIGHT OF THE LONG KNIVES

1. Godin, *René Lévesque*, p. 172.
2. Ibid.
3. Trudeau, *Memoirs*, p. 321.
4. Sheppard and Valpy, *The National Deal*, p. 293.
5. Peter Meekison, interview with author.
6. Davis, interview with author. Davis didn't know what the prime minister was thinking until then. Blakeney remembered relaying proposals to Davis by phone all through the evening: "He kept indicating that some provision was, or was not, acceptable. I did not know, and to this day do not know, to what extent, if any, he was in touch with Mr Trudeau, Mr Chrétien, or Premier Hatfield." Blakeney, *An Honourable Calling*, p. 188.
7. Chrétien, *Straight*, p. 185.
8. Trudeau, *Memoirs*, pp. 324–25; Clarkson and McCall, *Magnificent Obsession*, p. 383. "That was the most categorical, definitive, direct, precise Davis had been in the entire negotiation with Trudeau over several years." Segal, interview with author.
9. Hoy, *Bill Davis*, pp. 368–69. "Trudeau wasn't enthused, but he came to the conclusion after our discussion that my assessment was probably correct. If we didn't do this, the whole thing would fall apart." Davis, interview with author.
10. If convention required Westminster to rubber-stamp Ottawa's request, as Trudeau argued, didn't convention also require Ottawa to get the support of a substantial number of provinces, as the Supreme Court stated? Conversely, if Trudeau could stick to the letter of the law, couldn't the British MPs claim their legal right to interfere?
11. Trudeau, *Memoirs*, p. 324.
12. Chrétien, interview with author.
13. Chrétien, *Straight*, p. 185.
14. Leeson, "First Ministers' Conference," pp. 6–7.
15. Montreal *Gazette*, November 7, 1981.
16. Leeson, "First Ministers' Conference," p. 8.
17. Ibid., p. 9.
18. Lévesque, *Memoirs*, p. 332.
19. Leeson, "First Ministers' Conference," p. 7.
20. Blakeney, *An Honourable Calling*, pp. 188–89.
21. *Canada by Night*, produced by Luc Cyr and Carl Leblanc (Montreal: Ad Hoc Films, 1999). Peter Meekison, for one, was surprised that Morin hadn't picked up on the many signals of more talks to come that evening. Morin rarely missed a trick and had regularly phoned his contacts in the other delegations to ask what was going on. "I can only conclude that Quebec was sure it was going to fail and didn't want to be blamed for bringing it down." Meekison, interview with author.

According to a report in *Le Devoir*, November 6, 1981, "[A] senior Quebec civil servant, when asked why he did not make a last attempt to keep the provinces together as he had done in September 1980, replied in a disenchanted tone, 'We no longer have any credibility after what happened at noon.'" Quoted in William Johnson, *A Canadian Myth: Quebec, Between Canada and the Illusion of Utopia* (Montreal and Toronto: Robert Davies Publishing, 1994), p. 182.

22. Morin, correspondence with author, November 12, 2009. Also Godin, *René Lévesque*, p. 173.

23. Davis, interview with author.

24. Duart Farquharson in Southam, *Remembering Richard*, p. 63; Roy McMurtry in ibid., p. 48.

25. Michel Cormier and Achille Michaud, *Richard Hatfield: Power and Disobedience* (Fredericton: Goose Lane Editions, 1992), p. 94.

SIXTEEN: A MEAN PROCESS

1. Chrétien, *Straight*, p. 186.

2. Romanow, Whyte, Leeson, *Canada … Notwithstanding*, p. 210.

3. Chrétien, *Straight*, p. 187. See also Trudeau, *Memoirs*, p. 325.

4. Chrétien, interview with author.

5. Sheppard and Valpy, *The National Deal*, p. 298.

6. Leeson, "First Ministers' Conference," p. 10.

7. Montreal *Gazette*, November 6, 1981. In fact, Manitoba hadn't signed by breakfast.

8. Meekison, *Constitutional Patriation*, p. 26.

9. Lévesque, *Memoirs*, p. 332.

10. Lougheed, interview with author. "Lévesque wasn't trying to improve the constitution—he was a separatist. The other premiers finally realized what I had known all along, that it was a matter of two totally conflicting visions of Canada and Quebec fighting it out." Trudeau, *Memoirs*, p. 326.

11. Meekison, *Constitutional Patriation*, p. 26.

12. Lougheed, interview with author.

13. Nate Nurgitz, interview with author.

14. Cormier and Michaud, *Richard Hatfield*, pp. 96–97.

15. Leeson notes, p. 42.

16. Ibid., p. 46.

17. Chrétien, *Straight*, p. 187.

18. McMurtry, interview with author.

19. Chrétien, *Straight*, p. 187; Sheppard and Valpy, *The National Deal*, p. 299; Chrétien, interview with author.

20. Morin, *Lendemains piégés*, p. 309.

21. Leeson notes, p. 46.

22. A member of the Ontario delegation had woken Howard Leeson at 3:00 a.m. to ask about the possibility of removing the notwithstanding clause from fundamental

rights. Leeson's pessimistic response may have influenced Trudeau and Davis the next morning. Leeson, "First Ministers' Conference," pp. 9–10; Sheppard and Valpy, *The National Deal*, p. 298.

23. "Trudeau didn't say anything. Lougheed would have dropped it. He wanted to see if Trudeau was serious about negotiating. I think if Trudeau had pushed, and it was the only thing left, Lougheed would have said okay." Meekison, interview with author. Meekison didn't even know whether Lougheed had put it in as a bargaining chip. Thirty years after the fact, Premier Lougheed remembered that it was an important matter of principle for him and something he really wanted. In other words, though he might have dropped it if push had come to shove, he suspected by then how much Trudeau was prepared to give up for the sake of a historic agreement. Lougheed, interview with author.

24. Trudeau, in Axworthy and Trudeau, *Just Society*, p. 417. At the time, however, he sounded less concerned. "I must be honest and say that I don't fear the notwithstanding clause very much. It can be abused, as anything can, but ... I don't think the notwithstanding clause deters very significantly from the excellence of the Charter." Interview with Jack Webster, CHAN-TV, Vancouver, November 24, 1981, quoted in David Johansen and Philip Rosen, "The Notwithstanding Clause of the Charter," Background Paper, Parliamentary Information and Research Service, Library of Parliament, Government of Canada, October 16, 2008. Also: McWhinney, *Canada and the Constitution*, p. 128.

25. "Unlike Quebeckers," Trudeau later explained, "neither the native peoples nor the 'multiculturals' nor women are collectivities defined by a specific territory and enjoying executive, legislative, and juridical powers. Consequently, the constitution does not give them, as collectivities, any specific jurisdictional power to 'promote' their distinct societies." Trudeau, in Axworthy and Trudeau, *Just Society*, p. 435.

26. Leeson notes, p. 46.

27. Sheppard and Valpy, *The National Deal*, p. 299; Leeson notes, p. 47.

28. Leeson notes, p. 47; Sheppard and Valpy, *The National Deal*, p. 299.

29. Meekison, interview with author.

30. Leeson notes, p. 47.

31. Lougheed, interview with author.

32. Blakeney, *An Honourable Calling*, p. 189. It's hard to believe that Blakeney or Lougheed would have accepted an argument from Lévesque that the federal government could have arbitrarily reformed the energy sector just because Joe Clark and many in his Cabinet were from Alberta.

33. Trudeau, *Memoirs*, p. 325; Sheppard and Valpy, *The National Deal*, p. 301. "Had there been a referendum on the 1982 constitutional proposals, it would have represented a definitive judgement of their fate. If the proposals were rejected, there would have been no basis for proceeding any farther; had they been ratified, any objections would have been rendered irrelevant. Conversely, the fact that a referendum was *not* held meant that the federal government lacked the moral and political authority simply to ignore the objections of the government of Quebec." Monahan, *Meech Lake*, p. 21. On the other hand, it could be argued that the federal government retained its moral and political authority once the provinces

(including Quebec, by this point) refused to go along with Trudeau's offer of a referendum.

34. Reprinted in Hurley, *Amending Canada's Constitution*, appendix 13, p. 249. Trudeau's reply in ibid., appendix 14, p. 251.

35. Chrétien, *Straight*, p. 187.

36. Davis, interview with author.

37. As obvious and innocuous as this "continuity" clause might have seemed, it became the controversial loophole through which francophone and immigrant Quebecers sought to get their families into the English public-school system, by first putting at least one of their children into an English private school for a year or two. See, for example, William Johnson, "Quebec's English-language Education Bill Is Everyone's Villain," *Globe and Mail*, September 17, 2010.

38. Godin, *René Lévesque*, p. 183.

39. Sheppard and Valpy, *The National Deal*, p. 301.

40. Whyte, interview with author.

41. Burelle, *Trudeau: L'intellectuel*, p. 370, footnote.

42. *Globe and Mail*, November 6, 1981.

43. Blakeney, *An Honourable Calling*, p. 189.

44. Ibid., pp. 182–83.

45. *Winnipeg Free Press*, November 6, 1981.

46. Plecas, *Bill Bennett*, p. 169.

47. *Globe and Mail*, November 6, 1981.

48. Lougheed, interview with author. "From the perspective of regional politics in western Canada, the amending procedure reinforces the claim of provincial governments that they alone speak for their provincial electorates *in national affairs.* Ottawa cannot appeal directly to the people of the West over, under or around their provincial governments" (italics in original). Roger Gibbins, "Constitutional Politics and the West," in Banting and Simeon, *And No One Cheered*, p. 127.

49. Segal in Hoy, *Bill Davis*, p. 114.

50. Davis, interview with author.

51. Godin, *René Lévesque*, p. 189; Tremblay, *Derrière les portes closes*, p. 271. When Charron left Ottawa later in the day, he was still so numb that he forgot his suitcase in a taxi.

52. Godin, *René Lévesque*, p. 186.

53. Lévesque, *Memoirs*, p. 333; *Globe and Mail*, November 6, 1981.

EPILOGUE

SEVENTEEN: A BEAUTIFUL RISK

1. See www.collectionscanada.gc.ca/primeministers/h4-4024-e.html.

2. Montreal *Gazette*, November 7, 1981.

3. Duchesne, *Jacques Parizeau, Le Baron,* pp. 407–8; Tremblay, *Derrière les portes*

closes, p. 146. Parizeau undermines the accuracy of his recollections by also placing the Kirby report controversy at the start of the November 1981 conference, when in fact it took place at the start of the September 1980 conference. Duchesne, *Jacques Parizeau, Le Baron,* pp. 406–7. The error was compounded in Poliquin, *René Lévesque,* p. 172, which put the September 1980 conference in the spring of 1981.

4. Tremblay, *Derrière les portes closes*, pp. 271–72.

5. The first use of the expression has been attributed to the journalist Michel Vastel and the polemicist Pierre Bourgault. It immediately took hold, even in the English media. Poliquin, *René Lévesque*, p. 161. Of course, it's a flagrant misuse of history to equate what happened to René Lévesque that Wednesday night with Hitler's bloody killings in 1934. The essayist Gérard Bergeron preferred "Day of the Dupes." Bergeron in Banting and Simeon, *And No One Cheered*, p. 59.

6. Lévesque, *Memoirs*, p. 333.

7. "Lettre du premier ministre René Lévesque à Mme Margaret Thatcher, première ministre de Grande-Bretagne, le 19 décembre 1981," reprinted in Morin, *Lendemains piégés*, p. 360. My translation.

8. *Ottawa Citizen*, April 17, 1982.

9. *La Presse*, March 30, 1982; Trudeau, *Memoirs*, p. 327; Johnson, *A Canadian Myth*, p. 187, footnote 11. The March poll also revealed that 55 percent of Quebecers opposed Ottawa's decision to proceed without the Quebec government's approval. If so, they didn't seem particularly disturbed by that fact.

10. *Toronto Star*, May 27, 1987. Quoted in Johnston, *Pierre Trudeau Speaks Out*, p. 17; Trudeau, *Against the Current*, p. 234.

11. *Ottawa Citizen*, April 19, 1982.

12. At a premiers' conference in Halifax in August 1982, Roy McMurtry found Lévesque looking very glum and assumed the premier was still angry. As it turned out, he was unhappy because he was about to turn sixty. McMurtry, interview with author.

13. *Globe and Mail*, September 24, 1984; Fraser, *PQ*, p. xv.

14. Lévesque, *Memoirs*, p. 20; Fraser, *PQ*, p. xix.

15. The argument that Trudeau took advantage of Lévesque's weakness is an odd one, though it's often heard in nationalist circles. They weren't playing a friendly game of street hockey, after all, but were engaged in a form of civil war that threatened political, social, and economic chaos. And hadn't Lévesque tried to take advantage of Trudeau's weakness by delaying the referendum until after the 1979 election?

EIGHTEEN: POWER TO THE PEOPLE

1. Ron Graham, *The French Quarter: The Epic Struggle of a Family—and a Nation— Divided* (Toronto: Macfarlane Walter and Ross, 1992), p. 234.

2. Brian Mulroney, *Memoirs: 1939–1993* (Toronto: McClelland and Stewart, 2007), p. 305. "I wrote the speech as though I would be giving it myself, giving free rein to the indignation that I felt over Quebec's being pushed aside." Lucien Bouchard, quoted in Johnson, *A Canadian Myth*, p. 196.

3. Vastel, *Bourassa*, p. 216. "In fact, federalism is a technique of administration that can make it possible for us to garner important sums of money." Bourassa, quoted in Johnson, *A Canadian Myth*, p. 108.

4. It is interesting to note that the Quebec Liberals didn't object to the Charter of Rights and Freedoms or insist on changes to it.

5. "When I became leader again," Bourassa said, "I drew up a program that took into account both the referendum defeat and the *unilateral* patriation. While I couldn't ask for everything in every sphere, I summed up everything that I regarded as essential. But 'special status,' 'associated states,' and 'distinct society' are concepts that work together in a certain way" (my italics). Vastel, *Bourassa*, p. 94.

6. Proceedings of the National Assembly, June 18, 1987, p. 8708; Johnston, *Pierre Trudeau Speaks Out*, p. 140; Vastel, *Bourassa*, pp. 112–13. My translation. Although the PQ opposed the Meech Lake Accord, Parizeau saw its potential: "It's remarkable how much we could get through that clause if the courts say, well, yes, in some circumstances, it can overrule certain dispositions of the Charter of Rights. If the courts ever say that, my God, what a weapon it could be for people who have the sort of, shall we say, political project that I have." Parizeau, quoted in Axworthy and Trudeau, *Just Society*, p. 23; Johnson, *A Canadian Myth*, p. 211.

7. *Globe and Mail*, November 3, 1987, quoted in Cook, *Teeth*, p. 161. "The distinct society clause and the new role attributed to Quebec of promoting that distinctiveness are scarcely negligible. They conferred a special status on Quebec, at least potentially. In grey areas of the division of powers, where there are overlapping jurisdictions, the courts could have invoked the distinct society clause to rule in Quebec's favour. No other province would have enjoyed such treatment." Guy Laforest, *Trudeau and the End of a Canadian Dream* (Montreal and Kingston: McGill-Queen's University Press, 1995), p. 78. See also Fournier, *Meech Lake Post-Mortem*, pp. 21–24.

8. Johnson, *A Canadian Myth*, p. 212.

9. Graham, *French Quarter*, p. 241.

10. Quoted in Johnston, *Pierre Trudeau Speaks Out*, p. 131.

11. Ibid., pp. 87–88.

12. Ibid., p. 99.

13. The Supreme Court had ruled that the law violated the Charter's freedom of expression. Tellingly, Bourassa's intergovernmental affairs minister argued that "Quebec will be able to use its new status as a distinct society in court to defend laws that might be seen as contravening the federal Charter of Rights and Freedoms." Gil Rémillard, Proceedings of the National Assembly, June 19, 1987. As for Bourassa himself, he "hinted that, if the accord were ratified, and Quebec gained extra powers to protect its language and culture, it might be possible to repeal the notwithstanding clause." Monahan, *Meech Lake*, p. 161.

14. For example, Newfoundland held a referendum in 1995 on school secularization, New Brunswick in 2001 on video lotteries, Nova Scotia in 2004 on Sunday shopping, Prince Edward Island in 2005 on electoral reform, and Ontario in 2007 on proportional representation. British Columbia had referendums in 2002, 2005, and 2009, with another expected in 2011. "The idea that a constitution to be

legitimate must be derived from the people—a dreadful heresy to our founding fathers—has become constitutional orthodoxy for most Canadians. Indeed, it may be the only constitutional ideal on which there is popular consensus in Canada." Peter Russell, *Constitutional Odyssey: Can Canadians Become a Sovereign People?* 2nd ed. (Toronto: University of Toronto Press, 1993), p. 5.

15. Trudeau, *Memoirs*, p. 364.

NINETEEN: TO THE PRECIPICE

1. "Pierre Elliott Trudeau: Memoirs," vol. 3, ep. 5. Howard Leeson's notes also reveal how hard Trudeau fought for a veto for Quebec, to no avail.

2. As premier, Bouchard himself had to petition Ottawa to amend the new constitution to establish language-based school boards in the province.

3. In 2006, in a desperate bid to build up their support in Quebec, the Conservative government and the Liberal opposition felt trapped by the Bloc Québécois into passing a motion recognizing "that the Québécois form a nation within a united Canada."

TWENTY: CHARTER CANADIANS

1. *Toronto Star*, January 20, 2011.

2. Simpson, *Faultlines*, pp. 4, 66–67, 87, 96. Simpson attributes the expression "Charter Canadians" to Alan Cairns. See also McRoberts, *Misconceiving Canada*, p. 180; Russell, *Constitutional Odyssey*, pp. 115, 147.

3. Environics poll, Centre for Research and Information in Quebec, February 2002.

4. Howard Leeson, "Section 133, the Notwithstanding Clause: A Paper Tiger?" *Choices* 6, no. 4 (June 2000), p. 20. Leeson compared it to the disallowance power, available in law but unusable in practice. Perhaps, but it did create a political firestorm when Premier Bourassa used it in December 1988. "With the benefit of hindsight, it is now evident that the existence of the notwithstanding clause was a serious threat to the unity of the country ... Having provided the Quebec premier with a tool to promote the French language, you compel him or her to use it." Monahan, *Meech Lake*, p. 167.

5. Peter Lougheed, "Why a Notwithstanding Clause?" *Points of View* 6 (1998).

6. Trudeau, private conversation with author.

7. Trudeau, interview with author. By the time the documentary aired in 1994, Trudeau was ready to express his regret in public. "It's still my belief today that it would have been better if we had gone alone and had whatever difficulties we would have had in Britain rather than have one province out." "Pierre Elliott Trudeau: Memoirs," vol. 3, ep. 5.

BIBLIOGRAPHY

ARCHIVE COLLECTIONS

Edward S. Goldenberg Fonds. Library and Archives Canada, Ottawa.
Michael Kirby Fonds. Library and Archives Canada, Ottawa.
Howard Leeson Papers. Private collection.

BOOKS AND ARTICLES

Ajzenstat, Janet, Paul Romney, Ian Gentles, and William D. Gairdner, eds. *Canada's Founding Debates*. Toronto: University of Toronto Press, 2003.

Alberta, Government of. "Harmony in Diversity: A New Federalism for Canada." Government of Alberta Position Paper on Constitutional Change, October 1978.

Axworthy, Thomas S., and Pierre Elliott Trudeau, eds. *Towards a Just Society: The Trudeau Years*. Toronto: Penguin Books, 1992.

Banting, Keith, and Richard Simeon, eds. *And No One Cheered: Federalism, Democracy and the Constitution Act*. Toronto: Methuen, 1983.

Behiels, Michael D., ed. *Quebec Since 1945: Selected Readings*. Toronto: Copp Clark Pitman, 1987.

Blakeney, Allan. *An Honourable Calling: Political Memoirs*. Toronto: University of Toronto Press, 2008.

Brooks, Stephen, ed. *Political Thought in Canada: Contemporary Perspectives*. Toronto: Irwin Publishing, 1984.

Burelle, André. *Pierre Elliott Trudeau: L'intellectuel et le politique*. Montreal: Éditions Fides, 2005.

Cairns, Alan C. *Charter Versus Federalism: The Dilemmas of Constitutional Reform*. Montreal and Kingston: McGill-Queen's University Press, 1992.

———. *Disruptions: Constitutional Struggles, from the Charter to Meech Lake*. Toronto: McClelland and Stewart, 1991.

Canada, Government of. "Briefing for the Delegation of the Government of Canada." September 8–12, 1980. LAC MG32-G15, vol. 12, file 6.

———. "Charter of Rights." August 5, 1980. LAC MG32-G15, vol. 15, file 1.

———. "Constitution," June 23, 1981, LAC MG32–G15, vol. 13, file 11.

———. "Constitutional Strategy, August–September 1980." August 20, 1980. LAC MG32-G15, vol. 8, file 6.

———. "Re Discussions with Saskatchewan Officials on Patriation Resolution." October 17, 1980. LAC MG32-G15, vol. 15, file 5.

———. "The NDP Position on the Constitution: Premier Blakeney and the NDP Caucus." January 16, 1981. LAC MG32-G15, vol. 15, file 8.

———. "Notes of Events Surrounding Negotiations with the Province of Saskatchewan in the Period from Thursday, January 22 to Tuesday, January 27, Inclusive." January 31, 1981. LAC MG32-G15, vol. 12, file 19.

———. "Patriation of the Constitution: Validity of Unilateral Action." August 26, 1980. LAC MG32-G15, vol. 15, file 4.

———. "Patriation, including Amending Formula: Notes for an Introductory Statement by the Prime Minister." September 5, 1980. LAC MG32-G15, vol. 12, file 7.

———. "Prime Minister's Briefing Book—Meeting of First Ministers—November 2, 1981." October 30, 1981. LAC R12685, vol. 5, file 2.

———. *A Preliminary Report of the Royal Commission on Bilingualism and Biculturalism*. Ottawa: Queen's Printer, 1965.

———. "Report to Cabinet on Constitutional Discussions, Summer 1980, and the Outlook for the First Ministers' Conference and Beyond." (The Kirby report.) August 30, 1980. Kirby Fonds, LAC R12685, vol. 5, file 14.

———. "Report on Mr. Chrétien's London Trip." March 27, 1981. LAC MG32-G15, vol. 15, file 9.

———. "Results of a Survey on Attitudes to Constitutional Change." July 18, 1980. LAC MG32-G15, vol. 15, file 6.

———. *Royal Commission on Bilingualism and Biculturalism*. Book 3A, *The Work World*. Ottawa: Queen's Printer, 1969.

———. "A Scenario for the FMC." October 31, 1981. LAC MG32-G15, vol. 15, file 7.

———. "Strategy Paper Re. Quebec," September 23, 1981, LAC MG32–G15, vol. 13, file 11.

———. "Towards a New Canadian Constitution: Federal Position on the Priority Items." June 16, 1980. LAC MG32-G15, vol. 16, file 4.

Charron, Claude. *Désobéir*. Montreal: VLB éditeur, 1983.

Chrétien, Jean. *My Years as Prime Minister*. Toronto: Alfred A. Knopf Canada, 2007.

———. *Straight from the Heart*. Toronto: Key Porter, 1985.

Clarkson, Stephen, and Christina McCall. *Trudeau and Our Times*. Volume 1, *The Magnificent Obsession*. Toronto: McClelland and Stewart, 1990.

Connors, Richard, and John M. Law, eds. *Forging Alberta's Constitutional Framework*. Edmonton: University of Alberta Press, 2005.

Cook, Ramsay. *Canada and the French-Canadian Question*. Toronto: Macmillan of Canada, 1966.

———. "Civic Nations and Distinct Societies." *The Literary Review of Canada* (July–August 1994).

———. *The Maple Leaf Forever: Essays on Nationalism and Politics in Canada*. Toronto: Macmillan of Canada, 1971.

———. *The Teeth of Time: Remembering Pierre Elliott Trudeau*. Montreal and Kingston: McGill-Queen's University Press, 2006.

Cormier, Michel, and Achille Michaud. *Richard Hatfield: Power and Disobedience*. Fredericton: Goose Lane Editions, 1992.

Craig, Gerald M., ed. *Lord Durham's Report*. Toronto: McClelland and Stewart, 1963.

Djwa, Sandra. *The Politics of the Imagination: A Life of F.R. Scott*. Toronto: McClelland and Stewart, 1987.

Doern, G. Bruce, and Glen Toner. *The Politics of Energy: The Development and Implementation of the NEP*. Toronto: Methuen, 1985.

Duchesne, Pierre. *Jacques Parizeau*. Tome 2, *Le Baron, 1970–1985*. Montreal: Éditions Québec Amérique, 2002.

Dunsmuir, Mollie. "Constitutional Activity from Patriation to Charlottetown (1980–1992)." BP-406E, Parliamentary Research Branch, Library of Parliament, Government of Canada, November 1995.

Elliott, David R., and Iris Miller. *Bible Bill: A Biography of William Aberhart*. Edmonton: Reidmore Books, 1987.

English, John. *Citizen of the World: The Life of Pierre Elliott Trudeau*. Vol. 1, *1919–1968*. Toronto: Alfred A. Knopf Canada, 2006.

———. *Just Watch Me: The Life of Pierre Elliott Trudeau*. Vol. 2, *1968–2000*. Toronto: Alfred A. Knopf Canada, 2009.

Fournier, Pierre. *A Meech Lake Post-Mortem: Is Quebec Sovereignty Inevitable?* Translated by Sheila Fischman. Montreal and Kingston: McGill-Queen's University Press, 1991.

Fraser, Graham. *PQ: René Lévesque and the Parti Québécois in Power*. 2nd ed. Montreal and Kingston: McGill-Queen's University Press, 2001.

———. *Sorry, I Don't Speak French: Confronting the Canadian Crisis That Won't Go Away*. Toronto: McClelland and Stewart, 2006.

Godin, Pierre. *René Lévesque: L'homme brisé (1980–1987)*. Montreal: Boréal, 2005.

Goldenberg, Eddie. *The Way It Works: Inside Ottawa*. Toronto: McClelland and Stewart, 2006.

Graham, Ron. *The French Quarter: The Epic Struggle of a Family—and a Nation—Divided*. Toronto: Macfarlane Walter and Ross, 1992.

———. *One-Eyed Kings: Promise and Illusion in Canadian Politics*. Toronto: Collins, 1986.

Gwyn, Richard. *The Northern Magus*. Toronto: McClelland and Stewart, 1980.

Holmes, Nancy. "Human Rights and the Courts in Canada." Law and Government Division, Government of Canada, November 1991. Revised October 2001.

Hoy, Claire. *Bill Davis: A Biography*. Toronto: Methuen, 1985.

Hurley, James Ross. *Amending Canada's Constitution: History, Processes, Problems and Prospects*. Ottawa: Ministry of Supply and Services, 1996.

Ibbitson, John. *Loyal No More: Ontario's Struggle for a Separate Destiny*. Toronto: HarperCollins Canada, 2001.

Jeffrey, Brooke. *Divided Loyalties: The Liberal Party of Canada, 1984–2008*. Toronto: University of Toronto Press, 2010.

Johansen, David, and Philip Rosen. "The Notwithstanding Clause of the Charter." BP 194E, Parliamentary Information and Research Service, Library of Parliament, Government of Canada. Revised October 16, 2008.

Johnson, William. *A Canadian Myth: Quebec, Between Canada and the Illusion of Utopia*. Montreal and Toronto: Robert Davies Publishing, 1994.

Johnston, Donald, ed. *Pierre Trudeau Speaks Out on Meech Lake*. Rev. ed. Toronto: General Paperbacks, 1990.

Laforest, Guy. *Trudeau and the End of a Canadian Dream*. Montreal and Kingston: McGill-Queen's University Press, 1995.

Latouche, Daniel. *Canada and Quebec, Past and Future: An Essay*. Toronto: University of Toronto Press, 1986.

Leeson, Howard. "Memorandum from Howard Leeson: First Ministers' Conference on the Constitution, Ottawa, November 2–5." Government of Saskatchewan, November 16, 1981.

———. "Memorandum: Negotiations—January 20 to January 27, 1981—Sequence of Events." Government of Saskatchewan, February 5, 1981.

———. "The Patriation Minutes." Unedited notes.

———. "Section 133, the Notwithstanding Clause: A Paper Tiger?" *Choices* (Institute for Research on Public Policy) 6, no. 4 (June 2000).

Lévesque, René. *Memoirs*. Toronto: McClelland and Stewart, 1986.

———. *An Option for Quebec*. Toronto: McClelland and Stewart, 1968.

Lipset, Seymour Martin. *Agrarian Socialism: The Cooperative Commonwealth Federation in Saskatchewan, A Study in Political Sociology*. Toronto: Doubleday/ Anchor Books, 1968.

Lougheed, Peter. "Why a Notwithstanding Clause?" *Points of View* (Centre for Constitutional Studies, University of Alberta) 6 (1998).

Lyon, Sterling. "Notes for a Statement on the Entrenchment of a Charter of Rights." September 9, 1980, document 800-14/072.

MacDonald, L. Ian. *From Bourassa to Bourassa: A Pivotal Decade in Canadian History*. Montreal: Harvest House, 1984.

MacLean, Angus. *Making It Home: Memoirs of J. Angus MacLean*. Charlottetown: Ragweed Press, 1998.

———. "Notes for an Address to the First Ministers' Conference." September 8, 1980, document 800-14/015.

Macpherson, C.B. *Democracy in Alberta: Social Credit and the Party System*. Toronto: University of Toronto Press, 1962.

McMurtry, Roy. "The Search for a Constitutional Accord—A Personal Memoir." *Queen's Law Journal* 30 (1982–1983).

McRoberts, Kenneth. *Misconceiving Canada: The Struggle for National Unity*. Toronto: Oxford University Press, 1997.

McWhinney, Edward. *Canada and the Constitution 1979–1982: Patriation and the Charter of Rights*. Toronto: University of Toronto Press, 1982.

——. *Quebec and the Constitution 1960–1978*. Toronto: University of Toronto Press, 1979.

Meekison, Peter, ed. *Constitutional Patriation: The Lougheed–Lévesque Correspondence*. Kingston: Institute of Intergovernmental Relations, Queen's University, 1999.

——. "The Amending Formula." *Queen's Law Journal* 30 (1982–1983).

Milne, David. *The New Canadian Constitution*. Toronto: James Lorimer and Company, 1982.

——. *Tug of War: Ottawa and the Provinces Under Trudeau and Mulroney*. Toronto: James Lorimer and Company, 1986.

Monahan, Patrick J. *Meech Lake: The Inside Story*. Toronto: University of Toronto Press, 1991.

Monière, Denis. *Ideologies in Quebec: The Historical Development*. Toronto: University of Toronto Press, 1981.

Moore, Christopher. *1867: How the Fathers Made a Deal*. Toronto: McClelland and Stewart, 1997.

Morin, Claude. *L'Affaire Morin: Légendes, sottises et calumnies*. Montreal: Boréal, 2006.

——. *Les choses comme elles étaient: Une autobiographie politique*. Montreal: Boréal, 1994.

——. *Lendemains piégés: Du référendum à la nuit des longs couteaux*. Montreal: Boréal, 1998.

Mulroney, Brian. *Memoirs: 1939–1993*. Toronto: McClelland and Stewart, 2007.

Nemni, Max, and Monique Nemni. *Young Trudeau 1919–1944: Son of Quebec, Father of Canada*. Translated by William Johnson. Toronto: McClelland and Stewart, 2006.

Nurgitz, Nathan, and Hugh Segal. *No Small Measure: The Progressive Conservatives and the Constitution*. Ottawa: Deneau Publishers, 1983.

Pearson, Lester B. *Mike: The Memoirs of the Right Honorable Lester B. Pearson*, Vol. 3. Toronto: University of Toronto Press, 1975.

Peckford, Brian. *The Past in the Present: A Personal Perspective on Newfoundland's Future*. St. John's: Harry Cuff Publications, 1983.

Pelletier, Gérard. *Years of Impatience, 1950–1960*. Translated by Alan Brown. Toronto: Methuen, 1984.

Plecas, Bob. *Bill Bennett: A Mandarin's View*. Vancouver and Toronto: Douglas and McIntyre, 2006.

Poliquin, Daniel. *René Lévesque*. Toronto: Penguin Canada, 2009.

Quebec, Government of. "Constitution Express, No. 3." Department of Intergovernmental Affairs, Quebec, November 19, 1980.

———. "Opening Statement by the Quebec Minister of Intergovernmental Affairs, Claude Morin." July 8, 1980, Continuing Committee of Ministers on the Constitution, Department of Intergovernmental Affairs, Quebec, LAC MG32-G15, vol. 17, file 6.

Radwanski, George. *Trudeau*. Toronto: Macmillan of Canada, 1978.

Robertson, Gordon. *Memoirs of a Very Public Civil Servant: Mackenzie King to Pierre Trudeau*. Toronto: University of Toronto Press, 2000.

Romanow, Roy. "'Reworking the Miracle': the Constitutional Accord 1981." *Queen's Law Journal* 30 (1982–1983).

Romanow, Roy, John Whyte, Howard Leeson. *Canada ... Notwithstanding: The Making of the Constitution 1976–1982*. Toronto: Carswell/Methuen, 1984.

Russell, Peter H. *Constitutional Odyssey: Can Canadians Become a Sovereign People?* 2nd ed. Toronto: University of Toronto Press, 1993.

Saul, John Ralston. *Louis-Hippolyte LaFontaine and Robert Baldwin*. Toronto: Penguin Canada, 2010.

Scott, Frank R. *Essays on the Constitution: Aspects of Canadian Law and Politics*. Toronto: University of Toronto Press, 1977.

Sheppard, Robert, and Michael Valpy. *The National Deal: The Fight for a Canadian Constitution*. Toronto: Macmillan of Canada, 1982.

Simpson, Jeffrey. *Faultlines: Struggling for a Canadian Vision*. Toronto: HarperCollins Canada, 1993.

Smith, David E. *The Regional Decline of a National Party: Liberals on the Prairies*. Toronto: University of Toronto Press, 1981.

Southam, Nancy, ed. *Pierre: Colleagues and Friends Talk About the Trudeau They Knew*. Toronto: McClelland and Stewart, 2005.

———, ed. *Remembering Richard*. Halifax: Formac Publishing, 1993.

Starr, Richard. *Richard Hatfield: The Seventeen-Year Saga*. Halifax: Formac Publishing, 1987.

Steed, Judy. *Ed Broadbent: The Pursuit of Power*. Toronto: Viking, 1988.

Thomson, Dale C. *Jean Lesage and the Quiet Revolution*. Toronto: Macmillan of Canada, 1984.

Tremblay, Martine. *Derrière les portes closes: René Lévesque et l'exercice du pouvoir (1976–1985)*. Montreal: Québec Amérique, 2006.

Trudeau, Pierre Elliott. *Against the Current: Selected Writings 1939–1996*. Toronto: McClelland and Stewart, 1996.

———. *The Essential Trudeau*. Edited by Ron Graham. Toronto: McClelland and Stewart, 1998.

———. *Federalism and the French Canadians*. Toronto: Macmillan of Canada, 1968.

———. "Lettre ouverte aux Québécois." *La Presse*, July 15, 1980.

———. *Memoirs*. Toronto: McClelland and Stewart, 1993.

Vastel, Michel. *Bourassa*. Toronto: Macmillan of Canada, 1991.

———. *Trudeau le Québécois*. Montreal: Les Éditions de l'Homme, 1989.

Waite, P.B. *The Life and Times of Confederation 1864–1867: Politics, Newspapers, and the Union of British North America*. Toronto: University of Toronto Press, 1962.

Webber, Jeremy. *Reimagining Canada: Language, Culture, Community and the Canadian Constitution*. Kingston and Montreal: McGill-Queen's University Press, 1994.

Weiler, Joseph M., and Robin M. Elliot, eds. *Litigating the Values of a Nation: The Canadian Charter of Rights and Freedoms*. Toronto: Carswell, 1986.

Wiseman, Nelson. *In Search of Canadian Political Culture*. Vancouver and Toronto: UBC Press, 2007.

Wood, David G. *The Lougheed Legacy*. Toronto: Key Porter, 1985.

Young, Walter D. *The Anatomy of a Party: The National CCF 1932–61*. Toronto: University of Toronto Press, 1969.

INTERVIEWS

Blakeney, Allan—May 6, 2009; November 25, 2010

Broadbent, Ed—June 22, 2010

Carver, Horace—November 24, 2010

Chrétien, Rt. Hon. Jean—May 2, 2009

Davis, William—June 16, 2009

Dawson, Mary—December 20, 2010

Kinsella, Noel—September 30, 2010

Kirby, Michael—June 3, 2009; November 24, 2010

Leeson, Howard—October 21, 2009; May 14, 2010

Lougheed, Peter—May 29, 2009; January 10, 2011

Matkin, James—September 23, 2010

McMurtry, Roy—May 7, 2009

Meekison, Peter—October 20, 2009

Morin, Claude—November 12–13, 2009 (email correspondence)

Nurgitz, Nathan—September 30, 2010

Romanow, Roy—May 5, 2009; November 22, 2010

Segal, Hugh—June 2, 2009

Spector, Norman—June 23, 2010

Tassé, Roger—November 26, 2010

Trudeau, Rt. Hon. Pierre Elliott—May 4, 1992

Whyte, John—October 19, 2009

WEBSITES

Canadian Legal Information Institute, Federation of Law Societies of Canada. www.canlii.org/en/ca/scc/doc/1981/1981canlii25/1981canlii25.html.

CBC Digital Archives, Canadian Broadcasting Corporation. archives.cbc.ca/politics/constitution.

Centre for Constitutional Studies, University of Alberta. www.law.ualberta.ca/centres/ccs.

Library of Parliament, Parliament of Canada. www.parl.gc.ca/information/library.

Le Secrétariat aux affaires intergouvernementales canadiennes, Government of Quebec. www.saic.gouv.qc.ca.

Studies on the Canadian Constitution and Canadian Federalism, Marianopolis College, Montreal.faculty.marianopolis.edu/c.belanger/quebechistory/federal/index.htm.

ACKNOWLEDGMENTS

I am deeply grateful to Eddie Goldenberg and Michael Kirby for allowing me access to their restricted files at Library and Archives Canada (LAC). Their fonds are an invaluable trove of federal and provincial documents, memoranda, and correspondence relating to the constitutional negotiations. The LAC staffers, in particular George Bolotenko and Maureen Hoogenraad, were consistently helpful.

Equally valuable were the memoranda and documents in the possession of Howard Leeson. As far as I could discover, his notes are the only detailed record of the discussions that took place the week of November 1981. My research—and this book—benefited from the access he generously gave me, as well as the permission to quote from the material in advance of the publication of his own account, *The Patriation Minutes*, by University of Alberta Press, in 2011. Roy Romanow was kind enough to give me a photocopy of the "Kitchen Accord" from his private papers.

All histories are indebted to many primary and secondary sources. The one owes much to the excellent work of Robert Sheppard and Michael Valpy; Roy Romanow, John Whyte, and Howard Leeson; Graham Fraser; Pierre Godin; and Claude Morin. I also learned a great deal from those participants who gave me interviews; those who wrote memoirs; and those who reported on the story at the time. Thanks.

I would also like to thank George Anderson, Graham Fraser, Eddie Goldenberg, Charlotte Gray, and Roger Tassé for bringing their expertise and advice to earlier drafts of this book. Of course, the mistakes and judgments remain entirely mine.

Thanks, as well, to Margaret MacMillan and Bob Bothwell for including me in their important series on Canadian history, for their astute reading of several drafts, and for their constant support. At Penguin Canada/Allen Lane, I owe much to the professionalism and guidance of Diane Turbide, Janice Weaver, and Mary Ann Blair.

Last but not least, in this project as in all things, my enduring gratitude to my wife, Gillian, a superb editor, a patient companion, a *dhamma* traveller, and the love of my life.

INDEX